SRI is in orbit; it's our job to keep it there.

greater understanding among the nations.

ONWARD COURSE

SRI should play a role in its future.

AREA OUTPOSTS

search techniques …

VILLAGE HOME

We must grow; we must earn a surplus.

TAL

There are many ways to grow; the best of all is in quality.

First study science and then follow the practice born out of that science.

Cover design — Evolution of SRI Colophon during ''The Take-Off Days.'' ———— **SRI** International 1986 Colophon.

SRI

The Take-Off Days

MID–1900s

SRI

The Take-Off Days

THE RIGHT MOVES
AT THE
RIGHT TIMES

By

WELDON B. GIBSON

Publishing Services Center   Los Altos, California

My good friend, Dr. Weldon B. ''Hoot'' Gibson has written accurately about SRI in its early days. We have known each other very well since the Institute's beginnings. Throughout this time, he has played a key role in its rise to worldwide prominence.

— D. J. RUSSELL - 1984*

* A founding director — deceased, 1985.

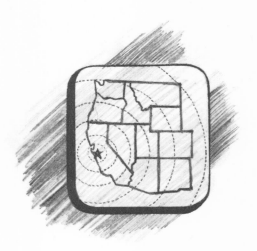

Library of Congress Cataloging-in-Publication Data

Gibson, Weldon B., 1917–
   SRI, the take-off days.

   Includes index.
   1. Stanford Research Institute—History   I. Title.
T178.S754G53   1986   607'.20794'74   86-12392
ISBN 0-86576-103-5

Publication — Private Auspices

Table of Contents

Chapters

SRI
GUIDING THEMES

———————————— for Volume 1 ————————————
The Founding Years*

IN CONCEPT .... VISION

IN ORIGIN .... INSPIRATION

IN CREATION .... PERSERVERANCE

IN PURPOSE .... DEDICATION

———————

* Published 1980

———————————— and for Volume 2 ————————————
The Take-Off Days**

ON PROGRAMS .... CREATIVITY

ON PURPOSE .... ELABORATION

ON GROWTH .... STIMULATION

ON RESOURCES .... GENERATION

———————

** Published 1986

SRI and Stanford

SRI was founded as Stanford Research Institute in 1946 by the Trustees of Stanford University in cooperation with a group of western US business executives. The basic idea originated within the University in the mid-1920s.

The basic purpose was to apply science for useful purposes. Although the concept was promoted in various ways through the 1930s it did not take form until 1939. The Great Depression was a deterrent.

As a Stanford Trustee, Herbert Hoover strongly supported the early idea. This continued during and after his United States presidency. Later, the outbreak of World War II put everything on the shelf, so to speak. The momentum gained new force in 1945 and into 1946. This was when the group of western executives entered the picture. Thus, the founding years were spread over a couple of decades.

An earlier book on SRI carries the subtitle A Significant Step at the Golden Time. These words arose from a Stanford Committee report in 1945 and Dr. Donald B. Tresidder's comment at SRI's first board meeting in early 1947. Tresidder was Stanford's president and first SRI chairman.

During its first two and one-half decades, SRI was, in effect, a nonprofit subsidiary of the University. By mutual agreement, the two institutions separated in 1970 but with no change in SRI's structure or purposes. Its name was changed to SRI International in 1977 but the acronym is still widely used.

The names "SRI," "Stanford Research Institute" and "Institute" are used interchangeably as they were during the final founding years, through the Take-Off Days and into an Upward Surge that followed. This is the title for a third book.

HIGH HONOR	HIGH RECOGNITION
— The Founding Years —	— The Take-Off Days —
Robert Swain .... Proponent	Jesse Hobson .... Instigator
Alvin Eurich ..... Architect	Charles Blyth .... Facilitator
Atholl McBean ... Founder	J. E. Wallace Sterling ... Presider

The Institute owes a great debt of gratitude to Stanford University. It was the "father" of SRI that has since become a far-flung and well-known organization, one of the largest of its kind in the world.   □

Public Service*

- Promote the educational purposes of Stanford University through research in the physical, life and social sciences, engineering and the mechanic arts.

- Extend scientific knowledge in the several pursuits and professions of life and assist Stanford University in extending learning and knowledge.

- Apply science in developing commerce, trade and industry and in improving the general standard of living and peace and prosperity of mankind.

- Publish research results deemed to be of general public interest.

The highest purpose of research is the enhancement of knowledge and understanding, and thereby the advancement of productivity, human relations, and man's progress in all respects.

— E. Finley Carter - SRI

* The essence of SRI's basic purposes. See also chapter ''A Search for Purpose''

Dedication

The institution is everything.

—ATHOLL McBEAN - 1950

THE LEADER OF SRI's FOUNDERS — AND INDEED THE TRUE FOUNDER — was fond of putting his views even on complex matters in a few words. He did this in such a way as to drive home what he felt were cardinal points.

Thus, during SRI's early days he would often say such things as ''we are here for a great purpose'' or ''never falter in the Institute's dedication.''

He often gave short shrift to anyone or anything raising any doubts about moving ahead quickly for the future of the Institute.

To McBean, SRI was ''everything.'' Its dedication in his view was complete. He urged its leaders to ''keep their eyes on the ball'' and asked Stanford's Trustees and their elected SRI directors to ''keep faith'' with the whole initiative.

Some — both inside and out — might question his ''directness'' and ''persistence'' at times but never did anyone doubt his intense dedication to the Institute. He insisted that all of SRI's senior people be as dedicated to its long-range welfare as he knew himself to be.

The history of any institution is significant when events of certain times greatly affect its future. There can be ''trial and error'' but in a young organization things must be set in motion at some point if there is to be success in the years or decades to come. As McBean once said about SRI in the mid-1900s, ''the greatest risk is to let nature take its course.''

Our founder's urge to move ahead in cohort with others on a collective vision is much in the forefront in an earlier book on SRI's founding years. It was clear from the outset that the new institute was to ''apply science for useful purposes'' in service to business, industry, and, by implication, government and other public institutions.

The title and subtitle of this book suggest that some things happened soon after SRI's founding that were to have lasting impacts on the fledgling organization. This was indeed the case with two basic dedications very much in the background.

- A growing force in developing useful research programs.
- A rising devotion to public service including assistance in various ways to our parent, Stanford University.

Over the years these dedications have provided an underpinning or principle for SRI. They have helped make it unique, strong and important as well as dynamic, exciting and productive. The origins of these ends lie not alone in the founding years. Their main impetus arose during the institution's Take-Off Days.

Several specific events and trends in SRI's subsequent development were set in motion during its second stage beginning in the main in mid-1948. They greatly affected all that was to happen during a following Upward Surge and even beyond into succeeding phases of the Institute's history.

Thus, as the 40th Anniversary of SRI's creation is observed in 1986, it is altogether appropriate and timely to outline a few highlights from the Take-Off time.

- Selection of our main ''research areas'' — the physical and life sciences, engineering and economics/management sciences, the latter having been entirely new ground for research institutes of SRI's type.
- An early thrust that brought the organization from an uneconomic scale to a ''critical mass'' within a few years.
- New ''dimensions'' in scope from the American West to the nation and then to the world beyond.
- An ascending but never ending elaboration on ''purposes'' based on the founding charter.
- A drawn-out process leading to a site for our ''permanent home'' in Menlo Park, California.
- A long-delayed Associates Plan to provide more capital for an under-financed institute.
- A group of area offices away from Menlo Park as part of a plan to maintain physical presence in economic communities important to SRI's future.
- An expanded board of directors with broader representation both geographically and by types of business.
- A more stable system of guidance with the chairman's post being filled by one person for several years.
- First policy attention to a variety of operating matters — growth rate, self-sufficiency, government/commercial ratio, self-sponsored research, patents, pricing, project administration, and so on.

These and other key features were set in motion during the Take-Off Days. They merely illustrate what was happening. Perhaps even more important in the longer run, was an intangible — an infusion of ''high energy and entrepreneurship'' — which caused SRI to move ahead successfully in a way unparalleled then and later within the family of independent institutes. Fortunately, the time was right. In retrospect, the right moves were made even though they were hesitant and tentative in some cases.

There is another aspect of dedication involving SRI. Many have spent long years during ''the first forty'' in helping build SRI. I am fortunate to be among them and the time continues. My view, however, is one of appreciation for the opportunity and a salute to others who have done and are now doing so much in a great cause.

In any case, I fully agree with what our founder had to say in 1950. The Institute is ''everything'' to all who are dedicated to its welfare. This is one reason why it has become one of the world's leading institutions of its type. □

Appreciation

THIS BOOK HAS BEEN MADE POSSIBLE by many people within and outside SRI. As the author, I am indebted to them. Although too numerous to mention all by name, they include:

- Some fifty colleagues who were staff members during the late 1940s and in the 1950s and who reviewed chapter drafts in the 1960s and 1970s.
- About twenty-five persons who were directly involved in various events depicted in the book and who read later drafts of the pertinent chapters.

The latter group includes, for example, George R. Herbert, former executive associate director, and Morris M. Doyle, director emeritus, (and an author in the mid-1940s of our founding charter), and William E. Rand, assistant director during the Institute's earliest days.

Three other persons, all of whom have died since final drafts of the book were written, must be singled out for special credit. They read each and every chapter and provided helpful counsel on facts and interpretations.

- Donald J. Russell, one of the Institute's eleven founding directors who then served SRI for almost forty years.
- Dr. J. E. Wallace Sterling, president of Stanford University and SRI's chairman during most of the period covered by this book.
- Dr. Frederick E. Terman, a long-time Stanford faculty member, then Provost, as well as an Institute director and our vice chairman.

I am indeed most grateful for all the help and advice given by these people. We enjoyed many close associations during our Take-Off Days. Each contributed greatly to the Institute's early development.

Another note of appreciation is to SRI itself and the staff who helped build it during the formative years. I feel honored in having had the opportunity to work with this dedicated group.

My appreciation goes also to Dr. William F. Miller, SRI's current president and chief executive officer, for the Foreword and to Charles N. Kimball, president emeritus of Midwest Research Institute, for the Preface.

Finally, my thanks extend to several other people who have added to the book in particular ways: Dennis D. Maxwell — Manuscript review, Wilbur ''Will'' Ashworth — Design/Graphics/Production, Galina Tahir — Word processing, Ronald J. Moore — Sketches, Helen M. Gibson — Watercolors.

Names of many persons appear on the pages of this book. In addition to appreciation, the author is most grateful for the personal relationships that were involved.

This book deals mainly with the time between SRI's founding years that ended in the late 1940s and the upsurge years that began in the mid-1950s.

It has been written primarily for an ''SRI audience.'' but hopefully it may be of some interest in other circles.

WELDON B. GIBSON

Menlo Park, Calfornia - 1986

The Institute's growing strength through its early years is on the record. As the years pass, more and more credit for all that was done must be given to George Herbert for his steadying hand.

— JOHN F. FORBES - 1958

Foreword

ENTERPRISE*

ONLY A CONCEPT IN THE MINDS OF ITS FOUNDERS forty years ago, SRI is now one of the largest research and consulting institutes in the world. It is a product of the business enterprise system. Created and operated under private auspices, the entrepreneurship of an able staff is its driving force.

A university strives to enhance the capabilities of individuals. SRI works to strengthen the institutions it serves while solving complex problems and contributing to knowledge.

SRI benefits today — and for the future — from a vigorous start. With constantly increasing quality, it gained maturity and achieved self-sufficiency in less than a decade.

This book deals with that vigorous start, the formative first decade. It supplements ''SRI — The Founding Years,'' an earlier book by the same author on the beginnings of SRI.

Dr. Weldon B. Gibson (known as ''Hoot'' by government and industry leaders around the world) writes with the authority of one who was there. As program leader, associate director, executive vice president, member of the Board and now, senior director, Hoot has long been an ''abiding force'' in SRI affairs.

He created and for many years led our programs in economics-management and other social sciences as well as SRI's international operations. These were new areas for organizations of our type.

Hoot founded our International Associates Program with its business and economic activities in more than fifty countries. He originated the International Industrial Conference in San Francisco. Also, he later organized and

WORLD HEADQUARTERS
Menlo Park, California – 1986

directed major SRI events in Moscow and Hangzhou (China).

Held every four years, the prestigious SF meeting is one of the leading business conferences in the world. A dramatic symbol of that international spirit can be seen in ''The House of All The Lands,'' the SRI International Building, dedicated in 1969. That building

*WILLIAM F. MILLER - SRI President and CEO, Menlo Park, California - 1986

came to be through the unique combination of Hoot's global friendships and firm leadership.

An early proponent of economic progress in the Pacific Basin, he was one of the founders of the Pacific Basin Economic Council and of the Japan-California Association. In addition, Hoot is a director of several companies and serves as a trustee for several universities, foundations and other public service organizations.

One of the first persons to join SRI, Hoot symbolizes the professionalism and spirit of enterprise that are central to success. A plaque mounted in our International Building says it best:

Dr. Weldon B. "Hoot" Gibson

With appreciation for his distinguished contributions to the world business enterprise and especially for his foresight and dedication in developing the International Associates Program at SRI International. September 15, 1985 — Menlo Park, California.

As dedicated today as forty years ago, his closing words in the Epilogue of this book show strong faith in and support for the cornerstones which are the basis for SRI's further development in the 1980s and beyond.

"THE HOUSE OF ALL THE LANDS"

AN EXCHANGE ON THE FUTURE
Left: William F. Miller, president and CEO (1986), and the author discussing some SRI plans.

On growth . . . let it first be in quality.
— J.E. WALLACE STERLING

Preface

UNITY IN PURPOSE[*]

THE PERIOD FROM 1948 THROUGH 1955 was one of the most exciting of this century. The nation launched a rapid and sustained economic expansion. R&D spending was growing apace. Certainly, the time was an exhilarating one for the independent research institutes. They moved upward in size and outward in scope faster than even those involved in leadership roles may have fully recognized.

All of the institutes were busily engaged in defining their roles and fields of service and in creating viable financial structures. Although the nonprofit applied research institutes taken together accounted for only a small fraction of the nation's R&D — as is the case today — they nevertheless had a definite impact on national research.

The institutes were not well known except within highly specialized R&D circles. One sometimes encountered the question, ''Just what is a research institute anyway?'' Yet the leaders were fairly clear in their own minds as to what they were trying to do. We felt this way at Midwest, and I know there was a similar unity in purpose within SRI.

The mix of public and private research varied greatly among the nine leading institutes: Mellon, Battelle, Armour, SRI, Franklin, Cornell, Southern, Southwest and Midwest. It soon became obvious that some of the institutes, for example SRI, would flourish while others would grow at a slower pace. Their circumstances, including location, sponsorship and management philosophies varied greatly.

SRI and Midwest had one basic characteristic in common. They were dedicated to the geographical regions they served — the West by SRI, and the American Heartland by Midwest. They were striving to provide a broad range of public services, along with research assistance to business and government.

There was, however, a particularly significant thrust within SRI. Its leaders visualized that industrial economics, the management sciences and indeed other areas of the social sciences were fruitful fields for an independent research institute. They might not have known where all this would lead but were confident that an appropriate path could be forged within a scientific research organization.

While being intensely proud of the success Midwest has enjoyed over the years, I have always been envious of SRI to some extent. The two ''grew up'' together and shared many common experiences. I know, too, that SRI was often envious of some of the things that were done at MRI. The important point is that we tried to help each other.

I often look back on the late 1940s and early 1950s as a time when many able scientists, engineers and other research specialists were anxious to move westward. They were seeking better climates, higher pay, more-exciting work, and a sort of special access to the future.

Being situated in one of the nation's most attractive areas, SRI had much to offer to competent men and women in the wide spectrum of research it was developing. Moreover, SRI had a valuable relationship

*CHARLES N. KIMBALL – president emeritus, Midwest Research Institute, Kansas City, Missouri - 1986.

with Stanford University, one of the country's great educational and research institutions. And from the very beginning, SRI aspired to become an internationally-oriented institute. Its plans and steps in this direction were bold and decisive.

Those of us at Midwest often contrasted SRI's rapid growth with our own slower but measured growth. We had some early difficulty in attracting the best scientists to the Midwest, even those who had lived here before earning their degrees elsewhere. In those years Kansas City greatly needed an urban revival program; it certainly was not ''a San Francisco Bay Area'' in attraction. Furthermore, the nearest university of Stanford's status was in Chicago.

All this has changed, of course, and in many ways both SRI and Midwest have prospered. But, on our part, there are fond recollections about ''ties of affection'' between the two organizations, especially during the early years. I have ample reason to believe that the same attitude toward MRI still exists at SRI, especially on the part of those who were among its early leaders. The point has been emphasized to me over the years by Hoot Gibson, the author of this book.

In glancing toward the SRI of that time, I recall many key events and contributions to the research institute movement. Here are a few that come readily to mind.

- The pioneering work in techno-economics and the management sciences.

- The famous ERMA computerization project for the banking business.

- The small-industry research projects in India, Pakistan, and elsewhere, one of the beginnings of a wide ranging international operation.

- Early work on the problems — and possible solutions — involving smog and air pollutants.

- Major efforts in evaluating and perfecting the nation's civilian defense program.

- The Western Resources Handbook, the first really comprehensive compendium on western resources.

- The highly-successful Chemical Economics Handbook that contiues to this day as a prime source of technoeconomic information on world chemicals.

- Dr. Thomas Poulter and his work in geophysical exploration.

- Regional offices in Phoenix, Los Angeles, Portland and Hawaii dedicated to area development studies.

- Many comprehensive industry-wide studies illustrated by a classic report on forest products.

- And, finally, the energetic cast of founders, as well as early researchers and administrators typified by Atholl McBean, Jesse Hobson, Finley Carter, Paul Lovewell, Don Benedict, Tom Morrin, Thomas Poulter, and others, especially the author.

Another indication of SRI's contributions is that four of its staff members became presidents of other research institutes. One of them is John McKelvey at MRI. Another is George Herbert at Triangle. But, again alongside SRI, Midwest has done its share in this respect with two of its alumni in similar positions.

MRI has benefitted in other ways from SRI. SRI's early director of public relations was long a consultant to MRI. Four other SRI staff members moved into key positions at MRI, and other ex-SRI people have served as consultants in their special fields.

But there is more to the story. Throughout his stay at SRI, Jesse Hobson always championed the cause of MRI. And, for four decades our close friend, Hoot Gibson, has never wavered as a friend, supporter and helping hand when called upon by me and others at Midwest.

There is an excellent record of cooperation between these two research institutes. We have always been on close and intimate terms, and I think we always will be. That spirit of cooperation, right from the beginning, is my fondest recollection of SRI.   □

HONOLULU — HAWAII
A Western Outpost

ITALY
First Major Project Abroad

rcolors by Helen Gibson

TAKU GLACIER — ALASKA
A Project on the Ice Fields

ANGEL ISLAND — SAN FRANCISCO BAY
An early proposed home for SRI

Watercolors by Helen G

Prologue

Keep up the momentum; take off as quickly as possible.

— BERNARD BARUCH - 1948

ARTICLES OF INCORPORATION FOR STANFORD RESEARCH INSTITUTE were filed with the State of California on November 6, 1946. This was the culmination of a long series of events beginning in the 1920s when the concept of an SRI affiliated with Stanford University first arose within its faculty.

Robert E. Swain, a highly respected chemistry professor and later dean of the department, was the man with "an early vision" about a new applied research institute in the American West. During the late 1930s, a Stanford alumnus, Dudley Swim, and another chemistry professor, Philip Leighton. were attracted to Swain's initiative. They called themselves The Three Musketeers.

The Great Depression and then World War II brought an end to this first step in SRI's creation. In 1945, however, a group of western business executives under the leadership of San Francisco's Atholl McBean became interested in the idea and began working on it with Stanford's president, Donald B. Tresidder, and its executive vice president, Alvin C. Eurich.

In due course, Eurich became the architect and McBean the founder of SRI working in cooperation with the University's Trustees. Their efforts led to what Tresidder called a "significant event in economic development of the western part of the United States."

Even before the Institute was incorporated within the University's family of organizations, our first "executive director", William F. Talbot, was on the scene just as Stanford's academic year began in the autumn of 1946.

I have the honor of being one of the first persons invited by Talbot to join the fledgling organization. Quite understandably, he spoke about a temporary position but this did not matter. I was excited about SRI's prospects and remain so four decades later.

Unfortunately, it was soon clear that Talbot and Tresidder did not see eye to eye on how the new institute was to operate. As the senior officer, Tresidder considered himself the chief executive with Talbot as administrative director. Talbot had thought CEO was his role when accepting the position. In any event, he resigned in late 1947. One of the other first invitees, William E. Rand, together with Carsten Steffens, took over the reins temporarily.

Seventeen months after the Institute's incorporation, J.E. (Jesse) Hobson, was on the scene as our second director. At the time, SRI had fewer than 50 people, less than $21,000 in fixed assets and a net worth of only $10,500. But, unfortunately, as might be expected, there was something else - a deficit running at well over $50,000 per year.

The cash balance when Talbot left was only $450; the inventory also was a problem — $21.54!

Even so, a start had been made. Research projects were under way in chemistry and economics. The largest in the former involved an attempt to develop rubber from the guayule plant, and in the latter, an "expansibility" study on the nation's aircraft industry was being sponsored by the U.S. Air Force.

Having earlier been head of the Armour Research Foundation (an applied research institute in Chicago) Hobson was dismayed by the meager SRI operation and decided to do something about it quickly. He made a move with the eleven-man board of directors on April 6, 1948.

I feel it is quite important for an aggressive development program to be undertaken at the earliest possible date.

Indeed, he meant *immediately* and on *five* fronts — more staff, equipment, promotion, public relations and a business office separate from the University. Hobson asked for $325,000 to get the ball rolling. This was a large sum under the circumstances. The directors gave a "Go Ahead" knowing that the money would have to be raised somehow to repay Stanford's working capital advances — some $133,000 at the end of 1947 plus whatever additional might be drawn down in 1948.

A bold plan had been presented; an even bolder approval had been granted. Both steps were acts of faith. The Institute was on its way. The second stage was at hand.

For a single day, the decision on April 6 is more interesting by far than the organizing step in early November of 1946 or any other day leading to SRI's launching. I have always thought of it as the "take-off" start. It ushered in a vigorous thrust that was to be the theme for 1948. But, it was also to be the source of some "engine trouble" that would plague the organization during its Take-Off Days and beyond.

A full account of SRI's founding years appears in an earlier book under the same name. The last chronological chapter is aptly titled ''An Exciting Time'' covering the start of our ''aggressive program.'' It followed on the heels of a ''Gathering Storm'' during 1947 and the Quiet Transition under caretaking hands before April 1948.

Knowing that money could not be raised in a hurry and that Stanford's officers and Trustees were already worried about the future for SRI, yet seeing the apparent sudden spurt of new money, I wondered with pen on paper: ''Can it be late April Fool's news?''

Having been involved in helping prepare the plan and seeing the action, a few of us knew the step was for real even though surprising. Thus it was that the Institute's directors rallied around and supported the cause as they were to do on many future occasions.

Stanford was having its own money and programming problems at the time. While hoping for the best to happen on April 6, some of us thought the process would be much more difficult than was the case. However, in retrospect, we had not fully realized how persuasive Hobson could be when he thought action was necessary.

My impression — based on deduction without really inquiring — was that Hobson had an understanding with the directors when he accepted his position that some new capital would be inserted in the picture right away. Otherwise, how could he have been so confident? Later on, he said that everything had been vague, partly because he had not known what was needed.

Thus, as the Founding Years ended by steps in 1948, our second stage — all under Hobson's pushing and pulling — began step by step in the same year. Perhaps, the end of the that stage can be assigned with ample reason to the year 1955. The impetus had shown some rather remarkable results, bringing the Institute to a point when it would enter a longer Upward Surge, while earning its own way except for some capital.

By mid-1950, the staff had grown more than five times in a mere 27 months since the beginning of the Vigorous Thrust. The fixed investment had multiplied some thirteen times; monthly revenues were about six times higher. More important, the Institute broke even financially in July for the second time. However, a small net worth had become a red figure — about $430,000 before some $160,000 in contributions. Obviously, SRI had been spending for the future.

There were also changes and new developments on the research front, but these will appear later. One way to summarize the situation is that SRI was moving energetically for the first time toward its goal of becoming a significant research organization.

Midway through the Take-Off Days, the young Institute was to be engulfed in a financial crisis with everything invested in growth. A solution was found just in time to save the organization.

Along with some black ink on the horizon, June of 1950 brought a sudden change on the world scene that would soon pervade much of what happened during our later Upward Surge. The Korean War began; a step-up in U.S. military capabilities placed new demands on — or at least offered new possibilities for — the Institute's service to government.

The first few chapters that follow are basically in chronological order. However, for some, such as the one on Equity Capital, the time span is not continuous and overlaps to some extent with other chapters in the calendar flow. Some begin in essence as early as 1948 and some go beyond the Take-Off Days.

Hobson's leadership had an immediate as well as lasting impact on SRI. He set to work in 1948 with great energy and without delay to develop the Institute. He did this with few resources in prospect except for some working capital advances from Stanford. The whole process was quickly brought to high pitch. It was an exhilarating experience.

The most important research step taken during the early Take-Off times was the beginning of an engineering program, mostly electronics, in the autumn of 1948 — September 1, to be exact. This was to round out the Institute's later spectrum including the sciences and economics-management.

Although finances and a vigorous development program dominated the affairs of the Institute during the second stage, one movement was fundamental to the organization. Once it became apparent during the latter part of 1949 that we could — and hopefully, soon would — reach financial self-sufficiency, attention was focused on a new search for purpose. This was largely a further interpretation of our charter and was to be a never-ending process as times and circumstances changed.

In the course of lengthy discussions during the first half of 1950, Hobson's viewpoint came through loudly and clearly. Based on firsthand knowledge of our founders' intentions, I agreed fully with what he was saying. We were expected to serve business and industry — first and foremost. Whether right or wrong in whatever degree, service to government was secondary. This may have been an all-too-simplistic view but our directors had no doubts on the matter.

Thus, we chose not to equivocate on the point. The opening sentence in a new board-approved policy was quite specific: ''The basic purpose of our existence is to be of service to business and industry ... '' This was meant to include government if it served this purpose directly or indirectly as, for example, work with companies serving government.

This did not imply that the principals, including the directors, were unmindful of the Institute's obligations to assist Stanford University and to engage in other activities in the public interest. Nevertheless, as a matter of emphasis those pursuits were somewhat secondary at the time. We had to do something on contract research before anything significant could be done about the latter.

In retrospect, this line of thinking in 1950 was only a first step towards more elaborate attention to policies in 1954 and 1956, and then again in the 1970s and 1980s.

As Alvin Eurich points out in The Founding Years, a key Stanford reason in creating SRI was some possible revenue for the University. The need was indeed great in the 1940s.

Swain, the man with an early vision on SRI, chaired Stanford's Golden Jubilee in 1941. He knew the University urgently needed more money and hoped the 50th Anniversary would help bring more support.

ALVIN C. EURICH
Architect

One Trustee, Almon Roth, who later helped bring SRI into being, spoke about Stanford's necessities. Among other things, he had relationships with industry in mind. This was one reason why he thought Swain's idea of an SRI was a good move.

Although not involved during our second stage, Swain was greatly pleased about SRI's emergence at the time. He once said ''everything goes so much faster than I could have imagined.''

A prominent American on the East Coast also was enthusiastic about the new western institute and its future. He made this clear during a couple of 'park bench' talks in Washington, D.C. in mid-1948.

Bernard Baruch's advice was being sought during our participation in a Presidential Commission on The Air Age. He heard what was happening at SRI and said, ''Keep up the momentum; take off as quickly as possible.'' This *is* what happened.

1950 was indeed a busy time around SRI. Among other things, a consultant retained by the directors was preparing a report as background for a fundraising program being considered by the board. In addition, his report was meant to be an appraisal of the Institute's position.

Even Hobson, let alone others on the senior staff, felt that his friend from New York went overboard in laudatory comments. Nevertheless, Maurice Holland was correct on two points — the Institute's remarkable development in such a short time and greater things in the offing.

All agreed with the board's adviser that ''SRI apparently had met a need and that the time of its formation was pretty near perfect.''

Holland made several recommendations to the directors including the idea of inserting up to $700,000 of new capital in the Institute's treasury. He went on to say that ''SRI should do less flying by the seat of the pants and more instrument flying'' Perhaps he was right — but most probably wrong. We were still on the 'runway.'

At Hobson's urging the Institute had been highly opportunistic. Many believed this was necessary. Neither Hobson nor the directors paid much attention to Holland's report. One reason is that all eyes were fixed at summer's end on a possible loan from the RFC as a source of new capital. Furthermore, not enough time had passed, since SRI had begun operating with a monthly surplus, to convince the directors that a fundraising plan was feasible. The whole idea was put on the shelf even though nothing came from the RFC episode. The Institute ploughed ahead more or less on its own with one development plan after another in rapid succession.

In any event, the following points are clear about financial affairs within SRI during the second stage.

The first is Hobson's courage at the beginning in requesting and spending far more capital than the Institute was able at the time to provide from possible earnings. The second is borne out by the record as well as by my own recollections. Things were moving so fast that neither the directors nor the Stanford Trustees fully realized the extent of the development program and, as time went on, the amount of money being spent until after it had been spent.

The third highly-important point is simply that Hobson's regime accomplished more in

J. E. WALLACE (WALLY) STERLING
New Chairman

ATHOLL McBEAN
Founder

JAMES B. BLACK
CEO — P.G. & E., A New Director

30 months — and in a few years to follow — than he had set out to do and what he had promised the directors would be done. However, it seems clear that the Institute would not have been allowed to begin the ambitious program had there been a clear understanding of the prospective deficits.

This is not to suggest that the board was not kept advised on all developments. In fact, there were frequent progress reports. Events were moving apace and Stanford did not place strict limits on working capital advances at the very beginning. They had not thought this was necessary.

There were, of course, at least two ways to get SRI in being and in the black. One was to proceed slowly and methodically on a pay-as-you-go basis with a low allowance on initial working capital. This is, in effect, what was attempted at the outset. The red ink began to accumulate in 1948; at the end of 1947 it was only about $50,000.

Another approach in the mid-1940s would have been to plan an Institute some 3½ years later with a pro forma balance sheet along these lines:

Assets		Liabilities — Net Worth	
Cash	$100,000	Current	$140,000
Receivables	450,000	Reserves	18,000
Inventories	40,000	Bank Loans	600,000
Improvements	90,000	Stanford debt	500,000
Deferrals	27,000	Contributions	162,000
Fixed	285,000	Net Deficit	($428,000)
TOTAL	**$992,000**	TOTAL	**$992,000**

This was not the plan but it is what happened under the force of the Take-Off Days.

The Institute was and still is the beneficiary of an unlikely combination of circumstances and events between late 1946 and mid-1950.

- Stanford's willingness to create SRI but with no resources to spare — only a hope that western business would make things possible once an initial step was taken.

- Business assumptions that Stanford would find some way to handle the initial investment; raising money for a non-existing institute was not feasible.

- Faith by all parties that something good would happen even though no concrete financial plan was in place to support a ''go ahead'' decision.

- A slow start with minimal investment for the founding period(1946-1948) most of it by happenstance or promise rather than by plan.

- An energetic but unanticipated push during the Take-Off Days with steps rapidly following each other more or less on a ''no turning back'' and ''keeping up the momentum'' basis.

- An Upward Surge arising immediately from the organization's second stage with emphasis all along the way on quick actions rather than longer-range methodical planning.

The result of this rapid and often hectic process was a 1955 Institute of a thousand people and $10 million in revenues from contract research in the physical and life sciences, engineering, economics and management sciences, and social systems.

This rapid development along with more that followed was and still is remarkable. It is unparalleled within the nation's and the world's independent research institutes.

It is in this perspective that our second stage is highly important. A ''fork in the road'' was on the immediate horizon in 1948-1950 and, fortunately, SRI took the right path. In doing so, the right driver was in the seat at the right time, even though the flight plan was being sketched and laid out as we moved along. The crew was wholly supportive; each helped explore new routes and horizons.

Now and then, perhaps all too often, the onrushing Institute missed some turns, passed through some storms, took a few detours, ran out of gas, added a few too many passengers, sped up too much, hit some turbulence, and so on. But, it moved — past one milestone after another — on a productive course.

Perhaps another analogy is more appropriate. The second stage for SRI was a trip down the runway and a take-off in 1955. The flight plan was changed many times, but through the runway run our directors in the control tower never faltered in their support, nor did Stanford at critical times. Despite Holland's advice in 1950, there was still to be a lot more ''flying by the seat of the pants'' before instrument flying entered more and more in the flight plan.

Whether the analogy is movement by land or by air, SRI was on its way to becoming an important institution — both national and international.

Our first annual report in 1947 says that the Institute had been founded but was not yet established. By the beginning of the second stage the latter had been done. One of our directors — William Stewart in Southern California - said that "the right moves are being made at the right times."

Edward Pembray, a public relations consultant from earlier Westinghouse renown, spoke in mid-1948 about the second stage — or at least what he thought should be done: "We must wind up the spring for the future."

Rand, Steffens and I from the Talbot times were on hand as the second stage began. Several others arrived soon thereafter and took up key positions.

BASIC ORGANIZATION

Jesse Hobson	Executive Director
George Herbert*	Executive Assistant
Thomas Poulter	Associate Director
Cledo Brunetti	Associate Director
William Rand	Assistant Director
Ralph Krause	Director of Research
Carsten Steffens	Assistant Director
Louis Koenig	Chemistry
Thomas Morrin	Engineering
Edward Doll	Physics
Thomas Poulter	Geophysics
Weldon "Hoot" Gibson†	Economics/International
A.M. Zarem	Los Angeles

* Later associate executive director
† Also chairman-finance committee and later associate director, executive vice president, board member and then senior director.

All of us knew that things were happening. None of us knew how important they would become in time. ■

Murphy's Law Adapted

(SRI — 1948/1955)

"If all goes well, start worrying;
there must be a problem somewhere."

— ANONYMOUS

ONWARD AND UPWARD

— The Pilot —

There is no time to lose; we must rush along in building the Institute.

— J.E. HOBSON - 1949

IN AN EARLIER BOOK ON SRI's *Founding Years,* a chapter on ''An Exciting Time'' portrays some feeling about the energy, enthusiasm and excitement within SRI generated largely by Jesse Hobson in 1948 even during his first few months. There is no need to repeat this part of the story. Suffice it to say that he did even more during the next seven years. It is to his credit that he persevered expecially during The Take-Off Days when some, including several directors and Stanford Trustees, were not as confident about the trend of affairs.

Hobson was a master — almost a magician — in finding silver linings in stormy clouds, and in voicing optimistic plans towards clear weather. So it was in early 1949 when hearing some bad financial news while in a San Francisco hospital. He first shrugged off the problem with a statement about shortage of time in building SRI, and then urged that we ''rush along'' on some basis. Even with a severe cash crisis at hand and flat on his back, and with no immediate solution, he was not deterred from a wholly affirmative viewpoint.

Hopefully, this book portrays Hobson as an optimistic leader even in the face of cash flow problems that indeed troubled many others with more conservative and cautious leanings. He was insistent on positive thinking about new research programs that might help build the Institute. He urged all of us to think up new ideas and to gamble on our convictions. Nothing caused him to lose confidence in an associate more than when he saw ''undue'' hesitancy and caution in starting new lines of research within SRI.

When Hobson liked the idea of some proposed research endeavor, there was no holding him back in his support. No sooner were some plans for a Western Resources Handbook adopted than he began asking about progress and wanted to see some of the output. To him the project was the essence of public service for certain types of business, and he was impatient with what others might have considered reasonable progress. Hobson wanted rapid movement in whatever his enthusiasm embraced.

There is no question that Hobson was controversial in many quarters. He had an image among some of the directors as being ''too expansionist'' in concept; he sometimes impressed business executives as being ''too promotional.'' Some Stanford Trustees thought that on potentially controversial projects he was often willing to walk where angels feared to tread!

Several Stanford officials and faculty members wondered now and then if he was devoting sufficient emphasis to quality. And, although many people (including some of his co-workers) often saw an undue impulsiveness, no one questioned his devotion to SRI's welfare.

Although there were individuals around the country who did not like Hobson, the reason almost always was traceable to his impulsive habit of being too critical of people who sometimes heard indirectly what he had said. Also, towards the end of his time at SRI he did a few things both in and out of character that were not helpful to him as an individual. For example, he once drove his car when he should have been a passenger, and on more than one occasion he skirted on thin ice with scanty information.

But his batting average was high and this was clear for all to see in the early 1950's. Moreover, Hobson was well liked by the vast majority of people with whom he came in contact, and, as the years passed after he resigned in 1955, practically everyone inside and outside SRI who knew about his early role at the Institute realized he had been a bundle of energy and ideas.

Within an environment of respect (and even applause at times) for his courage and strong leadership, many of his close associates were, nevertheless, often exasperated by his impulsiveness. But all this was set aside or handled in the normal course of operations without any basic change in attitude towards our good friend in the front office.

By and large, he inspired confidence, loyalty, dedication and hard work. Among his associates he instilled pride in the Institute, particularly because he preached a public service philosophy and a dedication to Stanford University, even though some faculty members were not aware of his commitment in this respect.

Fred Terman, head of engineering at Stanford, raised questions now and then about SRI and its director. Among other things, he thought too little attention was being given to government and to the Institute's role with Stanford.

However, thirty years later (on July 15, 1978) after having been University Provost and the Institute's vice chairman, Terman referred to Hobson as a "builder" and a man with "definite goals." Terman, also, was a builder and always felt that some "good opportunities were lost" in developing various joint SRI-Stanford programs. Some joint activities, particularly in engineering, were pursued. However, given our financial constraints and diverse objectives it was not easy to do more. SRI's attention was centered on rather immediate problem-solving work.

Hobson knew and gave voice to the idea that SRI's sole ultimate reason for existence as a non-profit, tax-exempt organization was to provide a unique public service and to assist Stanford in its pursuits. Throughout his term and especially toward the end he was anxious to do more in helping Stanford. This included, for example, a proposed gift program beginning at no less than $250,000 per year and moving upward beyond $500,000 as soon as possible. An initiative along this line was, in fact, taken after he left SRI.

But now, back to a few incidents, humorous and otherwise, in what some of his associates called "Life in the Putty Knife Factory" with an engaging and able executive director. Some of us have since looked back on these years as "Onward and Upward" having in mind an immediate surge that Hobson generated as well as an environment of energy and enthusiasm that carried over into The Take-Off Days.

On many occasions, Hobson was overly impulsive in selecting people. He would sometimes return from a trip with a long story about " ... meeting one of the ablest young men who has ever come to my attention. ... " We all knew this signalled a staff addition for a role undetermined

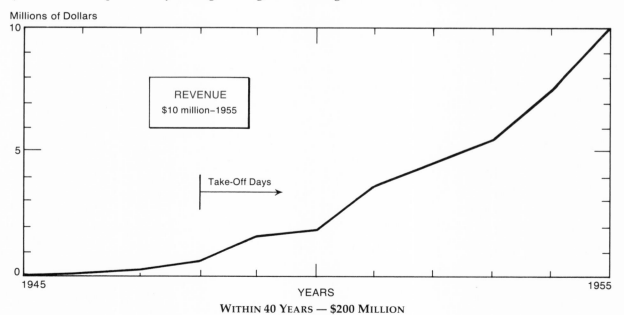

WITHIN 40 YEARS — $200 MILLION

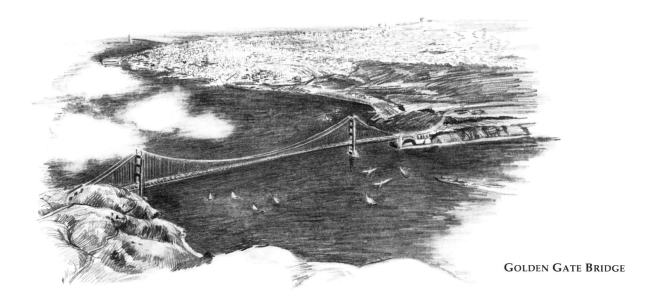

even by Hobson. On occasion, he would ask one of his associates to create a position taking advantage of the man's "great abilities."

This happened once with a chaplain he met during a visit aboard an aircraft carrier. We did our best to develop some sort of research program on "ethics for industry" but to no avail. Even Hobson soon agreed that a parting of the ways should be arranged, but he left the task to others. He simply did not like the "undoing" in such situations. Although some of his impulsive actions worked out very well, as might be expected others did not.

For some time after Hobson's arrival, he was quite alone outside the office while going through a divorce and remarriage. This often led him to suggest evening meetings with some of his associates. Although much got done during these apartment gatherings, they often went on until the wee hours of the night. No one objected particularly; we were all quite young and eager to move things along on a new, exciting — even though uncertain — path. No matter what the hour of "adjournment" might be, all were on hand early the next morning for an interesting and challenging time.

Hobson did not like pipe-smoking and, in his mind, questioned people who drove sports cars. He was expounding on these themes one day when all became quiet as we saw one of our senior associates drive up in a newly-purchased sports car. Later, we moved into a conference room and Hobson began his remarks while looking through a cloud of smoke rings coming from another

associate whose seating was, to say the least, inadvisable.

Towards the end of Hobson's tenure he was involved in an Arizona incident that both irritated and amused him no end. One of his associates was making a report on a study covering the San Carlos Indian Reservation in Arizona. The ex-tribal chief was present and took umbrage at a statement in the report about prior leadership. He implied that SRI was calling him a dictator. Hobson explained the passage as being a compliment rather than a criticism. Nevertheless, the ex-chief stood up, turned his back on Hobson and refused to talk to him. Upon returning home, Hobson kept complaining that he had almost been scalped and asked that no other such invitation be extended to him in the future! However, all soon passed over in a light vein; Hobson had a good sense of humor even when adversity came his way.

Our director was always urging unity of purpose among his associates. But he had a pet suspicion about any sort of club activity involving wives of staff members. Somehow, he looked upon such gatherings as "gossiping sessions" with a diversionary potential. His uneasiness was not helped by the fact that an SRI Women's Club was quite active at the time in arranging parties for husbands and wives and various other programs for its members. A quiet truce emerged in time; Hobson sort of gave in, and the women took pains to stay far away from any Institute matters. In fact, they never had an inclination to be so involved in the

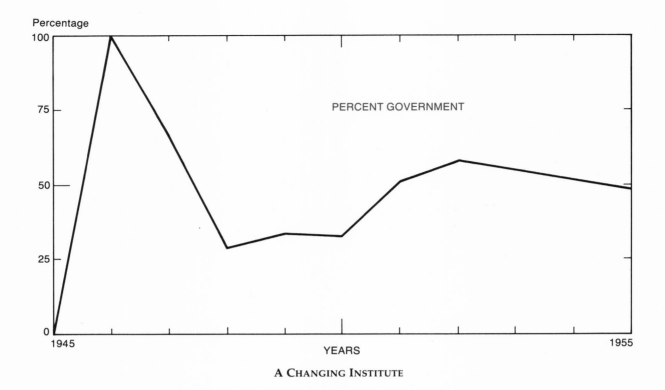

Percentage

PERCENT GOVERNMENT

1945   YEARS   1955

A Changing Institute

first place. Part of Hobson's feeling probably emerged simply because his new wife was busy with her professional work as an interior decorator and had little time or interest in such sideline social activities.

Midway during Hobson's term an unsettling incident occurred that he escaped but others did not. He was planning a talk in San Francisco on one of his favorite topics — a forseeable energy shortage. He asked for help on the speech and several of his associates spent time on it. Soon after the appearance he was "raked over the coals" by a P.G.& E. executive and one of our directors, who took great exception to the thrust of his speech. McBean was even more upset.

Hobson simply asked some of us to see them one by one and explain the speech. We explained but probably did not convince anyone. Finishing in mid-afternoon one day, we sympathized with each other and jokingly decided to use the rest of the day in seeing what else — with or without Hobson — we could help unravel. It really was no consolation to read a few months later that the Standard Oil tanker "McBean" had arrived in San Francisco just in time to avert a temporary oil shortage in Northern California.

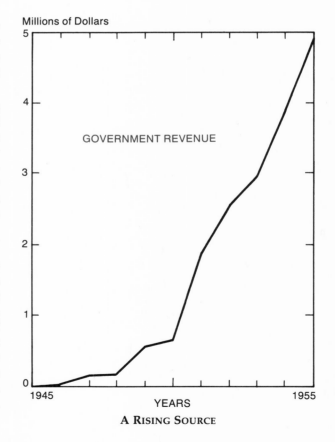

Millions of Dollars

GOVERNMENT REVENUE

1945   YEARS   1955

A Rising Source

In late June 1950, Hobson and three of his associates were in the Biltmore Hotel in Los Angeles. As chairman of our finance committee, I was assuring him one evening that SRI would break even in its July operations. He probably agreed but continued to argue against any forecast by an ''economist'' saying that as an ''engineer'' he did not like to predict.

We decided to take a late evening walk in Pershing Square, a favorite forum for soap box speakers on various causes. As we stood side by side listening to a man lecture on the Townsend Plan (a sort of ''painless'' economic welfare program), Hobson asked us for a reaction and heard a negative response. So did the nearby speaker who stepped forward and said, ''Well, it's plain to see you are not an economist.''

Hobson never let us forget this evaluation by an obviously well-informed ''expert'' and often speculated (humorously, we chose to believe) about relying on economists' predictions rather than on safer, conservative forecasts by engineers! The truth, of course, is that Hobson was not conservative and was always predicting, often with no points on a curve, so to speak, to guide him.

There is another interesting sidelight on Hobson's appraisal of his promotional work. During his early years at SRI, he would often talk about having to sell ''blue sky,'' meaning an Institute with only the bare beginnings of research programs. But on occasion he would call for harder work to support the ''blue sky'' activity. During a Christmas gathering, he spoke about the situation and thanked the staff for backing him during the year. The result was rising loyalty, harder work and greater enjoyment. Hobson knew very well how to sell his colleagues on a movement at hand. He was always ''onward and upward'' and most of the time we believed in him. One of his senior

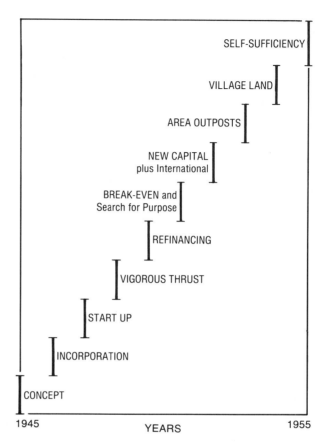

TEN EARLY INITIATIVES

associates still ''believed'' some three decades later.

Jesse was good at taking and keeping the initiative. When SRI was in a predicament (and it usually was ... in cash flow or unwise staffing on his part ...), he had a flair for shifting the discussion to an arena where he could take charge. He always seemed dedicated to SRI's advancement.

Even so, as indicated elsewhere in this book, there were some people outside SRI during the Hobson years who were not so convinced about his role. In retrospect, however, he was the right man for the time, but he was certainly on a fast track. His contributions were very great indeed but, as might be expected, he often generated an image of moving too fast. There is no point in examining the situation further. As time passed, all turned out in good fashion. □

THE FIRST FEW *
– From 1946 –

William Talbot †	James MacLeod
William Rand	Emo Porro
Paul Magill	Weldon Gibson ‡

* I.D. order first issued early 1947
† Resigned 1947
‡ Employed third

May this modest gift be a symbol of a future SRI on a world scale.

— MARIO CAMERINO (Italy) - 1952

A NEW DIMENSION

SRI WAS CREATED IN 1946 with a prime dedication to the American West. However, it soon became national and then worldwide in scope.

The first principal projects outside the United States were in Italy in the early 1950s. One was a study on the nation's mechanical industries. The other was part of a mission on European research organizations; it included a team from SRI and two of our sister institutes.

While in Venice in 1952, the SRI group visited Salviati and C., a ceramics and glass company. Its chief executive was much interested in our international aspirations. Thus began a long friendship.

Mario Camerino graciously presented some Venetian glass with a hope that it might be a symbol of a future SRI operating around the world. Several more pieces came seventeen years later when our International Building was dedicated. Now, another seventeen years later, all are on display in our "House of All the Lands."

Maurizio Camerino was a good friend of Mr. and Mrs. Stanford, the University's founders in the late 1800s. His son Mario was pleased to hear that Stanford was SRI's parent.

In 1903, Jane Lathrop Stanford wrote to the elder Camerino thanking him for his interest and friendship in sending a collection of glass and mosaics for the University's museum. The company produced the well-known Stanford Mosaics.

By train, ship and gondola, her letter reached Salviati in a mere 20 days. Another arrived in 19 days and still another in 21 days.

Although some 80 years later, there is a time saving on letters from the U.S. West to Italy, the number of days is open to question!! The earlier "special delivery" was quite remarkable.

One by-product of our first Italian projects was that they soon led to an SRI Office in Milan with Dr. Lorenzo Franceschini as the first director. The office is now part of a world network for "SRI International."

In one respect, then, our friend in Venice was prescient in 1952.

The Sister Institutes

A new force is rising in industrial research.

— HAROLD VAGTBORG - 1948

IN SOME RESPECTS, THE TAKE-OFF TIME FOR SRI during the 1948-1950 period, was part of a broader emergence of research institutes as the American economy moved from World War II into an upward course .

When SRI was conceived in 1945 as a partnership between business and Stanford University, there were three eastern institutes more or less of the same type already in existence. Two of them, the Mellon Institute in Pittsburgh and Battelle Memorial Institute in Columbus, Ohio, were the forerunners of what later were called "the independents and the nonprofits."

Mellon was founded in 1911 and Battelle in 1929. Armour Research Foundation in Chicago was created in 1937 and was known initially as ARF. It later became IITRI (Illinois Institute of Technology Research Institute).

There was a direct connection through three people between ARF and SRI in their early days. Thomas Poulter was the first scientific director at ARF; Harold Vagtborg was the first executive director. When Vagtborg left in early 1945 to become head of the new Midwest Research Institute (MRI) in Kansas City, Missouri, he was succeeded by Jesse Hobson who, later, along with Poulter moved to SRI.

As pointed out in an earlier book, the CEOs of both Mellon and Battelle were consulted by the principals involved in SRI's creation. Also, Vagtborg was close to SRI through Hobson and the author during the former's days at Southwest Research Institute (SwRI) in San Antonio, Texas, where he was its chief executive officer. SwRI was founded in 1947.

Hal Leedy succeeded Hobson at ARF while Charles Kimball followed Vagtborg at MRI.

Three other independent research institutes of SRI's type were founded in the mid-1940s. Two were in the East — Cornell Aeronautical Laboratory in Buffalo and Franklin Institute in Philadelphia; the third, Southern Research Institute, was in Birmingham, Alabama.

Thus, with SRI's formation the so-called "nine independents" were in place as The Take-Off Days for the new Stanford Research Institute got under way in the spring of 1948.

Six of the nine were young with little operating experience. Four of the institutes, Midwest, Southern, Southwest and SRI had special regional dimensions.

In this setting, the first of a later series of meetings by executives of the institutes was held in Chicago in the summer of 1948. The other independents were interested in hearing about "the new SRI." Vagtborg, Leedy, Hobson and Clyde Williams (Battelle's CEO) and the author were present.

Close informal relationships have continued over the years among the nonprofits. George Herbert is President of Triangle; John McKelvey is head of Midwest; both were from SRI.

Vagtborg was a leader among the research institutes in 1948. He was a strong promoter of the institutional concept with unbounded faith in its future. He even exceeded Hobson in this respect. Seeing the recent creation of Midwest, Southwest, Southern and SRI, it was at Chicago that he spoke about a "new force" in industrial research involving the so-called independents. He believed, however, that contrary to the ARF and SRI pattern, the best course was to be "truly independent" even from universities.

Vagtborg maintained that the real new force in the making had to do with their interdisciplinary concept and promoting industrial research rather than merely their volume of work. Their revenues were and have continued to be less than 2% of national R&D spending in the United States. Even so, at the time and in retrospect, it appeared that the group of independents was entering some sort of "take-off" on the burgeoning scene.

Mellon and Battelle were in a special class of endowed institutes. The others were to be developed more or less on a self-promoting or self-financing basis with some capital contributions. It was already obvious that the key to their success would lie in vigorous promotion.

This was one reason why Vagtborg and Hobson had a close affinity for each other; both were strong "builders" at heart. Of the two, however, Hobson had the greatest courage in forging ahead even with scant resources in sight.

It was already clear that he wanted SRI to be out in front in all respects. He was greatly attracted to what Vagtborg called "the art of selling research."

In any event, the nine independents were entering what Vagtborg would later call a period of "stabilizing, looking ahead, diversifying and maturing." This is an apt phrase in a backward glance, even if not fully evident in mid-1948. Certainly, SRI was in the midst of an upward movement even though its base was small.

Although Mellon and Battelle had their own traditions, the other non-profits were launching their operations along lines that were being called "The Armour Plan for Industrial Research" featuring contract work for business, industry and government with no endowments (or the equivalent) of consequence. It was a right move at the right time. SRI both helped push the initiative along and greatly benefited from its rising acceptance in the market place.

From the very beginning, Mellon had a special mission in life somewhat different from the other institutes that were to follow. It featured both basic and applied research and a system of industrial fellowships. The concept of industrial research under contract was not initiated until 1927. Mellon later was affiliated with the University of Pittsburgh and then was moved into Carnegie-Mellon University when the two institutions merged in 1967.

During the early 1950s, a movement was afoot at SRI's initiative to merge or affiliate with Mellon, but for various reasons nothing came of the idea. It was part of a rising Institute attempt to become more fully involved in basic research along with its applied pursuits.

In most respects, Battelle and Armour were the real forerunners of SRI in concept. They were really quite young as the group assembled informally in Chicago in mid-1948.

THE CHAIRMAN'S HOME — STANFORD
Late Afternoon Talks on SRI

MT. LEE — HOLLYWOOD
SRI Antenna Laboratory

rcolors by Helen Gibson

MEMORIAL HALL — STANFORD
Meetings for a Growing SRI Staff

A VILLAGE BUILDING
From Student Housing to SRI Use

- Although carrying out work under contract for American companies, Battelle's first government contract (on armor-plate) was not started until 1939. It was for the U.S. Army (at cost) and ushered in later strong programs in metallurgy at the Ohio institute.

- The first noteworthy project at ARF was started in 1939 on development of a snow cruiser for Admiral Byrd's expeditions to the Antarctic. Poulter, later to join SRI, was in charge.

- The first public disclosure of Battelle's soon-to-be famous Xerox process was made on October 22, 1948, *after* the institute group met in Chicago and *while* SRI's first vigorous thrust was still in process. We heard from Williams of Battelle that ''something significant'' involving the Columbus institute would soon be announced at an Optical Society meeting in Detroit.

The so-called ''nine institutes'' are more symbolic than literal. First of all, many other institute-like groups connected with universities were created during the late 1940s, the 1950s, and thereafter. The key point is simply one of convenience, — a close relationship from 1948 onward among the nine. Also, the number became ten with advent of Triangle Research Institute in North Carolina in 1958.

In any event, SRI was not alone in ''taking off'' during the late 1940s and early 1950s. All were very small in 1948. ARF had only some 450 people and a revenue of $2 million. It had doubled in size during the war years. SRI was to reach the $2 million point in 1950.

Another way to look at the emergence of the ''nine'' as a group involves their volume. Mellon had revenues of about $600,000 in 1935, about the same as for SRI in 1948. Volume for Mellon, Battelle and Armour considered together was about $2 million in 1940.

Revenues for the nine rose to some $24 million by 1950. They moved up 2½ times to about $65 million by 1955 while SRI's revenues alone increased five times to some $10 million during the first half of the 1950s.

Size, of course, is only one measure of the rise of any organization or group of institutions. The really big event of 1948 was a collective move. At mid-year, an upward view on the institute concept was certainly in the offing.

Perhaps, this was an inevitable result when two such ardent ''promoters'' of the whole idea came together. We saw this happen and, in fact, added something to the optimistic view by outlining some thoughts about the new economics/management dimension arising within SRI.

Even before going to Chicago, Hobson was a strong proponent for this move. Vagtborg was at first ''lukewarm'' but soon became an enthusiastic advocate. In any event, we came away from the meeting with an even higher enthusiasm for SRI's future.

During the one day and evening discussions at ARF, there were various exchanges on the future. Although for Midwest and SRI some capital from an Associates-type plan would be needed ere too long, no one questioned the idea that the nonprofits could operate in the long run on a financially self-sufficient basis.

One topic at Chicago had an interesting twist and some later impact on SRI. Vagtborg was much interested in the international field. Upon hearing that we wanted to do something in this direction, he proposed that some sort of informal collective endeavor among the non-profits be set up, thus adding expertise in various fields beyond what one institute alone might be able to provide.

This was in fact done within a couple of years on a project in Cuba and again soon thereafter on a study of research organizations in Europe. However, as ARF, Southwest, Battelle and SRI grew in size and diversity of skills, the idea faded away. Meanwhile, we became more and more dedicated to international work and proceeded on our own as did the other institutes.

By far the most important outcome of the Chicago talks was the cementing of relationships. They were informal but nevertheless were effective from time to time during later years when consultation appeared desirable. One such occasion arose early in the 1950s concerning the tax status of contract research institutes. Another occurred later when SRI in particular was mounting an eventually-successful effort to obtain a fixed fee on government projects.

A keynote on the exchanges was later outlined by the author in a few words solely of personal interest:

> *"Unless something unforeseen happens, the institute movement will be successful. We have a marvelous opportunity to be a part of a growing surge. We need more and better programs and the same for people. Everything is and should be great fun — and important."*

Hobson had an additional idea. He was highly motivated to get SRI in a number 1 position among the institutes and not merely a late addition to the family. His competitive instinct was heightenend.

At the time, SRI stood a bit in awe of Mellon and Battelle and looked upon Vagtborg as a special friend and ally. The same view soon applied to Kimball, Midwest's chief executive. Quite understandably, Hobson thought of ARF's leaders as being his "pupils." Edward (Eddie) R. Weidlein at Mellon was certainly the "dean" or elder statesman.

Hugh Burnham, a fund-raising adviser, who was already giving some help to Midwest and who would soon be an SRI consultant, spoke about the "explosive growth" of applied research institutes. He and Vagtborg wrote along the same lines in 1976. A sort of "explosion" most certainly was involved. Their volumes rose rapidly; their contributions multiplied; their impacts spread; their dimensions expanded — at home and abroad.

Being endowed, the first two institutes, Mellon and Battelle, operated somewhat differently during the pre-World War II years, at least from what Battelle was to do after the war. They engaged in project research, but did not emphasize the contract approach with business and industry that was to become central to the independent institutes.

Battelle's main development began as World War II ended. As the first non-endowed institute, ARF moved at the same time from a highly government-oriented organization to the industrial scene based on the contract concept.

In the main, Battelle was diversifying from a metallurgy-based operation to one involving many disciplines and industrial fields. Under Vagtborg's leadership, ARF was featuring its own plan on research for industry. It included the key principles on which the contract institutes operate today.

The prime emphasis in both Battelle and ARF was on *promoting* industrial research in general and contract research in particular. Many years later, Vagtborg referred to Williams as a "scientific research salesman extraordinaire." The phrase certainly applied to Vagtborg himself.

In great measure, Hobson absorbed energy and enthusiasm from them during his ARF days prior to joining SRI. They also influenced McBean's thinking in many ways as SRI was being founded.

THE REGIONALS

More must be said about emergence of the four regional institutes during the early post-World War II period. Entirely aside from how each developed during the next four decades, the regionals had four things in common at their outset:

- Dedicated to further development of a geographical region.
- A strong proponent or founder in each case within the region's business community.
- Heavy emphasis on concepts of public service
- Self-financing beyond some early capital contributions.

Midwest came into being on June 17, 1944, based on a 1943 Continental Congress of business executives in the area who believed that some sort of research organization should be created to help stimulate its further industrialization.

These leaders were concerned that the area's population gain was less than one percent per year. Emigration was reducing its economic strength.

MRI's formation attracted nationwide attention. For example, both Manufacturers Record and Science Illustrated featured articles in 1946 on the new research institute. One of them went directly to the point: " ... Midwest fosters area development ... " in mid-America. Governors of all the states in the area were solidly behind the initiative.

The new Missouri institute soon came to President Truman's attention who twice — in 1946 and 1947 — strongly endorsed its endeavors.

The principal southern states also were beset at the end of World War II with emigration problems and their impacts on economic performance and prospects. Southern Research Institute arose from an even earlier initiative in Alabama that by August 1944 had been expanded to a regional basis. As in the case of MRI, the aim was to harness science for the region's economic betterment.

Southern's first home was indeed modest — a residence in Birmingham; its first expansion was into an adjacent carriage house. It had no benefit from the equivalent of a Stanford Village.

The story of SRI's founding in the autumn of 1946 has already been laid out in a 1980 book. The basic concern in the U.S. West was not emigration but quite the opposite. Its business leaders who cooperated with Stanford University on our formation wanted to stimulate further industrialization and thus accommodate the region's rapid population growth.

Southwest Research Institute's creation on September 4, 1947, arose largely from the energies and dedication of Tom Slick, a well-known name in the oil business. He was concerned about uneven economic progress in the Southwest.

In 1946 Texas had a per capital income of only some $970 compared with the national average of about $1,200. Although Texas was gaining people at a healthy rate, Oklahoma was experiencing great losses. As did his forerunners in the Midwest, South and West, Slick thought that more scientific research in the region could be helpful in creating jobs and income.

As time passed, the "regionals" took on new dimensions, geographic and otherwise. The point, however, is that during the 1948-1950 period they were championing area development as a key mission. Midwest and SRI were the most vocal in this respect. ☐

It might appear now that SRI simply began moving along the Battelle-ARF-MRI paths. This is true in one respect, the basic idea of contract research, but not in another. Battelle and ARF were still rather small; MRI had only a few people; SRI was tiny in staff and facilities. Contract research was an infant business and practically non-existent in economics and related fields.

Thus, if SRI was to prosper, both contract research *and* the Institute as a new entity had to be ''sold'' to prospective clients. Furthermore, there were all too few candidate companies in the West. Someone said at the time — ''new ground must be ploughed even while the fields are being prepared.''

In this setting, it is not surprising that the new director from ARF was so dedicated to promoting SRI. He had been doing just that at ARF; he was indeed in a hurry — as was McBean.

THE WORLD OUTSIDE

WHEN SRI OPENED ITS DOORS IN 1946 the American economy was just beginning its war-to-peace conversion. Industry was making some ambitious plans for the future.

Although there were plenty of problems, by and large the environment within which the independent institutes moved upward during the balance of the 1940s and into the 1950s was upbeat.

The nation's civilian population when World War II ended was about 140 million with a labor force of some 54 million. Unemployment was less than 2%.

With demobilization, the civilian population grew almost 9% in five years and by some 19% in a decade. The labor force rose about 16% in a mere five years; unemployment also moved up to around 5% but then began coming down.

In any event, things were looking up on the economic front. Industrial production rose 15% in five years and almost 50% in a decade. One result was a one-third rise in GNP by 1950 and almost a doubling within ten years in current prices.

But, alas, there was too much money for too few products and too much pent-up inflation following the war. Thus, real GNP stood steady through the last half of the 1940s. Nevertheless, higher prices did not dampen the buoyant mood. Even in real terms, the rate of business investment tripled by the end of the 1940s and by the mid-50s had almost quadrupled.

Inflation pressures were intense as the war ended. On August 18, 1945, President Truman issued his famous ''Hold the Line'' order on prices, but the American people (except labor) were in no mood for a controlled economy. They pressed hard on lifting price controls. Finally, Truman gave in; the Washington Times carried a story in October about the end of the New Deal concept.

There is much more to recount — strikes, housing, Truman's face-down with John L. Lewis (the labor leader), his attack on Wall Street and a ringing call to give the country back to the people. In due course, things were put in better shape. With occasional setbacks the economic curve moved upward for four straight years.

In early 1949 during a session in which SRI was involved, Truman said that ''great things are in prospect.'' However, he may have been reflecting to a great extent on his recent upset election!

Business was quite good in 1950. Profits set a new record and so did dividends. Confidence in the future was growing. Economic conversion was virtually complete. Companies were looking more and more to the future with new enthusiasm.

Early in the year, Life magazine called the 1950s a decade of opportunity and urged its readers to start planning for the greatest ten years of business in the nation's history.

Another national trend had an impact on SRI and the other institutes. Total R&D spending was less than $1 billion per year when World War II began; the rate was about $1.5 billion in 1945; it

A personal note from shortly after the 1948 meeting with Hobson, Vagtborg, Williams and others in Chicago portrays one aspect of the situation:

"There is not much to go on. But, first, we have to catch up and go from there. Wonder how long it will take?"

Almost four decades have since gone by. Thus, some rewording seems in order:

- Our forerunners gave us a lot to go on; the independents have prospered.
- The real "catch up" is with challenges and opportunities.
- We (SRI) have gone from "there" and now go from "here."
- Wonder how long it will take; to do what?
- SRI has plans for its future.

had tripled by the end of the decade and doubled again by 1955.

Of greater significance is that by 1950 industry was appropriating more than a third of the nation's R&D money while some two-thirds of the grand total was being spent within business. More than $300 million, a threefold increase in five years, was being spent in universities and other research organizations. Thus, the R&D trends were upward and would remain so.

Several events on the global scene during the late 1940s and early 1950s would soon affect the institutes and in particular SRI. The Marshall Plan and European Community movements were launched as was Japan's economic recovery. SRI was already making some moves in these directions.

Then, finally, the outbreak of the Korean War in mid-1950 would soon accelerate the American economy and R&D spending in particular.

On the global scene, trade and investment was to increase rapidly for many years to come within the Bretton Woods system of fixed exchange rates.

MID-1980s*

Overall, non-profit research institutes as defined by the National Science Foundation receive about $785 million annually from the fed-

* Testimony in 1985 by Dr. William F. Miller, president and CEO, SRI International, before the U.S. House Subcommittee on Science, Research and Technology.

A NATIONAL EVENT
L to R: Donald J. Russell — SRI Founding Director in his S.P. capacity — Army temporarily takes over railroads on May 10, 1948.

eral government for research and development. The roughly one-third of (their) R&D devoted to basic research is 8% of the national total.

Their impact over the years has far outweighed their size. In the years ahead, (they) will continue to cover the technological spectrum from laboratory to market place.

Approximately 20% of SRI's work is in basic research ... another 10% is commercialization where we help in the final stages of product development. The other 70% is applications research.

CLYDE WILLIAMS
Battelle

HAROLD VAGTBORG
Southwest

TWO LEADERS AMONG THE INSTITUTES
– The 1950s –

COLUMNS APLENTY
New Mellon Home – 1937

The Nick of Time

The banks think SRI is important; they will help us out.

— CHARLES R. BLYTH - 1948

THE SECOND STAGE IN SRI's EMERGENCE as a dynamic research institute got under way in the spring of 1948 with a vigorous thrust at Jesse Hobson's initiative. Events moved quickly and successfully — perhaps too much so. By early autumn it was obvious that a new plan was needed; we were running out of resources and our future was threatened. Something had to be done; there was no time to lose.

The work began at a September management meeting in Aptos, California. Along with Hobson, several of us worked feverishly on a possible solution. One result was a paper dealing not so much with a severe problem but with another expansion program. We thought this might be necessary even when the first plan was being launched.

Several reasons were given for a spectacular jump in staff and revenue. The first and most important was industry's long unanswered ''need'' for a western research facility. But this did not just happen; it had been promoted. So, the report said the obvious — more staff was needed because projects had resulted in more work than had been expected.

A vigorous campaign had indeed been carried out, especially among industrial prospects, to increase volume. Expansion was the keynote — projects first and then staff plus equipment.

Our message to the directors was quite simple, the problem was success with demand running ahead of capacity. Thus, the solution was to build up capabilities. Nothing was said about spending having been far above the first development budget. In other words, SRI was a victim and not a cause of the problem!

Since early spring the staff had grown twofold to about 125 with 70 full time. Revenue had more than doubled to $600,000 per year. During the last three months alone, it rose some 10%. The race was on; the pace was quickening.

Meanwhile, the government portion of our work had dropped from about 30% to around 20%. This was a good trend at the time and the decline had occurred while other research institutes had ''succumbed to the demands of the Federal government.'' This was the first time serious attention had been given to the government/commercial ratio, but it certainly was not to be the last. Our directors were not enthusiastic about government work with its cost-recovery limitations.

The new plan, prepared under Hobson's watchful eye, then came to the main point: '' … the earlier estimate of a million-dollar research volume by 1950 had been far too conservative.'' (This rate was already in sight.) The stabilization point (or optimum size) was said to be far above the million dollar mark.

Questions about our size were to come up many times during the next ten years. As revenues continued to expand through new targets ($3, $5, $10 million, and so on), some of the directors would recall a board decision, or a "plan" not to exceed a certain size. The million dollar figure from the spring of 1948 was often mentioned.

Long after he had left SRI, Hobson recalled this situation in a rather light tone. Mentioning that during the first two or three years he was often asked how large an organization was anticipated, he wrote:

> *I first told the Board about one million dollars annual volume and about*
> *100 people. That figure was later revised to about five million dollars and*
> *500 people. Later on we sailed right through that level of activity, and on*
> *several occasions I was kidded by the Board about my estimates."*

Some of the questions on size were far more serious than Hobson thought at the time and certainly more so than he later admitted. The Stanford Trustees were greatly worried about our rapid growth and deficits, and no one at SRI, including Hobson, looked lightly upon the quick move upward during 1948.

However, he became convinced — and sold others on the idea — that we could not operate properly with only a few million dollars of revenue. We often spoke about reaching the "critical mass."

Hobson was right in this respect, and, in addition, he had a burning desire to make SRI the best *and biggest* institute of its kind. It was part of his character to push ahead energetically even though this called for frequent and sometimes major raising-of-sights.

In a new plan presented to the directors in November 1948, Hobson tried to explain why the $1 million size was too confining. "To be restrained by that goal, it would have been necessary to reject the requests of a large number of industrial sponsors." At the time, no one — not even the Stanford Trustees — wanted to see us reject requests whether they had been promoted or not. So, the plan went on to say: "Had this course been followed, the Institute would have been building staff and facilities for only a small part of the available research volume ..."

The feeling in some quarters was that slower growth and less promotion would have already permitted self-supporting operations, but Hobson thought a longer-range view was imperative and that the market could — and should — be developed energetically and quickly.

THE DIRECTOR
Maybe we should issue
some common stock!

THOMAS H. MORRIN
Engineering begins
September 1, 1948

This line of reasoning was to be repeated many times by Hobson and others to the directors. Some wondered if it would ever have been necessary to reject projects if we had not been vigorously promoting them. This was indeed the case; a sort of "chicken and egg" situation was involved.

The late 1948 plan made it clear that SRI had been building staff and facilities for larger volumes of business. This, then, called for more investment in growth and laid the basis for a new two-point prediction. Self-supporting operations would be at "an intermediate point between a million dollar volume and January 1950." This sounded like apples and oranges!! Nevertheless, no one questioned it aloud.

The plan then got more specific and well it should have. An accompanying chart predicted $3 million in revenue by 1950 with a 9% earnings rate by year end. In retrospect, this was most unrealistic. More to the point, however, the plan called for break-even by July 1949, only some eight months away. This, too, proved to be unrealistic; it did not happen until the autumn and then was followed by deficits for another nine months.

Although the second plan included an array of supporting data, the prediction was made largely on faith and a feel of the situation. The growth line showed a smooth pattern laid out with the aid of a French Curve. Thus, it was really a target and not a forecast. Anyhow, the Institute was supposed to reach an annual revenue rate of about $2.5 million by mid-1949. The actual figure turned out to be about $1.6 million with a loss rate of some $265,000.

The base from which all this was to develop was hardly a comfortable one. The situation at the end of October 1948 was a red-ink net worth of $108,000 (after capital contributions of $63,000), a $369,000 investment by Stanford and a $1,300 cash balance. Obligations against the special April development budget stood at $276,000, far closer to the $325,000 requested than to the $100,000 approved. We had "jumped off" on a quick start in spending and expansion.

Results on the income-expense sheets were clear for all to see — a deficit running at some $180,000 per year — but improving. Even so, we were not high in Dunn and Bradstreet's eyes.

Meanwhile, earlier critical shortages of equipment had mounted. The per-capita investment was only some $690. This was nothing, even by standards of the late 1940s or earlier. It was our number one problem.

Another note on finances in the new plan involved some tortuous reasoning. The point was made that all but $83,000 of the Stanford debt was covered by assets on hand and that the deficit was "within the $100,000 approved in April" for vigorous development of the Institute.

This is equivalent to saying that upon liquidation Stanford could recover the working capital advances if the directors raised another $83,000. This might have been hard to do for a liquidated institute. Within this framework, the second plan turned to people and pro-

RALPH A. KRAUSE
Operations

grams. Krause was the principal author, but all the senior staff were involved. There were 180 people at SRI, but the curve pointed upwards. ''We can … expect … 200 by January 1, 1949, and 250 by July 1, and at least 300 by the end of the year.'' These estimates also were too optimistic; the actual number at the end of 1949 was less than 250.

In the autumn of 1948 SRI had a tiny electronics laboratory, some chemical research facilities, and a very small economics group. A soils laboratory was in the offing. There was no equipment for physics or applied mechanics — only some plans. We were seeking additional chemical and animal laboratories and some electronic facilities. The principal bottlenecks were in these categories. We thought a land subsidence project in Southern California would soon require a soils laboratory.

Planning for a program in electronics had only recently been started. The first move was to create an electron tube laboratory. A situation had arisen at Harvard's electronics laboratory that suggested quick action on our part. It was brought up by Fred Terman and his associates at Stanford's Engineering School.

A new three-year limitation on non-tenure appointments at Harvard meant that some highly-qualified people on government projects were becoming available. The Navy was interested in transferring some of this work to the Institute.

Thus was born what later became a large and significant electronics program at SRI. Several key people at Harvard did in fact move to Menlo Park which simply added to the facility problem. Krause summarized the situation succinctly: ''Personnel and support are assured. We must obtain facilities. The project potential in engineering is a minimum of $250,000 per year and could run to $500,000 by the end of the year with double this amount available if and when we are able to handle it.'' These were big numbers at the time.

Facility and equipment problems existed all over the Institute. Every program, so it seemed, was severely limited. We were soon to be embarrassed by lack of drafting, engineering, mechanical and soil laboratory facilities. Severe shortages also existed in hydraulic and materials laboratories and for geo-physical equipment.

A shopping list — part of a proposed buildup in the Institute's equipment — went on and on including facilities in such diverse areas as sugar, cancer, industrial hygiene, air and water pollution, radiation, medical electronics and mechanics, agriculture and food processing. Krause said that the Institute needed about four times its existing chemical laboratory to handle present and expected business.

The whole idea behind this line of argument was to show that SRI was already ''equipment limited'' and not ''demand restricted'' Again, the specter of rejecting projects was raised. '' … We have sufficient assurance to project a rate of business up to at least $3 million by the end of 1949 if we are equipped to do this amount of work.''

The late 1948 plan went on to say that SRI would have to ''call a halt immediately to the expansion program'' if facilities could not be provided for a $2 — $3 million volume by the end of 1949. A case was being built for more money to finance more growth in diverse directions and to support more and more promotion.

The track was a fast one and it ran in a tight circle. Hobson and others knew how difficult everything would be, but no one was fully prepared for the coming crunch.

Our second plan ended with a quotation attributed to a prominent West Coast industrialist whose identify now is unknown. Commenting on the swift pace of events at SRI, he said it was moving "the technical center of gravity a good step westward." Whoever he was, his words were certainly too expansive, but they did express a latent enthusiasm about SRI shared by many business executives, especially in the West.

All was in readiness by mid-autumn for policy discussion on the new proposal. Although no specific amounts of money were requested, the whole exercise immediately ran into trouble. The Stanford Trustees were unwilling to advance more working capital. The directors had a difficult problem. The Institute was fast approaching a cash crisis and its most critical period of the formative years.

A wave of doom quickly spread among the staff. Severe cutbacks were made on such things as travel, people, promotion and other expenses. Rumors persisted that Stanford was planning to liquidate the Institute. These stories were by no means confined to the staff. Word came in from the outside that SRI was in deep trouble and might be closed.

The year ended with a deficit of about $160,000 — four times that for 1947. After taking capital contributions into account, the negative net worth of $127,000 was more than forty times greater than one year earlier. Stanford's working capital advances had grown to $542,000. Revenue had reached an annual rate of $1.2 million; the deficit rate was some $200,000 per year.

We were working at the time for the Western Oil and Gas Association (WOG), on a study of the smog situation in Los Angeles . William Stewart, a Union Oil Company executive and one of our directors, was on the WOG board. Being concerned about our financial situation and ability to continue the smog project, Stewart suggested a $125,000 loan by the Association. There was a key condition; an additional $375,000 would have to be obtained from other sources.

Hobson liked this idea because it meant that a long-delayed fund-raising effort would have to be started. In fact, he had planted the idea in Stewart's mind. I saw this happen during a luncheon at the California Club in Los Angeles.

Meanwhile, McBean was saying forcefully to one and all that Stanford should continue providing working capital. One of the directors had agreed to follow up on possible contributions. Even so, bank loans seemed to be the only way to get funds in a hurry. The big question was whether or not any bank would loan money to a red ink, non-profit corporation. But, McBean thought something could be worked out.

In an environment of deepening concern the directors met in mid-December 1948. Hobson said that SRI was within a liquidation net loss of $100,000 but that immediate action was needed on new financing. He wanted to raise about $1 million to repay Stanford, provide more working capital, purchase equipment, and offset losses for at least six months.

CARSTEN STEFFENS
Sciences

Our problem, of course, was growth without an adequate financial base. The controversy — and there certainly was one — centered on the perils of success and on promotion. Forging ahead along an expansion path was already a familiar theme and would become even more so during the next seven years of Hobson's tenure. Here is what our new plan had to say:

A LATE 1948 PERSPECTIVE

"Our growth has been quite rapid due to demands for our services by western industry and due also to an effective program of promotion and publicity ...

"All phases of the development program have moved rapidly ... along the plan presented in April.

"The potential opportunities are indeed great. SRI can become a major institution among industrial research organizations ...

"Adequate planning and support for the next phase of ... development are urgently needed to provide ... facilities ... and to carry the Institute to the point where it can be self-supporting ...

"We are reaching the limit of funds advanced by Stanford University ... other support must be found if our progress is to continue..."

In this setting, one apparently had to be in favor of more growth or an advocate of holding back success. The Stanford Trustees wanted a solution. The directors were between a "rock and a hard place."

Hobson had a solution and his associates were solidly behind him. There was no real alternative — or so it seemed. The goal was to arrange an immediate $500,000 loan from Stanford plus a $125,000 loan from the WOG and launch a vigorous fund-raising program.

McBean wanted Stanford to do even more — a $1 million loan. Stewart was still saying that a WOG loan must come after some other financing. McBean thought at least $100,000 in contributions could be obtained within a few weeks. Unfortunately, there were no weeks to spare.

The directors were certainly not unanimous on a "forge ahead" policy. Some thought the expansion had been too rapid and that a break-even point should have been reached earlier. Nevertheless, they were reluctant to urge a negative policy.

Hobson argued forcefully that with more capital SRI could be operating on a balanced budget by mid-1949. But, even so, he was perturbed about loss of morale and efficiency during a time of great uncertainty on the future of the Institute. All of us were, in fact, very worried.

Hobson's idea on contributions — worked out with Eurich at Stanford — was quite specific for the short run. An Associates Plan would be created with three-year pledges from various companies for $5, $10 or $15,000 per year depending on their sizes.

We thought the expansion program could be continued at least until April 1949 on the basis of two loans totalling $625,000, advance invoicing of $50-$75,000 on a few research projects, and some contributions. In any event, it was clear that time was running out on working capital.

Although the next three months were critical, Hobson was also thinking about longer-term financing. "Ultimately, we will need contributions of $3 million to assure continued development, to provide financial security, and to provide for future permanent buildings." He thought a group of 100 Associate companies could easily give this amount. As events subsequently developed, about 150 companies did donate the first $3 million of capital.

Even though our situation was precarious, the directors did not approve a fund-raising program. They wanted a "break-even" first. But they did OK the idea of the WOG loan and a request to Stanford for $1 million. They did the latter with little hope the money would be forthcoming.

This was the last board meeting attended by Alvin Eurich who, as Stanford's acting president since Tresidder's death in early 1948, was also our chairman. Eurich had resigned to accept the presidency of New York State University. He had worked long and hard for the Institute since late 1945.

REPORTING ON THE PAST YEAR'S ACTIVITIES

There is no question that SRI today owes a debt of gratitude to Eurich. Hobson often gave voice to all he had done and some thirteen years later wrote: " ... one man really made possible the development of Stanford Research Institute, and that man was Dr. Alvin C. Eurich."

Hobson always felt that Eurich gave him great support and confidence in the face of "strong skepticism, doubt and, even, right-out antagonism." Eurich was especially helpful in relations with the Stanford Trustees. Hobson was to recall later: "There were two months in the Fall of 1948 when I did not know until the last day of the month whether or not we could meet our payroll.'' But he did know there was talk about closing the Institute, taking a loss of $400–500,000 and forgetting the whole affair. He was referring in the main to the Stanford Trustees and not to the Institute's directors — and certainly not to Eurich.

A plaudit by Hobson and his associates about Eurich was laid out more formally in the Institute's annual report for 1948. ''Special appreciation must be given for his assistance in encouraging development of the Institute.'' Thus, the ''architect'' had become one of the ''saviors.''

Our financial problem in late 1948 was made no less unpleasant by the Holiday Season, nor was it helped when Hobson had to enter the hospital early in the New Year. While there, he asked Brunetti to summarize majority views of the management group on the immediate financial outlook. The results were taken to Hobson in the Hahnemann Hospital in San Francisco. They called for a major retrenchment aimed at a quick break-even.

Even though plagued by illness (osteomyelitis) and having no real solution for our financial problem, Hobson reacted violently against this plan. He felt — and he was right — that such a negative move probably would spell the end of the Institute. In any event, he would have nothing to do with the idea, and in writing was highly critical of its authors. (The paper went into his safety deposit box.)

Hobson later wrote about ''the major crisis we faced in a room at the hospital.'' Then he went on to recall: '' … With the help of Charles Blyth and one or two others we completely reversed that philosophy and sailed ahead full steam.'' He always felt that his hospital stay came at ''a most critical period'' in our development. This certainly was the case.

By late January 1949 the problem had reached its peak. Something had to be done within a few days. Fortunately, a solution was near at hand. Blyth (a director and Stanford Trustee) had been working with the American Trust Company on a loan to be shared by six San Francisco banks. The directors met late in the month to hear his report. Louis Lundborg, Stanford's vice president for development, was in the chair. He and Hobson had already agreed we had to have new capital right away:

NEEDS

$	500,000	Repay Stanford
	100,000	Six-month loss in the offing
	170,000	Accounts Payable
	155,000	Equipment
	200,000	Working capital
$1,125,000		TOTAL

But where was all this money to come from? The WOG had agreed to loan $125,000 at 4% interest with repayment over an 18-month period beginning July 1, 1949. More importantly, Blyth and McBean had a tentative agreement from the banks for a $600,000 line of credit. Repayment was to be over a four-year period beginning 27 months later. Still further, the Stanford Trustees (at Blyth's urging) had agreed to convert $500,000 of the working capital advances into a loan at 4% interest. All this added up to the magic $1,225,000.

There were some conditions, however. We were expected to hold the Stanford loan to $500,000 and self-finance at least until mid-1949. Everyone hoped that not all the bank credit line would be used and that some of the withdrawals would not take place until after repayments had been started on the WOG loan.

An action then took place within the board — at Donald Russell's urging — that ended for the time being what later was known within SRI as ''the crisis of '49.'' The directors approved the scheme but stuck with a $1,125,000 maximum.

THE WRINGER

Atholl McBean thought that getting the banks involved with SRI was the key action. He was fond of saying: ''We will need money in time; keep their hands in the wringer so they can't let go. Earn a surplus and they won't even try to go away.''

This crucial step was taken only about eleven months after Hobson had taken over as executive director. He was obviously relieved. But, he was even more relieved and pleased when his appointment was extended for another year. Everything happened ''in the nick of time,'' so he said.

In due course, the Institute paid off WOG and drew the full line of bank credit. For policy reasons and as a symbol of the SRI-Stanford affiliation, the University loan was left intact for the long pull. Later liquidation of the bank loan ahead of schedule was a key step in the Institute's history. It removed any questions that may have remained about our financial strength.

ECONOMICS/MANAGEMENT/INTERNATIONAL
L to R: Weldon B. ''Hoot'' Gibson, Dexaix B. Myers and Paul J. Lovewell.

Although it is easy to look back to late 1948 and early 1949 with some amusement and nostalgia, there were no smiles at the time. The young institute was in deep trouble. It is understandable that Stanford did not want to make additional advances. Its investment was far beyond what the Trustees had expected at the outset. Whether right or wrong, they thought the time had come to take a firm stand.

Two or three of the directors — McBean among them — felt strongly that the Trustees should not take such a rigid position, but they did not take fully into account the limited funds available to Stanford (aside from the endowment) during the late 1940s. Furthermore, they were impatient with a general Trustee attitude that creating SRI had been a mistake.

In any event, the situation rose to fever pitch. Along with Hobson, Krause, Herbert and Brunetti (within SRI), I was heavily involved in the planning. The amount of money may not seem great in today's terms, but it was a large sum at the time.

Every day counted very much indeed. It was a tight squeeze, and we were buffeted from all sides — handling research projects, helping on a solution via further expansion, absorbing complaints on cutbacks, keeping McBean happy, and watching the cash flow hour by hour. It was good practice for problems yet to come.

The Institute and its senior people did their part at the time. We willingly agreed to have our pay deferred. There was no alternative; we could not meet the payroll. Fortunately, everything was put right in due course.

We must not let 1948 go by without seconding Hobson's tribute to Eurich. He fully deserves all credit given to him and more. There were days when Eurich must have wondered what he had wrought as an architect of the Institute. But, he stayed with the whole idea in fine fashion. He has not been forgotten; an SRI event in his honor was held on October 29, 1982.

I do not fault those who felt in 1948 that SRI was being expanded too rapidly, too soon and too much. I did not question growth decisions at the time and helped expand the operation. But the questioning view was and still is wholly understandable. Even so, once growth was started there was no viable alternative but to follow through.

Along with others, I have often wondered what SRI might have been in later years if the momentum had been lost in 1949. The impact would have been severe and it might have been fatal. Our supporting base was too small.

CLEDO BRUNETTI
Early Associate Director

The planning of late 1948 was certainly dominated by money and expansion. Financing had not been thought out prior to SRI's formation. No one had foreseen that it would grow so rapidly during the early days. The Hobson push was a success; it also was a problem.

EXCHANGES AT LUNCHEON – PACIFIC-UNION CLUB
San Francisco

Even in this setting, research programs were being developed. They fell into three groupings — engineering, physical & life sciences, and the social sciences (economics and management). This story appears elsewhere.

During the traumatic days in early 1949, word reached the Stanford faculty that SRI was ''getting more money'' from the University. Terman, a faculty leader, was very unhappy about such an idea, but in time he changed his mind and said: ''The loan was a good investment.''

Two brief exchanges at the Pacific Union Club in San Francisco on December 19, 1948, more or less opened the way to a solution for the money crunch. I happened to be present. McBean told Blyth (Stanford's Treasurer) that if the University made some move to help SRI further, he would ''guarantee'' the amount. Blyth then told a banker who was present that, in effect, Stanford's credit stood back of any bank loans to SRI.

The three agreed that nothing was to be said formally or put in writing; implications alone were to be sufficient. Apparently, they were. Everything moved quickly to a solution.

Although Blyth once used the words ''bail out'' in a light vein in referring to a bank loan, his reference to motivations was not in humor. Top executives of California's largest banks had indeed come to feel that SRI was important and that it should be preserved.

Some three decades later, the U.S. Government apparently felt the same way, in principle, about Lockheed, Chrysler and the Continental Illinois Bank. But, in our case, no government loan was involved. Behind the scenes, Stanford was, in effect, the ''guarantor.''

The ''bail out'' was certainly successful. Our Take-Off Days were given a great boost. A right move was made at exactly the right time. ∎

SPECIAL SERVICE
Thirty-five Years or More*

— The First Twenty as of December 31, 1985 —

Mary F. Armstrong	Richard C. King
Milton B. Adams	Roy A. Long
Betty P. Bain	Chester W. Marynowski
Lucien G. Clarke	Stephen W. Miller
Weldon B. Gibson	Arnold Mitchell
P. Roger Gillette	V. Lorraine Pratt
Jane Goelet	Shirley B. Radding
Nevin Hiester	Vincent Salmon
Raymond Irvine	Konrad T. Semrau
Fred J. Kamphoefner	Oliver W. Whitby

———
* Alphabetical order

SENIOR OFFICER

As president of Stanford University, Dr. J.E. Wallace Sterling served as SRI's chairman for 17 years from 1949 to 1966.

THE CHAIRMAN'S WORDS

Dr. Gibson's book about SRI during a time while I was chairman reflects the facts as I know them. He kindly asked me to read the chapter drafts as they came along. I am grateful for the opportunity this gave me to re-live some early days of what has become a magnificent institute.

— J. E. Wallace Sterling - 1983

Broadening the Base

Selectivity in growth must be the keynote.

— J. E. WALLACE STERLING - 1949

ONCE A TEMPORARY SOLUTION HAD BEEN WORKED OUT for our financial crisis in early 1949, the directors began to worry about the next six months or so. They finally decided to invest another $300,000 in the operation. This was to be our third plan. The main idea was to become self-supporting.

There was obvious concern at board level that somehow even more than the approved new money might be spent or committed thus re-creating the problems of late 1948. This was heightened by rumors coming from within SRI about a new expansion, more deficits, broadening the base and building the organization to a new level.

Although an Associates Plan for capital contributions had been formally launched, the directors said on several occasions that this unknown amount of money must not be committed before it was "in the till," so to speak. No one wanted to see the Institute stand still while concentrating on how to break even; nevertheless, restraint was a keynote among the directors.

Some were afraid that too much reliance might be placed on McBean's repeated assurances that gift money would soon be forthcoming from western companies. He kept saying this could be done in "90 days" or so.

Respect for Hobson was high, but everyone knew about his boundless enthusiasm and energy along with the staff's dedication to pushing ahead.

In this setting, Sterling felt a heavy load in taking up the reins of chairmanship on April 1, 1949. He had more than a full-time job in starting his presidency at Stanford but knew that as our chairman he was expected to keep a watchful eye on SRI. He was in the middle in many respects. The Trustees were worried; the directors had concerns; SRI needed the chairman's attention. But, even with the problems at hand, Sterling did not want to dampen the spirit of the place; dealing with McBean took time; but, of course, he had a special responsibility to SRI.

Thirty-five years later Sterling recalled his entry on the scene as Stanford's president and SRI chairman:

> *Why no Stanford Trustee ever mentioned the SRI responsibility before I took office (at Stanford) I shall never know ... I did discover it the hard way ...*
>
> *I spent more time on SRI that summer of 1949 than I did on Stanford, but at least we began to get matters turned in the right direction. And how it has matured and blossomed since then.*

The trend was certainly upward; but the problems were evident. Holding back would have been an easy decision, but Sterling did not want to throw a "wet blanket" so soon, if at all, over the Institute's first real momentum.

The directors were saying, "Let Wally handle the situation." However, he had a problem with a short fuse and little time to do anything about it. But, it was obvious that the status quo was not a solution. Fortunately, he took a long-term view.

Sterling knew full well that finance was a means to an end and not the end itself and that the real need in the long run was to develop strong research programs. These, in turn, would help solve the money situation. But Sterling and others were well aware that everything could not be done at once. So it was in mid-summer that the chairman gave voice to — "Selectivity in growth." The message came during an informal exchange following a board meeting in San Francisco.

This idea was equivalent to saying — "Growth seems inevitable" — and then asking — "But where and how?" Several times he was to say that expansion was needed, but there had to be a way to move along more conservatively. He had no short-term solutions. Even so, our new chairman realized that it was his duty to help set some course for the future.

He already knew Hobson was impulsive. Perhaps, he recognized that he, also, was "action oriented" in such situations. It was already obvious to him that Stanford needed a spurt of "expansion" of some sort or at least an upsurge in several areas. However, he was hearing from many quarters that our problem was too much growth too quickly. He felt that "buying a little time" was the right course.

GAME PLAN

Shortly after arriving at Stanford but before taking up reins as SRI's chairman, a reception was held in Sterling's honor.

An SRI guest asked the new chairman about a "Game Plan." His response was definitive if not reassuring. "I do not know the players except one (the author), have no playbook and do not know the quarter of the game."

Both men had a football background. They both realized that some points had to be "put on the board" very soon indeed.

One step taken during 1949 relieved the pressures on Sterling to a considerable extent. An arrangement was made with John Forbes, a business consultant and head of an accounting firm in San Francisco, to be a financial adviser to SRI and the directors. The Trustees liked this idea as did all the directors — and Hobson as well.

Forbes was well known in the business community as being highly conservative. Furthermore, his long friendship with McBean was a key asset. He served SRI and the directors very well indeed for several years and did so quietly, always in the background. It soon became standard practice to "talk things over with Forbes" on finances. His nod at a board meeting was the equivalent of saying "Yes" on any proposal at hand; his head being still meant "I say No."

JOHN F. FORBES
Stablizer

An overall plan was worked out during 1949 on the scope of five research departments. Chemistry and chemical engineering ranged across physical, analytical and organic chemistry, metals and minerals, experimental biology and chemical engineering. The electrical engineering group was devoted almost entirely to electronic circuitry, instrumentation, computers, communications, television, radiation systems and antennas, vacuum tubes, solid state physics, miniaturization, equipment engineering and related fields.

Geophysics and geology groups were concerned with petroleum engineering, primary and secondary oil recovery, soil mechanics, land subsidence, field geology, explosive materials and shock wave propagation. The applied physics department was directing its efforts to sonics, optics, nucleonics and microtime techniques.

Business and industrial economics covered the fields of production, marketing, finance, transportation and industrial planning. The group was emphasizing techno-economic research in which both economic studies and laboratory investigations were involved in particular projects both domestic and international.

Sixty-nine research projects were started throughout SRI in 1949. Thirty-four more were continued from the previous year. Sixty-one of the new projects were sponsored by fifty companies and individuals. The remaining eight were for Uncle Sam. Government revenue was about 35% of the year's total effort. Several more corporations became new clients including, for example, Carnation, Albers Milling, Hewlett-Packard and American Chicle.

Thus, after three years of operations, SRI was moving ahead quite well in getting new projects and clients. Perhaps more significant, however, a budding self-sponsored research program was taking shape. Seven such projects were active at year-end including work on continuous ion exchange processes, fluidized carbonization of redwood sawdust, field clays and aqueous foams.

With considerable fanfare, a Precision Gage Laboratory was opened during the year. The facility with a value of more than a quarter of a million dollars was loaned to SRI by the U.S. Army. Even though little research was involved, it provided a capability for precise instrument calibration, adjustment and measurement. In actual practice, the Laboratory was not used to any significant extent and later was returned to the Army. It did, however, dramatize at the right time the Institute's growing facilities.

By far the most important facility development was the launching of new laboratories for electronics work. A beginning was made on a general electronics laboratory, one for electron tubes and another for aircraft radio systems. These and other electronics facilities grew rapidly during the next few years and eventually were used in programs making up about half of the Institute's revenues.

One interesting — and newsworthy — project at mid-year involved geophysics and geology. As part of a program sponsored by the American Geographical Society, Poulter and a team of geophysicists spent three months on the Taku Glacier in the Juneau Ice Fields

SRI ON THE ICE CAP

of Alaska. Their objective was to apply a variation of the Poulter Method of Seismic Exploration to depth measurements on glaciers.

They charted ice thicknesses ranging from 400 to well over 1,000 feet. This was the beginning of several Arctic projects to be undertaken by SRI during the next decade. The Institute became involved on the Taku Glacier largely as an outgrowth of Poulter's earlier experiences as a senior scientist on Admiral Byrd's famous Expeditions to the Antarctic.

In the spring of 1949, the Institute formally announced its interest in the international field. This is significant because it marked the beginning of a worldwide orientation that steadily grew in scope during the years to come. The first idea called for work at home. ''In general, research investigations in the international field will be carried out at SRI where facilities and personnel are readily available.''

Our thought was that work might be undertaken for foreign as well as domestic clients This was soon to be the case with governments but industrial projects were not to come until the mid-1950s.

The announcement went on, however, to cover work in foreign locations. ''Wherever desirable, Institute personnel and facilities will be provided abroad, or arrangements will be made to utilize research facilities and personnel within the area involved.'' This approach was easily applied in the ''soft sciences'' but, except for a few U.S. Government projects, never materialized in the ''hard sciences.''

The third part of the international statement dealt with clients. ''The Institute is prepared to conduct applied research projects for American companies with interests abroad, for all governments wishing to encourage industrial expansion, and for private companies abroad with specific technical and economic problems ...'' All this was clear enough; both governments and companies at home *and* elsewhere were to be in our orbit.

The genesis of this announcement came from President Truman's ''Point IV'' program for aid to underdeveloped countries. There was rising public interest in international activities of a development nature. Thus, the time seemed right for SRI to announce its intentions. The statement went far beyond what any of the founders had visualized, but in early 1949 no one ''blew the whistle'' on SRI serving both governments and companies outside the United States. A bridge was crossed.

Although the new policy encompassed all of our research programs, it was clear that the main thrust would be in economics. For this reason, leadership was placed in the economics group. Thus, I was involved from the beginning. It was not long before project opportunities arose in Cuba and Italy.

In looking back from the 1980s, our new international horizon of 1949 may seem to have been a routine move, particularly in light of limited interest by American companies. The aftermath of World War II was present everywhere. U.S. firms were still in the peacetime conversion process.

Opportunities with companies abroad were practically non-existent at the time. The so-called "dollar gap" was at its height in Europe, Japan and elsewhere. Furthermore, SRI was an unknown entity beyond American shores.

In this setting, the only real opportunities for the Institute appeared to be with the U.S. government under its economic assistance plans for Western Europe and then the Truman program for newly-developing countries.

Thus, our spring, 1949, announcement was more a long-term hope than a signal for short-term action. Even so, it was a key policy move. One perspective at the time is pertinent.

A New Horizon

Our policy move abroad promises to be a major milestone in SRI's future. We may not see it clearly for some time to come, but geography is no longer a policy constraint ...

Hopefully, the day will come ere too long when we can and will serve on a considerable scale the rising world interests of American companies and the needs of foreign firms in their countries and elsewhere ...

Our immediate goal is to develop skills, knowledge and familiarity on an international stage. We can do this through government contracts and thus be prepared for industrial opportunities in the 1950s, 1960s and beyond.

Enthusiasm for an SRI international dimension was by no means unanimous among our program leaders. Some felt our new "intent" was impractical and maybe inappropriate. A few were talking about some far-away day when half of the Institute's work of a business and commercial character might be "international."

Point V !

During a 1949 meeting with President Truman on an Air Force sponsored project, the Institute's international announcement came to his attention. His response was encouraging "Action is my fifth point; the world needs SRI. Push ahead, don't hesitate!"

Meanwhile, of course, the American West was at the center of our attention as McBean and other directors kept reminding us of the purpose behind our formation. Even so, with McBean's support and at Hobson's urging there was much talk about "the West and the nation being inseparable — so we must be national." Fortunately, Hobson was a great ally to some of us even during the Take-Off Days in "thinking internationally."

A FUTURE V.P.
Donald R. Scheuch
(Joined Engineering, 1949)

Some said all this was wishful thinking and it was, in many respects, at least in the short run. The important point, however, is that the seeds were planted for a ''move abroad.'' It began sooner than any of us imagined at the time. A golden ring came around and we grabbed it, so to speak. The opportunity involved Italy, but more about this later.

Physical growth during 1949 was significant, although far less spectacular than in 1948. The value of laboratory equipment in place increased about 15%; occupied space rose some 35%. Our staff grew only modestly, but its diversity multiplied.

The year-end staff had been assembled from 65 companies, 46 universities and 14 research organizations. The key professional staff included 20 electronic engineers, 11 chemical engineers, 8 organic chemists, 6 physical chemists, 5 geophysicists, 5 mathematicians, 8 physicists, 11 economists, 6 industrial engineers, 11 market analysts, 8 statisticians and 5 electrical engineers. This diversity was soon to grow further and be a distinctive feature of the Institute.

AIRCRAFT ANTENNA WORK — 1949

Eleven companies and one individual joined the new Associates Plan in 1949. The companies were Bechtel, Columbia Steel, Gladding McBean, Newhall Land and Farming (a McBean enterprise), Pacific Clay Products, Pacific Gas and Electric, Richfield Oil, Standard Oil of California, Union Oil, Universal Rundle and W. P. Fuller. The individual was Atholl McBean.

The first Associates Day program was held at SRI in November; twenty-two executives of the new companies were present. The program included visits around the Institute's facilities, presentations on several research programs and a speech by Maurice Holland. He was an industrial research consultant from New York and Hobson's close friend.

Holland tended to the dramatic in speaking about SRI. He was one of the founders of the Industrial Research Institute (IRI), an association of research directors in American industry. Also, he had been retained by Hobson as an adviser and thus visited SRI from time to time. He liked to coin phrases and always spoke rapidly and at length.

He began his Associates Day remarks by emphasizing the value of industrial research. He likened it to insurance. His concept was that a company should spend for research as a form of technological protection. He credited "Boss" Kettering of General Motors fame with having originated the idea.

Holland went on to say that "research is a paying investment" and that more and more companies were establishing both internal and external research programs. Then he turned to the West — and to SRI in particular: "It took the march of progress of World War II to thoroughly establish the Pacific Coast as an industrial empire in the making. The resources are here. Industry support is evident at this meeting, and (by) ... projects ... at the Institute."

Holland said on this occasion, as he had before, that SRI obviously met a need and that the timing of its formation was "pretty nearly perfect." Then he turned to his often-repeated view about our development in so short a period being a remarkable series of events.

He thought our growth in only three years was "phenomenal" and called it "the most impressive single performance in industrial research during the last twenty-five years." He also referred to the staff as the most able group of people in "any similar institution in the United States." This sort of accolade was not new for Holland. He often used such words as distinguished, brilliant, young and aggressive in referring to SRI people. His enthusiasm for the Institute and its leaders was unbounded, and he often went way overboard on compliments as he did at the first Associates Day.

Holland took the occasion to champion an idea from the IRI. It was trying to convince the U.S. Treasury that capital spending for the "tools of research" should be directly deductible from federal income taxes. The association argued that this would lead to new industries, jobs and, eventually, higher dividends by American companies.

Needless to say, this concept was not fully embraced at the time by the IRS. Buildings and equipment had to be depreciated over long periods of time and not charged off like materials and services. The investment tax credit was yet to come.

One internally-sponsored project started in late 1949 on R&D management took a strange turn and created a severe problem within SRI. It was called a "Research Environment Study" but soon became a highly-negative influence. Hobson believed with some justification that SRI could make a contribution to research management by using its own operations in studying such things as staff selection, personnel policies, organization, leadership, fringe benefits and personal relationships.

His plan included addition of a consulting psychologist and, among other things, a series of confidential discussions with the senior staff — one by one — on a "self-help" basis. Through a case-study approach, the objective was to develop "concretions, not abstractions" in a "research-on-research" program.

Although the goals were laudable, the psychologist soon became involved in all sorts of personnel problems. Some staff members strongly resisted both the project and the psychologist. One unpleasant event led to another. Hobson was under pressure to do something about the "head shrinker" and "couch specialist." He finally gave in and brought the whole affair to an end. It was a misguided exercise from the very beginning. As someone later said, "It could not have happened — but it did."

This experience did not prevent the Institute from making good strides during 1949 in strengthening its research programs even with the concerted drive to break even on finances. A mood of rising confidence and some satisfaction pervaded the place as the 1950 decade began. A public report summarized the situation — '' ... 1949 was a year of accomplishment, progress, and realization of objectives.''

It went on to say that new laboratories had been established, staffed and equipped while older laboratories were strengthened and expanded. The main point was a shift in emphasis ''from rapid, over-all growth to integration, selective expansion and increased productivity.'' Much of this was true, but the Institute was soon to grow apace on several occasions. In fact, some plans were already in the works.

This appraisal of our position was written shortly after the directors had approved a third financial plan. It involved more growth and diversification but less selectivity than Sterling had in mind. Three trends were to help the cause. The first was some belt-tightening within American business at the time. It seemed clear that more emphasis was being placed on ''cutting costs to preserve profit margins.'' Thus, Hobson said that SRI was devoting more and more attention to projects along these lines.

The second trend had to do with industrial economics. Our feeling was that business was becoming more interested in ''applied research and scientific fact-finding'' in marketing, finance, economic planning, sales, transportation, and related fields. We were indeed expanding our work in economics, but this was more the result of vigorous promotion than an independent rise of business interest. In fact, the market was still quite limited.

We were giving major emphasis at the time to what we called ''techno-economics.'' Hobson said over and over that such programs were unique in the history of industrial research and that they held great promise for the future. We were gearing up for much more work in the field.

Also, the year-end report pointed out that plans had been drawn up to expand the new electronics program. This ran headlong into the equipment problem, especially in connection with aircraft antenna projects and work on a color television system.

The third broad trend at the end of 1949 was increasing national concern about problems arising from the polluted atmosphere. Having announced a new air and water pollution laboratory, everyone at SRI felt that many more projects would arise in this field. Again, equipment needs were paramount.

Hobson's message then turned to the Institute's overall objectives in light of perceived movements in the market place. ''Such broad trends as these will guide the Institute in its policy of selective expansion.'' This was a bow to the chairman's call. But another function — self-sponsored research — was to receive more attention.

We were gaining new confidence on the basis that more work of this type could be supported from Associate funds. The plan was to develop new ideas and processes with commercial promise or public good. Hobson and others felt strongly that industry would then look more and more to SRI for assistance.

The words ''fact finding'' and ''public good'' were signals of two messages to appear often in SRI's thinking and publications. The ''fact finding'' idea applied particularly to economics, the thought being that the Institute's role was to assemble and analyze facts and stay away from recommendations. In time this approach was gradually dropped as being far too restrictive and oftentimes less than helpful to clients. The idea of ''public good'' was to

DONALD L. BENEDICT
Engineering — Physical Sciences
(Later European Office)

be emphasized more during the 1950s under the concept of public interest and public service.

The final words in Hobson's message at the end of 1949 reflected the mood of the Institute as we completed our first three years and entered the 1950s. They breathed confidence, promise and eagerness: "With the continued enthusiastic support of industry, the future is bright indeed, with every indication that we will continue to move toward fulfillment of the Institute's objectives for industry, for the West, for government and for the nation." We should have added "the world."

There was much talk at the time among the staff about expanding the base of our research operations. Ample justification for this feeling was evident all around even though the organization was not yet in the center circle of domestic let alone world affairs. This was to come in the 1950s.

Another personal note may be appropriate. I admit to having been more euphoric at the time than the circumstances supported. But, others were equally enthusiastic. Perhaps one reason we felt this way is that (more than in 1948) we were heavily involved in the decisions and action. For example, I went through a baptism of fire as chairman of the Finance Committee while at the same time having a free rein in moving the economics program to a new and stronger base. Furthermore, all of us were enthusiastic about the potential in the new electronics operation.

Still further, I felt that our announcement on international research was a great step forward. Perhaps, then, it is wholly understandable why I fully supported the new thrust we were generating. Hobson could not have given more encouragement to the economics and international programs that were central to my interests. From a distant view backwards, this may not seem to be anything out of the ordinary, but, in 1949 both fields were new areas for research institutes.

We were also launching something new for research institutes in the area of electronics. As an electrical engineer, Hobson was closer to home in this field, but he also knew that we had to do more in the physical and life sciences. The key point is that he was pushing on all these fronts.

Along with Herbert, I knew at first hand that some of the directors were concerned about Hobson's drive for expansion. In 1949 he was constantly urging all of us to do more on research programs; thus, we were more concerned with action than with growth policy. Amidst the enthusiasm of the time none of us around Hobson fully realized that we had only taken the first steps in expanding SRI in all sorts of directions. Even more traumatic and exciting times were soon to emerge.

As the chairman had said, "selectivity" was to be the keynote. In fact, we more or less "selected" what could be done quickly. He knew our choices in time and substance were severely limited. There was no "Monday morning" quarterbacking.

The year 1949 brought several people to SRI who were later to play key roles in our development. Appointments in the growing electronics program included Donald Benedict and John Granger. Additions in physical and life sciences included, among others, Edward Doll, Louis Koenig and L. M. Swift. To the economics group came Bonnar Brown, Paul Lovewell, William Platt, Robert Shreve, Robert Smith, Kenneth Beggs and Eugene Staley.

In November, the First National Air Pollution Symposium was sponsored by SRI in Pasadena in cooperation with Cal Tech, the University of Southern California and the University of California. This was the first of many national and international, public service, scientific meetings under SRI auspices. The aim was to feature presentations by authorities in air pollution, to exchange ideas and techniques in pollution research and, in general, to stimulate interest in the field. About 400 scientists, business executives and civic leaders from the United States and Canada were present. The Symposium did much to focus national attention on our smog research in Southern California.

Some twenty papers were presented at the Pasadena gathering. The event was covered extensively by the press. One of the papers was on the economics of air pollution with an emphasis on losses and rehabilitation costs. This was the first paper on the subject to enter the literature; we were besieged with requests for copies and more information. Unfortunately, the work could not be continued for lack of sponsorship. My colleagues and I were greatly disappointed.

Late in 1949, Eugene Staley of the new international program was invited by Secretary of State George Marshall to join a group of 25 university, business and military leaders to participate in three days of closed-door discussions in Washington on U.S. policy in the Far East and particularly on the China situation. At the time, Staley was affiliated with both the Hoover Institution at Stanford and SRI. The Marshall appointment was an honor, and we were pleased to see the recognition. But, it was to produce a problem.

During the McCarthy days of the 1950s, Staley was brought into the national controversy partly because of his advisory role on China. We stood by him and helped in every way we could. In due course, his loyalty and integrity were confirmed and reaffirmed and he went on to become an international authority on economic problems of developing countries. Nevertheless, the McCarthy experience was traumatic for both Staley and SRI. But in a way it signalled the Institue's entry onto the broad stage of international affairs. ∎

TWO EARLY INTERNATIONALISTS
L to R: Harry J. Robinson and A. Eugene Staley.

A New Drive

SRI is on the right track.

— M. E. "MONTY" SPAGHT - 1949

EVEN WITH A LONG VIEW BACKWARDS, January 25, 1949 is a red letter day in SRI's early years. At a meeting in San Francisco (as portrayed earlier), the directors found a short-term solution to our financial crisis. This meant that the Institute was soon to broaden its base and then begin a new surge.

A wave of enthusiasm and energy swept the organization. The target had been to break even by mid-year. However, more than four months had gone by since serious work on a new development plan had started. The rallying call soon became "Break even by October!" However, we knew some key directors realized the target would have to be moved back. Even so, they were not unanimous in this view. Nevertheless, everyone felt a welcome relief from the severe pressures since mid-autumn 1948.

After about two years of discussion, the management and directors were at last developing plans for some fund-rasing. Lundborg and Hobson took the lead with help from McBean. Arrangements were made for Carl Titus of the Armour Research Foundation to join SRI as an assistant director to work on the project.

The emerging plan called for memberships by companies and individuals based on annual subscriptions. In return, as Associates, they would be invited to an annual meeting featuring new fields of research and be listed in Institute publications. Also, wherever possible, Associates would receive early information on our research programs and copies of various reports. The Stanford Trustees were willing to approve a special class of membership in the Institute to make all this possible.

The origin of the word "Associates" within SRI is somewhat obscure. It was suggested once or twice in 1947 but nothing was done at the time. Following a visit to Cal Tech in 1948, Ed Pendray (our public relations adviser) suggested that some modification of its Associates plan be created. When a name was being sought as part of the Lundborg-Hobson plan, Pendray's idea was picked up — at Joe Lovewell's urging in our Economics group.

The target set by Lundborg and Hobson was $3.0 million including $1.5 million within 12 to 18 months. An additional $1.5 million was included for a building. Both men emphasized over and over that success in the drive would depend on cooperation by all the directors.

Our first development plan — The Vigorous Thrust — was history by the end of 1948. Some $325,000 had been requested in April; $100,000 had been approved. By year end, $326,000 had been spent or committed.

As 1949 began, there were other things afoot at SRI in addition to financial planning. The new year began with 80% of revenues coming from industrial projects. Most other institutes had a far lower proportion of their revenues from business. But a quiet move was on within SRI to get more government contracts.

This triggered an internal policy discussion as well as one with the directors. Hobson and his colleagues clearly saw both sides of the budding controversy. Among the disadvantages were some derailment in pursuing the industrial purposes set by the founders, a longer collection period on receivables, and overhead recovery rates set by the military somewhat below actual costs. Principal among the advantages visualized at the time were enhancing our prestige in government circles, access to some federal laboratories, and participation in important defense programs.

Hobson, in particular, thought these would be of great value in the event of a national emergency with a heavy emphasis on research for the defense effort. This point was soon to come into play with advent of the Korean War in mid-1950. However, the government-commercial ratio was destined to come up many times in later years.

The tight financial situation in late 1948 and early 1949 focused attention by both management and the directors on pricing policies. The existing system was one used by the eastern institutes. Invoicing was based on costs for time, fringe benefits, materials and other direct expenses plus overhead recovery at a percentage of time charges.

The audited or maximum rate for government contracts at the time was 80%; the rate for commercial projects had been set more or less arbitrarily at 100%. Actual costs were higher. Hobson felt that billing rates for commercial projects should vary according to project size.

SRI entered 1949 with a staff of 210 including 71 administrative, clerical and service people. About half the staff were in professional categories with 13% in semi-technical groups. The professionals numbered 114 including 30 with Ph.D.s and another 37 with Masters degrees. One-fifth of the professionals were from Stanford. The total staff included graduates of 47 universities. This was a surprise to many who thought SRI was heavily populated by Stanford alumni.

As 1949 got underway, one of the principal research events had to do with the Poulter Method of Geophysical Exploration, a technique involving shaped explosive charges developed by Thomas Poulter. On January 5 the system was demonstrated near Bakersfield, California. Some 200 geophysicists, petroleum engineers and oil company representatives were on hand.

The event was newsworthy and brought SRI's program to the attention of many science groups. However, the petroleum industry remained doubtful about Poulter's technique, believing it to be effective only under ideal conditions.

The first Annual Northern California Research Conference was held in San Francisco on January 12. It was attended by about 275 business executives. Although originated by SRI, the meeting was jointly sponsored with the San Francisco Chamber of Commerce, the University of California and Stanford.

The event contributed greatly to a wider understanding about SRI, especially among Northern California business executives. A similar session was being planned for Los Angeles. These events were the forerunners of many other public conferences sponsored by the Institute in later years.

Whiskey Gulch!
Good space for Lease?

Our third year also began with some space additions. With all available Stanford Village buildings occupied, the small economics group moved to a leased building in East Palo Alto. Several bars and liquor stores were in the area. Thus, the new location soon became known internally as Whiskey Gulch — and sometimes as "The Hootstitute" based on the nickname of the director.

By 1958, when the group returned to Menlo Park, it had grown to several hundred people. More important, however, a new field had been created for the Institute'e future.

Also, in early 1949, the question of sponsoring basic research in the public interest came before the directors. Some felt that such programs would be helpful in fund-raising. The directors agreed that the Institute should do all it could as funds became available. In due course, this was to be a major goal.

During the Christmas season of 1948, Hobson gave a lot of attention to the Institute's organization as preparation for a new development program. He finally decided that the existing plan was appropriate for the coming year. There were eight administrative posts and six research leaders. An applied mechanics program had been added; an applied biology operation was being planned.

Late in January, 1949, both management and the directors moved quickly on our second development plan. Hobson lost no time in telling the directors that recent restrained promotion meant that future operations would run at least two months behind schedule. This was later to be extended somewhat.

Within a month after the new 1949 break-even plan was launched, the government-commercial and pricing questions again came to the forefront. Also, again, Hobson was saying that government projects would put SRI in a better position in the event of a national emergency and that they would be helpful in obtaining experience, facilities and staff. But by this time he was also stressing a patriotic obligation. This was not altogether convincing to the directors.

A graduated overhead recovery rate system on commercial projects was launched early in the year but soon proved to be administratively impractical. The whole matter was resolved with a flat rate of 125% on direct labor.

Hobson and Lundborg were devoting a lot of time to fund-rasing ideas. They considered a system of scale of contributions by company size but soon discarded the approach in favor of $15,000 units spread over three years. They hoped some companies would subscribe for multiple units.

The new Associates Plan called for outright gifts from industry. In order for the donations to qualify as tax-deductible contributions, all quid pro quo features were carefully avoided. However, the basic idea was that several general and indirect benefits would accrue to Associate Companies.

Both Hobson and Lundborg had in mind two broad purposes for the fund raising. The first was to retire loans, increase facilities, finance research in the public interest, and provide working capital. They suggested $1.5 million in this category and $1.5 million to be used later for a new building. Basically, the overall plan was the same as had been discussed earlier.

In creating the Associates Plan, the Institute had the benefit of experience on similar programs at Southern Research Institute, Midwest Research institute, Cal. Tech., University of Chicago, Harvard Business School and MIT. The whole plan was discussed with the directors during February, 1949. There was widespread agreement that the campaign should get underway. Shortly thereafter, the U.S. Treasury Department notified SRI that contributions received would indeed be deductible by the donors on tax returns. Everything seemed to be in readiness, but this was soon to be illusory.

Two other events in February, 1949, reflected to some extent our growing confidence in SRI's future. The directors looked with favor on a long-delayed retirement plan for staff members. Also, some general plans were evolving to extend the Institute's activities abroad. The board viewed the idea favorably and agreed to invite James Drumm, a retired executive of The First National City Bank of New York (now Citibank) to assist in developing some plans.

Our second development plan had a much more diversified based upon which to build than was the case a year earlier. At the beginning of 1949, about 40% of the research effort was in chemistry and chemical engineering, almost all for commercial clients. Another 42% in geophysics (under Poulter's direction) was for government. Industrial economics accounted for some 14%, again mostly for government. Work in electronics was just beginning at around the 4% point. Economics and electronics were to expand rapidly in revenue, staff and space during the next several months.

Throughout the first quarter of 1949, Charles Blyth continued discussions with six San Francisco banks on a $600,000 loan. By the end of the quarter all was set with five of the banks. But the need for cash was now urgent in the extreme. So, Blyth arranged for American Trust to loan the Institute $100,000 for sixty days with repayment when the full credit line was set up.

As the first quarter came to an end, the directors were moving along on the fund-raising plan with a list of 400 possible Associates in hand. Luncheon meetings to launch the campaign were being set up in Los Angeles and Portland.

In March, however, several directors began asking questions about whether or not the Institute would in fact break even on schedule. Everyone felt this was vital to the fund-raising effort. But, for a variety of reasons, revenues had dropped and losses had risen. To say the least, this was unsettling. Hobson, however, took it in stride, saying that all was moving ahead satisfactorily. He blamed a higher-than-expected loss on various curtailments at year end and again predicted that performance would run only two to three months behind earlier forecasts.

This was not a wholly-convincing response to rising questions from the directors. So, Hobson arranged a board presentation by one of his associates (the author) who was heading the internal Finance Committee. I also said that operations were two or three months behind the earlier predictions but added two more — $200,000 in monthly revenue by September and a net loss for April–September of only $59,000. A break-even point was not pinpointed. A new budget was in the works. October was the real target in my case.

The Institute was in a highly volatile state. The so-called "two-way stretch" was critical. When less time went on sponsored projects, revenues dropped not only by the labor value but also by the amount of overhead recovery not generated. Also, overhead costs went up to cover the unsold staff time. The "stretch," of course, worked in the opposite direction (as "time sold" increased) with highly-favorable results. This was the big hope in March of 1949.

In the meantime, a threat to the Institute's image and the fund-raising program had come to the forefront. A project was under way for a group of oil companies and public agencies on land subsidence in the Long Beach (California) area. There was a possibility the subsidence was being caused by oil extraction. Needless to say, this was a sensitive issue. In seeking the cause, SRI was in the middle.

It appeared that, indeed, oil recovery was one, but only one, of the explanations. The SRI team proposed that a test hole be drilled at a cost of about $300,000. Instead, the oil companies decided to being the project to an abrupt end along with considerable criticism of SRI's handling of the endeavor.

> *The Institute has already drilled a hole for itself — !!!*
> — William L. Stewart, Jr.

Hobson jumped into the picture immediately. Some of the criticism was justified. But he and others maintained that the Institute was being unfairly criticized, since work had gone ahead rapidly at the sponsors' urging even with no clear-cut answers on what was causing subsidence.

The project continued to be controversial for several months but in time came to be recognized as competent but uncompleted work. However, the experience was a lesson in showing that large and complicated projects (particularly those with multiple sponsors) must be followed closely by top management. It was not the last time this lesson was to be learned.

Also, in early 1949 a situation arose that resulted in a basic policy on patents. Based on his experience at Armour, Hobson felt strongly that SRI should not get involved in patent licensing and that the best policy was to get patents in the hands of industry as quickly as possible. (Armour had found itself on "both sides of a lawsuit" in a case involving licensing of its magnetic recorder patents.) Hobson's view was an overreaction but it was a fact of life in SRI for some time.

Being unable to find a sponsor for work on an idea involving sawdust fluidization, the Institute invested $5,000 of its own funds in the research. A California timber company then became interested in the project. The situation was discussed with the directors following which a project was accepted with a "finder's fee" of $7,500 and a one-third SRI interest in any future patent income. Although the research did not produce the expected technical results, a general policy of retaining some interests in future patent income first emerged.

Some tidying up in the Institute's organization took place in the spring of 1949. SRI had no treasurer; Blyth was elected to the post in May. Also, Hobson's title was changed from executive director to director in a step that later led to a more conventional corporate setup.

By late spring, a budget for the 1949 development plan was ready. It was aimed specifically at break-even in October and had been developed by the internal Finance Committee. Hobson told the directors that it represented a "turning point" in the Institute's operations following low periods earlier in the year. He said specifically that the self-supporting point would be reached in October.

This budget was a crucial one in the eyes of the directors. It was based for the most part on funds known to be available not including possible Associate contributions. The amounts included the last $275,000 from the bank loan, $20,000 in working capital advances from Stanford (thus leaving the loan at $500,000) and $5,000 more from client advances.

Several miscellaneous sources brought the total up to $309,000. This meant that since the beginning some $1.3 million in capital funds would have been invested in SRI.

FOR THE AEC
Ion Exchange Project – Shirley Radding.

The Finance Committee was specific on how these funds were to be used — accounts receivable, $116,000: inventories, $10,000; leasehold improvements, $35,000; fixed assets, $74,000; operating deficit, $89,000 (of which $50,000 were development costs); fringe benefit reserves, $4,000 — all this offset by some $16,000 in miscellaneous asset reductions. The total was $312,000.

The directors had many questions about this break-even plan. They wanted to know more about possible effects of a business recession, the feasibility of changing plans to meet shifting conditions, and internal expense controls. But they did approve the plan with emphasis on a break-even point by October. From then on everything was focused on this target. A slippage would be most embarrassing.

By the end of May, the fund-raising program was on the street, so to speak. Two directors, Paul McKee and T. H. Banfield, had hosted a luncheon in Portland (Oregon) attended by some ninety business executives.

William Stewart had done the same thing in Los Angeles. The Associates Plan was described at both events. In addition, each director had been asked to make one contact each month with a prospective Associate company. Written invitations had been sent to Northrup, General Petroleum, Bechtel Corporation, Joshua Hendy, Fullerton Oil, Lyon and Lyon, Richfield, and Edward Lyman (an attorney and board member in Los Angeles).

Having in mind the financial impact brought about by sudden termination of large projects (e.g., the one on subsidence), Hobson asked the directors for advice on how such situations should be handled. He proposed board discussions on contracts involving time charges of more than $5,000 per month. Several directors thought the size should be $20,000 or a grand total of $100,000. The matter was left dangling but would come up many times as the years went by.

One of the major research efforts in 1949 involved the smog problem in Los Angeles. In view of the relatively large size of the project and its sensitive nature, Hobson and other key administrators spent a great amount of time on the program. The directors were kept informed. Hobson reported in early summer that "the smog project is in good shape" and pointed specifically to work on the visibility problem. He went on to emphasize that the Institute's most important contribution had been "the development of techniques and instrumentation."

The project was supposed to end on October 31, 1949. Thus the Institute was busily at work during the summer trying to develop other work in the field. The program was continued in various ways under other auspices after the Western Oil and Gas Association ended its project. But by the end of the 1950s most of the remaining staff and facilities had been moved to other programs.

Having resolved the financial crisis in early 1949, the directors began to feel that a smaller executive committee should be formed to work more closely with management. By late spring, the board had been almost tripled in size, primarily in preparation for the fund raising. Sterling was asked in May to appoint the executive group. This was the first significant change in functioning of the board since SRI's formation in late 1946.

When the directors met in June, the main question was centered on whether or not the Institute would in fact break even in October. Hobson was on a eastern trip, so the responses fell on Brunetti and the finance committee chairman. We were quite specific — " ... the Institute will break even ... in October ... " This was what the directors wanted to hear, but even so not all were reassured by our confidence.

They wanted to know if there was any possibility the capital and expense budgets would be exceeded. As chairman of the finance committee, I tried to be specific, saying "The budget *cannot* be exceeded." Based on experience, the directors were still not convinced.

I had meant that in this instance operations would *have* to be kept within available funds. There was to be no alternative. It was clear that no more outside money would be available except from Associates and no commitments could be made on this possibility. However, invitations had been extended to 26 companies.

A new problem had arisen by midsummer, this time with Stanford. Our rapid growth and widening scope had led to faculty questions. Some felt that SRI was seeking and getting projects that otherwise might have gone to the University. Sterling was in an awkward position but said that "such apprehension is unhealthy and feeds on rumor rather than facts."

He thought, quite rightly, that something should be done to keep the faculty better informed about SRI.

His idea was to create a faculty committee and through it acquaint the faculty at large with the Institute's operations. Also, he asked the Institute to pay special attention to "source of projects" so as to minimize any competition with the University. Sterling decided later not to create the committee but rather to review SRI operations himself from time to time at faculty meetings.

Various approaches were tried during the ensuing years but no fully satisfactory system emerged. Many associated with SRI felt the problem was more apparent or possible than real. But, the faculty image was real, and it did cloud the picture.

We must grow; we must earn a surplus.

— ATHOLL McBEAN

Major efforts were made during the summer months to bring SRI to the break-even point by October as had been promised. Spending for promotion and public relations was sharply curtailed much to Hobson's regret. A physiology laboratory was closed; the applied mechanics program was terminated. The finance committee met almost daily. As mentioned, the May-September forecast on losses was $89,000. The final result was $67,000. Things were at least moving in the right direction.

For the month of October, a surplus did indeed appear for the first time in our existence. Although the amount was small, the impact was great. A new wave of enthusiasm and high spirits spread around the organization and among the directors. The surplus was only $1,518.35. Nevertheless, Hobson was already thinking about a new development plan.

Almost everyone knew that while the break-even target had been met, the organization was not yet in a stable financial situation. Everything possible and feasible had been done to achieve the break-even goal. Urgently needed expenditures had been postponed. The per capita equipment investment was still less than a meager $2,000. Variable expenses had been cut by more than 15%. Fixed expenses were rising. The situation was tight.

In effect, the Institute was operating at "about a break-even point" with no cushion on finances. It was apparent that several more months would be needed to stabilize operations. A November deficit of $142 illustrates the precarious circumstances.

McBean added a wry note — "looks like the November figure is a clerical error." Hobson felt — and others agreed — that the time had come to develop still another plan aimed at putting SRI on a permanent self-supporting basis with adequate safety margins.

Management was so engrossed in the drive to break even by October that little thought was given to a follow-on plan. In September, the directors were asked to approve a stand-by scheme for September–December, thus giving time for one plan to cover a "stabilization period."

No new money was requested; some reallocations were proposed. No expansion was planned; break-even for October through December was predicted. A December surplus of about $7,800 gave some comfort to the staff and directors alike.

The Institute ended 1949 in a financial situation vastly different from a year earlier.

Total revenue was $1.76 million, almost three times greater than for 1948. The deficit was about $183,000, some $23,000 above the previous year. However, the red ink had fallen from 27% to 11% of revenue. Even more significant, only 10% of the 1949 deficit occurred during the last six months. The curve was moving in the right direction.

The Institute's assets at year end stood at $964,000, more than double a year earlier. With almost three time more revenue, the investment in receivables increased less than two-fold. Associate contributions provided $58,000 in capital with some $42,000 pledged for later payment.

The most notable improvement was in the cash situation — $120,000 at year end, all but $14,000 arising from client advances. The bank balance exceeded current liabilities, and current assets were five times greater than current liabilities.

By year end, the full $600,000 had been received from the bank loan. The $500,000 in working capital advances by Stanford had been converted into a long-term loan. Our cumulative deficit was $393,000 but after capital contributions the negative net worth was only $251,000. Perhaps more significant, the staff grew only slightly during the year to some 250 people.

In many respects the Institute's growth during its first three years, especially in 1949, was remarkable. Armour had taken ten years to reach the same level. Battelle had taken fourteen years and Mellon thirty-four. Midwest had been in existence six years but was at a revenue level about one-third that for SRI.

Although a fund-raising program had been launched during the year, the Institute moved slowly in soliciting new Associates. Both management and the directors felt that things would move along much better once SRI demonstrated its ability to operate in the black. However, the need for Associate funds was increasing rapidly. A per capita equip-

FIRST COMMUNICATIONS EQUIPMENT LABORATORY — 1949

ment investment of $5–$6,000 — instead of $2,000 — was insufficient but in the right direction. A few projects in the electronics field were turned aside late in the year simply because there was no way to get the necessary equipment.

The year ended with a new board operation. Sterling had asked McBean, Blyth, Fuller and Stewart to serve with him on the executive committee. Also, just before year end a Technical Advisory committee was created to assist both management and the directors in guiding our research programs. This move grew out of Sterling's increasing concern about relationships between Stanford's faculty and the Institute.

Members of the new group were Dr. M. E. "Monty" Spaght, president of Shell Development; Dr. F. C. Lindvall, dean of engineering at Cal. Tech.; George Parkhurst, president of Oronite Chemical; Dr. Paul Wilbur, director of research at Food Machinery; Dr. Douglas Whitaker, Stanford's vice president; Dr. F. E. Terman, dean of engineering at Stanford; Dr. Philip Leighton, head of Stanford's chemistry department; Dr. Irving Leverson, dean of mineral sciences at the University; and Dr. Merrill Bennett, executive director of the Food Research Institute at Stanford.

This new committee met a few times and was helpful to the Institute in some ways. But it was soon disbanded primarily because of the wide spectrum of our activities and difficulties in generating meaningful technical discussions among members with such diverse backgrounds. It did not contribute much in strengthening SRI-University relationships.

The year 1949 brought new features in the Institute's research programs, especially in economics and electronics. This was made possible by improving finances. A new decade had arrived. SRI had ample reasons to take stock and look to the future.

A personal note brings the New Drive to an end. For the second time, Hobson had demonstrated his zeal for growth and development. But this time the drive involved more people, and the emphasis was on getting in the black and broadening the base in substance. The days were busy ones as many did double duty leading research programs and working on finances including the Associates Plan.

Much of the load fell on Herbert, Rand, Brunetti, Krause and myself with Hobson urging us on for both growth and earnings. We met practically everyday, and no expense was too minor for scrutiny. Along with Hobson, I went on line as a "spokesman" in trying to reassure the directors that we would break even in October. It is best not to think what might have happened had we been "way off" target. As Spaght said, we were on the "right track".

For Sterling, this first year in the chairman's seat was obviously a troubling start. He had a post not bargained for in accepting the Stanford presidency. Thus he said one midsummer day — "We must get rid of the red ink." This hit the nail on the head.

Looking back, it may seem that everything had to do with finances. This was not the case. My note from '49 is revealing.

> *The pressure is on; we turned it on; we are on double time; we are building our programs.*

No one knew what the future might hold, but the days were exciting and the work was fun. Even so, the directors — an expanded group — were worried — but not McBean. He thought we were on the right track and urged Spaght to say so. Both were looking far ahead.

■

An Expanding Board

The Finest … in the West …
— PAUL C. EDWARDS - 1949

A N EARLIER BOOK ON SRI's FOUNDING YEARS gives high credit to the Institute's eleven founding directors — ten of whom served through 1947 and 1948 and nine through The Take-Off Days and into later years of The Upward Surge. They were indeed leaders in the cause and SRI must always be grateful for all they did.

Donald B. Tresidder, Stanford's president and first SRI board chairman, was the only founding director who was not among the group in 1948; he died on January 28 of a heart attack while in New York City. Eurich resigned later in the year. Also, the book on the Founding Years pays special tribute to one other early director, S.D. Bechtel, Sr., who joined the board at the beginning of 1949.

Although these ''leaders among leaders'' in the American West during the middle years of the 1900s were men with vision and foresight, they probably never suspected that forty years after they ''took the step'' on SRI's creation their names would appear on a plaque at its world headquarters.

Throughout the second half of 1948, the early directors discussed the possibility of expanding their numbers. The basic purpose they had in mind was to broaden representation both geographically and by types of business. They felt this move would be helpful in a fund-raising campaign then under consideration.

The result was election of twenty-three new directors during the first quarter of 1949. Bechtel agreed in 1948 to join the group and was the first new director to be elected a month later. Within about two months, the size of the board was increased two and one half times.

The new roster included men of great accomplishment in western business and academic affairs plus one prominent executive in the Southwest and one in the East. The contingent prompted one of the first new board members, Paul C. Edwards of the San Francisco Chronicle, to say — ''I am honored to be among a group of thirty-three men who unquestionably make the SRI board the finest governing body of any institution in the West.'' It was indeed a distinguished assembly as seems evident from the account in this chapter.

THE FOUNDING DIRECTORS	
Charles R. Blyth	Atholl McBean
John E. Cushing	Paul McKee
Paul L. Davies	Donald J. Russell
Alvin C. Eurich	William L. Stewart
W.P. Fuller, Jr.	Donald B. Tresidder
James D. Zellerbach	

An aid to fundraising 59

Edwards joined the board not only in his capacity as a senior newspaper executive in San Francisco, but also as a Stanford Trustee who was greatly dedicated to both the University (of which he was a graduate) and to SRI. He had been a student at Stanford during the great earthquake and fire early in the century and was one of the first persons from the Stanford area to reach the City following the disaster.

THE EARLY 1949 BOARD EXPANSION
(January-March Additions in Order of Election)

Directors	Served Until
S.D. Bechtel, Sr.	March 1975*†
Paul C. Edwards	December 1961*
F.C. Lindvall	November 1970
Louis B. Lundborg	November 1970
Garrett W. McEnerney	March 1953
Alden G. Roach	December 20, 1956‡
Roland Tognazzini	March 27, 1970‡
Brayton Wilbur	March 1960
T.H. Banfield	May 1951‡
R. Gwin Follis	March 1975*
Mark R. Sullivan	September 1962
Clarence H. Faust	May 1949
W.W. Valentine	December 1957
Paul Pigott	January 23, 1961‡
Tom Slick	September 1957
Donald W. Douglas, Jr.	September 1967
James F. Crafts	March 1964
J.H. Drumm	September 1954
Lingan A. Warren	November 1955
A.G. Budge	April 1951
Edward D. Lyman	November 12, 1962‡
J.E. Wallace Sterling	June 1970*
Douglas W. Whitaker	October 1958
S.W. Royce	December 1964*†

---

* Bechtel, Edwards, Follis, Sterling and Royce retired as directors in the months indicated.
† Bechtel and Royce were elected directors emeriti.
‡ Roach, Tognazzini, Banfield, Pigott and Lyman died while serving as directors.
  Others resigned from the board in the months shown.

Follis was involved with SRI long before he became a director in 1949. McBean talked with him many times in 1945–46 about the proposed institute at Stanford. He joined McBean in guaranteeing an initial $50,000 for the plan. Follis later served at various times on the board's executive, development, membership and international committees and for several years was chairman of the latter group.

A quiet, highly-respected and internationally well-known chief executive of Standard Oil Company of California (SOCAL), one of the world's major oil companies, Follis had a greater impact on SRI matters than even he may have known. McBean was constantly seeking his views on diverse matters and relaying his comments to management and the directors. It was Follis who in 1959, following the first SRI-Time sponsored International Industrial Development Conference in San Francisco, suggested that future events be co-sponsored with The Conference Board of New York. This proved to be a very sound suggestion. He was always most emphatic about the highly favorable impact the several major IICs in San Francisco had on SRI. These worldwide events with some 500 senior executives from 65 or more countries have since been held every four years.

Follis chaired many meetings of the board's international committee during the 1950s and 1960s. Before most of these sessions, we would meet with him at SOCAL and discuss the agenda. He was a ''clean desk'' executive, and in many respects was rather formal in manner. He would usually glance over papers handed to him and then return them with, ''Tell me about the contents.'' He often looked to McBean for advice.

Roach, the chief executive of United States Steel on the west coast, also was one of the group that joined the board in 1949. One of his contributions was gaining Big Steel's interest in SRI. An early project was set up to help the company on plans for its next twenty years. Roach was killed in a private airplane accident in 1956.

''Les'' Worthington was soon appointed to the Colombia-Geneva position in U.S. Steel and at McBean's and Bechtel's initiative became a director in late 1953. After Worthington became president of U.S. Steel, his successor on the west coast, J.D. McCall, was elected to our board.

Worthington was faced with an awkward situation in the late 1950s when we were planning our first new building. A Japanese company proposed to provide the steel at a substantially lower price than the bids from American steel companies, including U.S. Steel. But he did not hesitate — ''Take the Japanese steel even though it is a signal of more bad news to come for our country's steel industry.'' Subsequent events proved him right.

Another of the early appointees was Mark Sullivan, then chief executive of Pacific Telephone and Telegraph Company in San Francisco. Being a member of the PT&T board, McBean thought Sullivan would be a good board member. Sullivan served until 1962, by which time he had retired from his PT&T position. During part of his board tenure, Sullivan was a member of its personnel committee and took a special interest in SRI's communications research programs.

In early 1964, the new PT&T chief executive, Carl Lindeman, at McBean's recommendation was invited to board membership. In due course, his successor at PT&T, Hornsby Wasson, became an SRI director and later board chairman and was elected director emeritus in later years. He was an able chairman and devoted a lot of time to the Institute.

Five other senior executives in the San Francisco area were appointed to the board in 1949. They were Roland Tognazzini of Union Sugar, Brayton Wilbur of Wilbur-Ellis, James ''Jim'' Crafts of Fireman's Fund Insurance Company, Lingan Warren of Safeway, and Garrett McEnerney II. Crafts served for several years as chairman of the board's personnel committee and was most helpful in working on our basic personnel policies and fringe benefit programs.

In an effort to strengthen our position in Southern California, the early 1949 board appointments included five persons from the Los Angeles area. They were Fred Lindvall, dean of engineering at the California Institute of Technology; Donald Douglas, Jr., of Douglas Aircraft; S.W. Royce of the Huntington Hotel in Pasadena; and Edward ''Ed'' Lyman, a prominent attorney. All were recommended by William Stewart.

Lindvall was proposed by Hobson who had known him since the mid-1930s when Hobson was a student at Cal-Tech. Lindvall had taken a special interest in our engineering and international research programs, serving occasionally as a consultant. In the early 1950s, he was a member of an SRI-organized mission to Italy on rehabilitation of that nation's industrial and scientific research institutes. He was the first SRI director from academic circles other than Stanford.

The 1949 appointments also included a few people from outside California. Paul Pigott, a Stanford graduate and head of Pacific Car and Foundry in Seattle, accepted membership early in the year. Two of his close friends on the board, Russell and McKee, urged him to join the group. Pigott served ably and with enthusiasm until his death in 1961. His son, Charles (Chuck), was later to join our ranks as a director. Tom Slick, of Texas Oil fame, was invited to memberhip largely at Hobson's recommendation. Slick had been a prime mover in creating Southwest Research Institute in San Antonio. He resigned from the board in 1957, having found it difficult (for various reasons) to participate actively in our affairs. He was then devoting a lot of time and energy to a search for the Abominable Snowman of the Himalayas.

A.G. Budge of San Francisco, chief executive of Castle and Cooke (one of the Big Five factors in Hawaii), served only about two years on the board, resigning in 1951. J.H. ''Jim'' Drumm of New York served until his resignation in 1954. Drumm was retired Vice President-Latin America of the First National City Bank (now Citibank). He was invited to the board at Hobson's suggestion with the thought that he could and would be helpful in our international activities.

The year 1949 also brought significant changes in board leadership. When Tresidder died early in 1948 Alvin Eurich became chairman. Then, when Eurich resigned from the University and from the board chairmanship later in the year, the directors were left with no chairman or vice chairman. Stanford's acting president, Clarence Faust, was elected to the board in January 1949, and promptly became chairman. He left the board in May of that year when Dr. J.E. Wallace ''Wally'' Sterling became the new Stanford president and, automatically, our board chairman.

Louis Lundborg, vice president for development at Stanford, was added to the board in early 1949 and immediately became vice chairman. He was particularly active with the Institute during the first few months of his tenure. These were critical times, and he helped hold things together. His own account of the situation appears in the accompanying text. Later, he served on the board's personnel committee and was much interested in our welfare.

In September, Lundborg resigned from his Stanford position to become vice president (later chairman) of the Bank of America. Douglas Whitaker of Stanford then became vice chairman of the board; he served until Frederick ''Fred'' Terman, university provost, was elected to the board and to the vice chairmanship in late 1955. Whitaker later resigned, but Lundborg remained as a member until 1970. Sterling automatically became chairman of the board's first executive committee when it was formed in late 1949.

The Lundborg Appraisal

(Lundborg became an SRI director while serving as Stanford's vice president for development. In January 1949, he was asked by Faust, acting president of the University and interim board chairman at SRI, to look into the situation at the Institute. Following is his account, from an autobiography - ''Up to Now'' - published in 1978.)

- … The Institute was on the verge of insolvency. Because it was a separate corporation without the credit of the University behind it creditors were growing uneasy and suppliers were starting to put SRI on a C.O.D. basis. …

- What remained — an open question in my mind — and in the minds of everyone involved — was whether all the elements of markets, costs, and prices could be pieced together profitably; whether the obvious potential market could be translated into reality, or whether the costs would break the University's back before the break-even point could be reached and passed.

- A powerful and vocal group among the University's trustees was convinced that backing SRI was a fool's game and should be ended at once. There was no doubt that this was the conservative, safe course and that probably a University should not be taking bold risks. But there were others among the Trustees, as well as among SRI's directors, who were equally convinced that the Institute was a sound, viable risk and that the University had an obligation to its broader constituency to see SRI through to vigorous health.

- Not because of my findings, but because they gave additional ammunition to those who favored that cause, the Board of Trustees voted to continue the support. Instead of advancing University funds, a loan of $600,000 was negotiated with the six principal California banks.

(Reproduced by permission of W.W. Norton & Company, Inc.

In accepting the Stanford presidency, Sterling was greatly concerned — and rightly so — about his added SRI burden, especially when he learned that we were cash-short, operating at a deficit and beset with many questions by University Trustees and others about our very existence. Also, he soon saw that McBean was, in effect, serving as an ''executive chairman without special portfolio.'' Nevertheless, Sterling plunged in and served ably as chairman within the constraints imposed by his time-consuming job at Stanford. In later years, he was always proud of the way SRI developed during his tenure as chairman.

In April of 1949, shortly after he had been elected as Stanford's president. We saw Sterling at a campus dinner in his honor. He posed an interesting question: ''What's this about my being chairman of SRI? I hear you may have some problems'' Sterling often made good use of understatements in the British manner, but in this instance he could have gone further. We did indeed have some growth and financial problems as he was soon to see at first hand.

Sterling's role in SRI gave him a difficult problem as Stanford's president. On occasion, some strong University alumnus would lodge a complaint about an SRI project on the basis that he disagreed with the results. Sterling felt, of course, that his first obligation was to Stanford, but he also accepted a strong responsibility for SRI. The dual task was not easy, but he handled it with skill and finesse. One of Sterling's problems on behalf of the board was somehow to apply some brakes on what many felt was "too much desire for expansion." Hobson, in turn, often said, "We are simply trying to respond to demand," and to some he would remark, "I am only trying to keep pace with Sterling at Stanford." Sterling was, indeed, a master builder, but felt that SRI was expanding too fast for comfort.

Only one new board member was elected in 1950. At a meeting of the executive committee in October 1949 there was a discussion on the contributions made in the way of patent counsel and advice by Leonard Lyon of Lyon and Lyon, a patent law firm in Los Angeles. At the year-end board meeting a resolution of appreciation to Lyon and his firm was adopted, and was soon followed by his election to the board.

Three new board members were elected in 1951. Fred Ortman and Monroe "Monty" Spaght (Shell Oil) were elected prior to a by-law change increasing the size of the board to 40 persons. The third board member was John McCone.

THE 1950–1955 ADDITIONS

Year	Name	Served Until
1950	Leonard S. Lyon	August 13, 1964
1951	Fred B. Ortman	February 26, 1961
1951	Monroe E. Spaght	November 1970
1951	John A. McCone	October 1958
1952	Robert C. Swain	May 1962
1953	Herbert T. Kalmus	July 11, 1963
1953	William R. Burwell	June 1954
1953	Lloyd W. Dinkelspiel	May 15, 1959
1954	John P. Weyerhaeuser, Jr.	December 8, 1956
1954	Henry Sargent	March 26, 1967
1955	Emmett G. Solomon	November 1970
1955	Walter R. Bimson	December 1964
1955	Frederick E. Terman	August 1965

Bimson was elected Director Emeritus in December, 1964.
Spaght, McCone, Swain, Burwell, Solomon and Terman (later vice chairmen) resigned in the months shown. Others died while serving as directors.

Solomon, president of the Crocker-Citizens National Bank, served for several years as chairman of the board's finance committee. He also served for some time on the building committee.

Bimson, chief executive of The Valley National Bank in Arizona, along with Sargent, played a key role in SRI's Arizona-based activities.

When Bimson was invited to become a director, he was well aware of the board's growth in size since the beginning of 1949. He also knew full well that the Institute had grown rapidly since 1948. Although quick in accepting the board's invitation, Bimson spoke in a light vein about "the board's expansion being even faster than SRI's growth."

All in all, thirty-seven new directors came into the fold from January, 1949, through 1955. There were six resignations and one death during that time (plus Tresidder's death in 1948), leaving a board of 40 in the mid-1950s.

VICE CHAIRMAN AND CHAIRMAN
L to R: Frederick E. Terman, SRI vice chairman, and
David Packard, chairman of executive committee.

For several years, it had been our good fortune to have a close relationship with McBean's long-time business colleague, Fred Ortman. Ortman was president of Gladding, McBean & Company at the time of his election, and a highly-respected member of the Southern California business community. He was a quiet, soft-spoken man with an excellent reputation among his business peers. Among other things, he was a great help behind the scenes in our sometimes erratic relationships with McBean. He had a keen sense of just when and how matters should be taken up with the founder. Upon retirement in 1957 from Gladding, McBean & Company he joined SRI as associate director in charge of our Southern California activities.

McBean was greatly pleased by this move. We had always looked upon Ortman as his protege. Some time later, it was Ortman who came up with the idea of working out a special gift-purchase arrangement between SRI and the Irvine Foundation and Company for some land south of Los Angeles, on which the Institute built laboratories for its Southern California operations. He performed ably for SRI until his death in early 1961.

At the time of Spaght's election to the board he was president of Shell Development Company in San Francisco. He was appointed late in 1949 to our Technical Advisory Committee which had been created to work directly with management in the development of research programs. Spaght later moved to New York and then to a higher position with Shell in London. Thus, he was unable to participate as actively as before in our activities. However, as a University Trustee, and through advice given in response to requests from individual board members as well as management, Monty Spaght played an absentee role in policy formulation on board matters.

At the suggestion of Bechtel, John McCone was elected while he was president of Joshua Hendy Corporation. Upon being appointed by President Eisenhower in 1958 to head the Atomic Energy Commission, he resigned from our board. He later became head of the CIA.

Our "expanded board" during the Take-Off Days was to be expanded further through the second half of the 1950s. Then, as before, the idea was to broaden membership both geographically and by types of business.

THE 1956–1960 ELECTIONS

Year	Name	Served Until
1956	Alfred B. Layton	June 1961
1956	E. Finley Carter	February 1965
1956	Edgar W. Smith	October 1961
1957	Arnold O. Beckman	November 1970
1957	William G. Reed	August 1964
1957	Edgar F. Kaiser	March 1979
1957	Leslie B. Worthington	November 1970
1958	David Packard	January 1969
1958	Edward W. Carter	December 1983
1959	Weldon B. Gibson	April 1982
1959	S. Clark Beise	November 1970
1959	James B. Black	April 1963
1960	Christian de Guigne III	November 1970

Black was elected Director Emeritus in April, 1963, Kaiser in March, 1979, and Carter in 1983.

Kaiser was a strong proponent for moves abroad in the 1960s and 70s, chaired the board's international committee for a time, and also was board chairman for four years.

He was general chairman of one of our world industrial conferences in San Francisco and of a major Institute event in Moscow in

1974. His wife died of a heart attack the first evening of this major worldwide assembly whereupon E. Hornsby Wasson, later to be our board chairman, handled the event in able fashion.

Packard was chairman of the board's executive committee during part of the Take-Off Days. As "Mr. Los Angeles," Carter has been a leading board member for almost three decades.

The Institute has benefitted enormously over the years from its board of directors. The composition has continued to change since the mid-1950s. In any event, the outside directors have provided wise counsel and policy guidance. They have been especially effective when key decisions were needed.

Many other national business leaders were elected to the board during the 2½ decades since 1960. Their names must appear in a later account on the Institute's upsurge years. Names of the chairmen during our first four decades appear on page 126.

These moves were successful, but as time went on the numbers were reduced primarily for efficiency in the decision-making process. This story must await another account.

THE MID-1980s BOARD

Year Elected	Name
1966	Daniel G. Aldrich, Jr.
1966	Ernest C. Arbuckle*
1981	Samuel H. Armacost
1949	S. D. Bechtel*
1975	B. F. Biaggini
1958	Edward W. Carter*
1947	Morris M. Doyle*
1981	Myron Du Bain
1982	Philip Hawley
1974	H. J. Haynes
1982	George Keller
1975	Richard G. Landis
1967	E. W. Littlefield
1985	Frederick W. Mielke, Jr.
1975	Arjay Miller
1979	William F. Miller
1985	Carl E. Reichardt
1946	Donald J. Russell†
1967	E. Hornsby Wasson*
1986	Paul J. Jorgensen

* Directors Emeriti (Arbuckle – deceased, January 1986).
† Founding Director (deceased, December 1985).

While President of the United States in the mid-1950s, Dwight D. Eisenhower looked over the SRI board list in connection with our international activities and made a short comment — "An A-number-one group." (He was referring to "outside directors.") This has always been the case. This is the case today for the full list. ■

SPECIAL APPRECIATION
LONG SERVICE

Donald J. Russell — Founding Director — 40 years.
S. D. Bechtel, Sr. — Director Emeritus — 37 years.

SRI must forever be grateful for their strong policy leadership and dedication from its earliest days.

THE FOUNDER

- Our eleven founding directors plus S. D. Bechtel, Sr., the first to join them in 1949, were forceful and colorful men in many ways. Their names appear in honor in our world headquarters buildings.

- A portrait of Atholl McBean, the leader of the founders, hangs in a special place at the center of SRI's main offices. He deserves all the credit that can be given to him. Donald J. Russell, one of his colleagues, often spoke about McBean's role.

    "SRI would not exist today (if it were not) for ... Atholl McBean."

- It is not easy to portray our founder's intense devotion to and involvement in the Institute. An attempt along this line appears in a chapter, "One of a Kind," in the 1980 book about SRI's beginnings.

- Much more could be written about him, but one characteristic must suffice at this point. Whatever the subject might be, his first impulse was always to seek help from persons in high places. He seemed to know someone everywhere. A personal note illustrates how he operated.

- In the mid-1950s SRI was seeking a role in the United Kingdom. In McBean's words—"the head man over there is a friend of mine; we must talk with him; I'll set it up."

- He did—and we talked. No affair of state was involved but the man at No. 10 Downing Street took the time to hear about SRI, how it was founded and what it could do.

- The action was in the business community. Even so, McBean spoke much later about how the PM had helped "clear the way." Whatever he did, if anything, is open to question.

- However, the "British Lion" remembered the exchange and later wanted to know if an SRI presence could be created in London.

- We opened an office in the early 1960's, some seven years after our "counsellor" had left his office. Meanwhile, McBean was impatient as he always was when things dragged out.

A STRONG MAN

- To all who knew him, Donald J. Russell, one of our eleven founding directors, was a "strong man." He was never in doubt about anything in which he was involved.

- With love and affection, a family member once said of him — "maybe not always right but never in doubt!!!"

- He was always immensely proud of the Institute he helped create. He read the first drafts of all chapters in this book. In his words, he helped "straighten things out" on a few interpretations. I always found him "right" on essential matters.

- However, he was "wrong" on one point — always saying he had merely "helped out." He did far more than help; he was a moving force.

- Don Russell left a message about the future — "take good care of SRI." He did just that for forty years. We owe him highest honor.

- This note is being written the day he died in mid-December, 1985 in San Francisco.

A New Target

It looks like another expansion is being planned ...

— PAUL DAVIES, SR. - 1950

ALTHOUGH THE INSTITUTE BROKE EVEN FINANCIALLY for the first time in October, 1949, there was a small deficit in November. Then, December brought a most welcome surplus. In the meantime, Hobson and the Finance Committee were thinking about a new development plan.

He was hoping it could bring another expansion based on new capital from the Associates Plan plus some earnings. He and others in the Institute knew the operation was on a tight wire with virtually no margin of safety. Nevertheless, Hobson wanted to expand revenues as quickly as possible from around $2 million to at least $2.5 million a year. This called for more staff, space and facilities — at least 25% in each case.

Some soundings among the directors convinced Hobson that this was a risky course. They wanted a continuing surplus before doing much more on the Associates Plan. It was during these reviews, one at a time, that Paul L. Davies, one of the founding directors, sounded a friendly warning — "It looks like another expansion is being planned ... even though there is no money to support it."

All this disappointed Hobson; he thought the time was at hand to increase the scale of the Institute. But, eventually, he acquiesced on some new guidelines. They would take the Institute to July 1950 — a target date that had not been forgotten by some of the directors.

Thus, work continued through much of December on another development scheme. The planning was based on two key assumptions; little additional capital would be available from Associates, and the first six months would be at the break-even point. As things began to settle down, the plan was really a holding operation. This was the only apparent way to get the Associates Plan under way by mid-year or so. Everything depended on capital.

The new plan was ready by year-end for discussion with the directors whose numbers had been greatly increased during the year. New capital was finally estimated at $148,500, higher than had previously looked possible. There were three main sources — some $79,000 in working capital from Stanford (bringing the loan up to a half-million dollars), about $57,000 from Associates with $17,000 already pledged, and $12,500 from new client advances. All this was to bring the Institute's total investment to about $1.4 million.

How to spread this money over so many urgent needs was no small problem. Some $31,000 was assigned to cover more accounts receivable, thus putting a cap on growth. Another $53,500 was to be used for building improvements, equipment and other assets. Three reserves for $54,000 were set up, and $10,000 was to be spent on self-sponsored research. The last amount was a key allocation; total spending for this purpose since our formation had not exceeded $8,000.

This combination of new capital and outlays along with a break-even operation was supposed to leave SRI with a cumulative deficit of $407,000. The idea was to start bringing it down at mid-year.

This conservative approach was what the directors wanted to see and they approved the plan. Meanwhile, Hobson was speaking optimistically on the outlook for new research projects — ''Generally, the picture is very good, with good contracts extending well into and through 1950.'' Events were to prove otherwise, however. We were not in a position to handle sudden revenue changes. Matters were not helped along by a $5,000 deficit in January.

This led right away to new questions from the directors and others about the Institute's financial viability. Some wondered why overhead rates seemed to rise along with revenue increases. The Stanford Trustees asked for more information about current and prospective operations. The directors wanted some assurance from Hobson that he and others at SRI fully understood the necessity for a new break-even as soon as possible. Hobson kept saying that everyone was conscious of the facts and working hard to reduce costs.

He also stressed now and then that SRI had been building for the future, that most investments had paid off, but, even so, investment in the future was no longer being made. Nevertheless, there was an underlying concern among the directors and Trustees that somehow SRI might be spending ahead of vital current needs. Hobson went on the line with a strong statement. ''There will be a surplus for the period ending June 30.'' We thought the deficits would be checked by early spring.

Although surrounded by a financial problem, the research operation moved ahead quite satisfactorily in early 1950. A large economics project was under way for Richfield. The smog project had produced some results; a public report at the turn of the year suggested that eye irritation was caused not by one pollutant (auto exhausts or refining affluents) but by chemical reactions among many substances. A project had been started on the feasibility of producing edible food by applying solar energy to chlorella algae.

The Second Annual Northern California Research Conference was held in San Francisco in February in cooperation with Stanford, the University of California and the San Francisco Chamber of Commerce. The growing importance of research in developing the U.S. West was emphasized in various ways by several speakers including Dr. M.J. Kelley, executive vice president of Bell Telephone Laboratories, and Fred C. Lindvall, chairman of the engineering division at Cal Tech. Kelly said — ''applied research ... provides the reservoir of knowledge that is the driving force of the creative technology of our industrial society.'' Dr. Cledo Brunetti, one of SRI's associate directors, gave an interesting and entertaining demonstration of small electronic devices including radio transmitters and receivers of wrist-watch size.

Throughout the spring as financial problems continued, Hobson worried, as he had earlier, about how to acquaint the directors more fully with the Institute. The board meetings in San Francisco were not very useful in this respect except for financial matters. Hobson was frustrated on how best to get over the full story as he saw it. This led to the annual board meeting being held at SRI in March where the directors could see some of the operations and meet more of the Institute's people.

Unfortunately, the financial news by March was not too good; the February deficit was $6,000, making a total of $11,000 for the first two months. Several economy measures had to be taken. But, Hobson was still confident about the near future, saying over and over again that there would be no net loss for the six-month period, January to June, 1950. Our government-sponsored work at the time was only 23% of the total. Hobson told the staff and directors he would not object if government volume totaled 35% to 40%.

The new electronics group was moving along quite well in the spring of 1950. But, it desperately needed more equipment. The directors were told that (with an investment of about $80,000) revenues could be doubled with only a minor increase in overhead costs. One possibility was to seek equipment gifts, if not cash, under the Associates program.

There seemed to be no solution to the immediate problem, but the directors did agree with an allocation of $15,000 in Associate funds to help ease the situation. This helped, but the basic problem remained and it grew larger day by day.

Knowing that Hobson was most anxious to expand the Institute, the directors began asking again about the ultimate size he had in mind. In March he said: "The most efficient size for the Institute would seem to be from one and one-half to twice the present size to absorb fluctuations without major effect on overall operations."

This meant he was suggesting something in the order of $4 million in annual revenues. Apparently, even his sights were too low; in a little more than a decade SRI was approaching a revenue rate twenty times the 1950 volume. In speaking about "fluctuations," Hobson knew, and was concerned, about the pending loss of a large economics project.

Even though the Associates Plan was on the back burner awaiting a surplus operation, Hobson wanted to get things moving again. Carl Titus had been employed to handle this work, but he was spending most of his time on project promotion. So, Hobson convinced the directors in March that a man by the name of George Keller, known to several board members, should be retained for the fund-raising post. He was persuasive and Keller soon joined the staff. But there were to be more delays.

Much to the concern of the directors, Hobson, and the staff, the financial situation went downward rather than upward in April. A surplus for the first six months seemed to be out of the question. Monthly revenue fell from the planned $175,000 to about $140,000. The result was an $11,000 deficit. In large part this setback was caused by termination of the Richfield marketing study on liquefied petroleum gas. The reason it came to an end was simple enough — the work was finished ahead of schedule and budget.

Losing $25,000 in monthly revenue immediately put the economics group in a loss position rather than its usual black figure. Several people had to be released. The swift turn of events could not have come at a worse time. Sudden ending of "Project Baker" — the Richfield Study, as it was called for confidential handling, was to demonstrate the hazards of having too many eggs in one project basket.

Hobson told the directors in May that this unexpected turn would mean some delay in reaching the break-even point. This was, of course, quite obvious. But he felt any further staff reductions would be unwise for the Institute's future. Although greatly disappointed, he exuded confidence that the situation would soon be brought into line. Sales costs were then running about 7% of revenue. Hobson's attitude was to increase rather than lower this spending. He was always at his best when things went wrong, and they surely did in the spring of 1950.

April and May were critical times within SRI. Even more reductions in the economics staff had to be made to compensate for Project Baker. However, by the end of April a turn-around had been made. The performance curve moved upward soon thereafter.

By this time, both Hobson and the Finance Committee had given up on break-even for the first half of the year. Their sights shifted to breaking even by July. Hitting this target was so important to the future of the organization that some drastic alternatives were considered — even though with great reluctance. Two possible lines of action, known simply as A and B, were worked out by the Finance Committee (Herbert, Rand and Gibson) and shared only with Hobson. Plan A was the most severe of the two. Another alternative labeled ''As We Are'' also was outlined.

All this was done in mid-April when the outlook was bleak. In retrospect, the differences between success and failure seem very small indeed. But, they were large for SRI at the time. Furthermore, rumors were circulating that Hobson might be in some jeopardy if things did not turn around quickly. This meant that some others might feel the impact. It was a tense time. In any event, the surplus possibilities were spelled out in detail.

THINK ABOUT THE FUTURE !

ONE EVENING, IN LOS ANGELES, in late June, 1950, Hobson enrolled one of his associates in a special prediction. They were elated about the breakeven at hand and this led to an exchange in a light vein at first, but then quite serious as the night wore on into the late hours.

It all began from earlier, humorous advice by a soap-box orator in Pershing Square.

Hobson's idea was to predict for five years ahead and then think about the longer term. This may not have been ''scientific'' but it was a welcome relief from the pressures at mid-year. The ground rule was to be specific on the first targets and then to generalize on some needed trends. Hobson took the lead.

Biltmore Forecast for 1955 !

- Quadruple the staff
- Increase revenue six times
- 50/50 government/commercial
- 5% surplus rate
- One-third each — sciences, engineering and economics
- 20% International
- Pay off the bank loans
- Get the red ink off the balance sheet

- $3 million new capital
- Begin paying Stanford up to $250,000 per year
- Some investment by Uncle Sam
- Five branch offices in the West
- A new building at a permanent home
- A Washington, D.C. office
- Get something going in Europe
- Expand the board again — by 20 or so.

Perhaps this might better have been termed a ''proposal'' rather than a ''forecast,'' but, in any event, it was a ''freewheeling exercise.'' How things actually turned out appears elsewhere in this book.

The Biltmore points, together with ideas on trends, are symbolic of the times. The thought that SRI was ''taking off'' pervaded the whole exchange as did a feeling that both the directors and the Stanford Trustees were beginning to breathe sighs of relief. The same existed internally.

With more capital, we should soon be able to move ahead under our own steam.
— SRI FINANCE COMMITTEE - June 1950

The night session then turned to some things that

Plan A was aimed at getting an immediate surplus and maintaining it indefinitely. Plan B called for break-even within a month and then a rising surplus. Both plans meant severe staff reductions including senior people. Among other things, the Los Angeles operation and all public relations activities were to be closed down. The payroll would have been cut sharply under both options. The "As We Are" plan called for only a few expense reductions and high confidence in the existing course.

Period	Plan A	Plan B	As We Are
First Quarter (actual)	$(15,350)	$(15,350)	$(15,350)
April Estimate	$(14,800)	$(14,800)	$(14,800)
May Estimate	$ 5,000	0	$ (9,100)
June Estimate	$ 8,800	$ 3,800	$ (5,300)
First Half 1950 Estimate	$(16,350)	$(26,350)	$(44,550)

Hobson and the finance group were extremely worried about the Plan A and B alternatives. Both would have turned the Institute in a downward direction. But the stakes were high. A decision on what to do was delayed on a day-to-day basis. When it began to appear

should be done during the longer term. They arose in no particular order except that finances came first.

- Maintain a rising surplus rate
- Create some "rainy day" reserves
- Tighter control on costs
- Get Associates Plan in high gear
- Invest more in equipment and public services
- Get more government business, especially in engineering
- Improve the balance sheet
- More attention to the Stanford affiliation.

All this was followed by some programmatic themes, such as, obtaining larger projects, particularly with involvement of all SRI divisions; thinking nationally and internationally (not just the West); improving quality; and attracting more able people.

There were all sorts of points on operations and the internal environment. The first was intended to soften the growth rate problem.

- Gradually slow down the expansion
- Decentralize decision-making as much as possible
- Make sure energy/enthusiasm remain high

- Do everything possible to make SRI a good place to work
- Get the name known worldwide
- Better planning, but remain opportunistic
- Improve systems, but nurture entrepreneurship.

Still another point was one of Hobson's favorites from the very beginning of his tenure — keep up a drive to make SRI #1 among its sister institutes! He also thought management should listen more to what our consultant-of-the-day (Maurice Holland) might say. Even his advice was "tongue-in-cheek," but somehow SRI agreed to "listen" but not necessarily "act."

Hobson recognized that the whole package might sound too expansionist, so he toned down an even higher prediction on growth rates and settled for the "slow-down" phase. Fifteen years later he talked about the Biltmore Forecast and did not blink an eye in saying that the growth dimension was too conservative. " ... We grew five times over, didn't we? More could and should have been done."

He could not remember who brought up the other points in the Forecast in mid-1950. Neither do I. It doesn't matter. As Hobson was fond of saying " ... some blue sky was involved." In any event, a lot was done during the next five years.□

in early May that the month's deficit would be no higher than the "As We Are" target, Hobson decided quite rightly to back away from the severe cutbacks. It was a crucial decision and took courage, but the Finance Committee was behind him to the hilt.

The directors next met in mid-June. By this time, some favorable financial trends had emerged even though the May deficit was almost $9,500. The backlog of research contracts was rising. It seemed likely the revenue rate for June would be back to the level predicted six months earlier. Overhead expenses had been reduced by 10%. The economics group was recovering quite well from the Project Baker problem.

In this setting, Hobson predicted a June deficit of only about $5,000. He went on to say " ... business prospects for the Institute are better than at any time in the past." His optimism proved to be right; the June deficit was only $1,000. The staff was elated about the trend; the directors were satisfied — but break-even was yet to come.

There was, then, some opportunity in June to think about future capital needs and the Associates Plan in particular. The idea of seeking contributions of equipment as well as cash was revived. Another proposal was to broaden the scheme to include some research projects. Still another was to apply one-third of a $15,000 Associate unit to reducing overhead costs for any projects the company might place at SRI during a three-year period. Nothing was decided; all the options were left open.

There was also another review on pricing policies and the government-commercial ratio. A general consensus existed within SRI and among the directors that the overhead recovery rate on industrial projects should be increased to 150% of project labor. The decision was promptly announced. Furthermore, Hobson was persuasive with the directors on government projects; they even urged the Institute to increase the proportion from the existing 25% level.

WILLIAM J. PLATT
Operations Research.

Although it seemed apparent in late June that the Institute would indeed break even financially in July, Hobson was worried and let his feelings be known. Then, once again, a mood of relief and even exhiliration spread around the staff when a surplus of $2,329.63 was announced for July. The deficit for the first six months was only $37,000, somewhat below the "As We are" estimate in April.

Even so, the record for the development plan was a reasonably good one. The ending capital investment had been estimated at $1,384,000; the actual figure was $1,353,000. A cumulative deficit of $407,000 was predicted; the result was $430,000. Negative net worth was set at $203,000; it turned out to be $268,000. Two shortfalls were largely responsible for the differences; new capital funds were $30,000 less than expected and the operating loss was $37,000 instead of zero.

The important point at the time was not so much a

MEETINGS WITH THE FOUNDER
McBean's summer home,
Woodside, California.

comparison between prediction and performance but rather the outlook. Basic trends were in the right direction. Revenue was moving upward from $160,000 per month. Overhead rates had dropped from 110% in January to 104% in June and on to 100% by July. At long last, there was good reason to believe the Institute could operate indefinitely with a surplus. This was welcome news to the staff, directors and Stanford Trustees. July of 1950 was soon to become a key milestone in our early history.

SRI might not have been able to sustain a profitable operation during the next 12 to 18 months had the Korean War not brought a rising volume of defense-oriented research. In any event, the financial situation continued to improve. The fact that the Institute benefitted from a new international situation is simply a part of history.

By mid-1950, several shifts had occurred in research operations. The electronics group was producing 25% of total revenue, based on its considerable growth during the first half-year. Economics was at about 20%, chemistry at 40%, geophysics at 15%, with only some 2% from applied physics.

Much of the new electronics work was sponsored by industry, especially by RCA on color television. Some new techniques of high-speed photography had been developed in connection with research on shock wave phenomena. An experimental biology group was beginning work on nutritional qualities of bread.

A major project on Italy's heavy mechanical industries was being negotiated at mid-year. Several directors were urging that many more foreign projects be brought into the fold. A flurry of activity was under way around the organization on plans for new and interesting research programs. Robert Smith of the economics staff was talking about possibilities for some sort of long range planning service for both American and foreign companies. Much more was to be heard about this idea. During all of this movement our Technical Advisory Committee met three times to discuss various facets of the research operation.

At mid-year, two endeavors aside from finances were occupying much of Hobson's attention. The senior management group was involved in both of them. One had to do with developing a more meaningful set of objectives for the Institute. The other was an upcoming review of our entire operations by an eastern expert on industrial research. The drive to break even had been successful. Thus, it was quite in order to look more carefully to the future.

A personal note is now added to the story. The first half of 1950 was a most difficult time for Herbert, Rand and others as we struggled with finances. Since the Project Baker termination in the economics group created most of the problem, I felt badly about the whole situation. There was little comfort in that early success on the project — and not poor perfor-mance — was responsible for our woes. But we did vow never again to depend so heavily on one project in the soft sciences. My personal relief was great indeed when the "As We Are" plan won out over the drastic alternatives.

Perhaps it is not possible from a vantage point so many years later to portray fully the events of January to July of 1950. The story may seem to be exaggerated and even trivial. But it was not a minor matter at the time. In many respects, the Institute's future hinged greatly on the spring events. No one knows what might have happened had the May-June-July curve been downward rather than upward. I penciled a personal note at the time, "It was a tight squeeze; we are lucky in the result."

Hobson said a few years later: "I would rather not think about it." This is a good way to leave matters and move on.

SOME LINES FROM THE TIMES*
(Anonymous)

- **Client relations** — Talk often — but not too much — and listen.
- **Priorities** — People, able people and more of them.
- **Personnel** — The golden rule is policy #1.
- **Teamwork** — Set the example; practice what you preach.
- **Clients** — An organization is known by the company it keeps.
- **Oral commitment** — A promise is a contract.
- **Legalities** — Be alert in "tiger country."
- **Office politics** — Steer clear; be a "pro."
- **Performance** — It's the batting average that counts.
- **International** — There is a great potential "over there."
- **Finances** — Pull hard on the bootstraps.
- **Associate companies** — They are the source of "equity" capital.
- **High quality** — Everything else is secondary.
- **The West** — It begins at the Hudson River.
- **Hallmarks** — Pick a few and pursue them.
- **Economics programs** — Without the sciences, they are "uneconomical."
- **Governments** — Watch out for the camel's head.
- **Advice** — Seek informed counsel and try to follow it.
- **Growth** — Watch it carefully; it's fascinating.
- **Planning —** It's important but don't miss the train while re-studying the timetable.

---

*In a light vein but with meaningful implications. ■

A Search for Purpose

What are our purposes and what are our obligations to Stanford?

— J.E. WALLACE STERLING - 1950

EVEN WHILE THE INSTITUTE WAS LOSING MONEY IN THE SPRING OF 1950, with almost everyone working on the break-even problem, some were turning to the future. This did not happen entirely on our initiative nor was the timing accidental. Sterling, Stanford's president and our chairman, was concerned about working relationships between SRI and the University. This led him to raise some questions about why SRI was founded, its ultimate objectives, obligations to Stanford, and other basic points.

His questions could not be easily answered. Some of the founders were no longer on the scene. Tresidder was dead; Eurich had moved to New York; Swain was no longer involved; Talbot was gone; McBean was concentrating mostly on finances.

Hobson was already thinking about the Institute's long-term goals. With the help of a few others he prepared a draft paper and shared it with the directors. One draft after another was then circulated until a policy paper was ready for further discussion. It was, in effect, an interpretation of the Institute's charter purposes.

The main thrust was, of course, on contract research for industry. The opening paragraph went directly to the point:

> *"The basic purpose of our existence is to be of service to industry and*
> *business, wherever and whenever such service is not otherwise available*
> *in adequate quality or extent to meet the needs of industrial and business*
> *organizations."*

This, most certainly, was the intent of the founders. The directors had said from the outset that SRI was formed to serve industry. Little mention was made of government; it seldom came up as a policy matter during the Founding Years.

Perhaps, this first statement should have been more specific on the main pursuit. There was, of course, no question that the word "service" meant scientific research of a unique character. Some were to argue later that SRI was not to compete with universities and profit-making organizations but there was no intent at the beginning to rule this out on a policy basis, except for Stanford. In the 1950 policy paper, only price was involved.

> *"We do not compete on a price basis with other institutions, universities,*
> *consultants, testing laboratories, or with our sponsors "* ... *Research*
> *in a public service institute is not, nor has it ever been, cheap research."*

Hobson would say over and over that SRI should never be a "bargain basement" for research. Both he and the directors felt that the Institute should do a first-class job with ample reimbursement. Pricing for industrial projects had just been raised with backing by the directors. There were some objections to the move, so the pricing clause was intended to nail the matter down for all to see and embrace.

The paper then turned to SRI's main role in solving particular problems for its sponsors (clients, as they were later called.)

> *"Our task is to undertake specific research investigations, to do the highest quality scientific work possible, as efficiently and quickly as it may be done consistent with high scientific standards."*

The genesis of this point lay in a view held by some of the staff, as well as by the Stanford faculty, that our principal thrust should be on basic rather than applied research. The word *specific* was underlined for emphasis.

One paragraph in the new policy grew directly from Hobson's concept of an educational function within SRI:

> *"We recognize a basic obligation to train and channel technical and professional personnel into the laboratories of industry."*

The Institute's charter calls for maintaining a staff of qualified educators, scientists and research experts but does not mention an educational resposibility to business. Hobson thought we should encourage our ablest people to move into industry at the right times in their professional careers.

All agreed at the time that a relatively high turnover among professionals was to be expected and even desired in the interests of the staff, as well as the Institute. The idea was that SRI should bring in more able young people than it could possibly retain over the longer term. Hobson encouraged people to leave SRI when attractive posts were offered and often recommended his associates for good industrial positions.

Therefore, it is not surprising that he, and later others, looked askance at fringe benefit plans that seemed designed to hold people unduly within the Institute. As time went on, however, the idea of channeling people into industry became more of a vague idea than an obligation. The charter interpretation was far too literal.

The Institute's public service duty as a non-profit, tax-exempt organization was taken up in one section of the paper.

> *"We also have a responsibility to undertake the scientific solution of problems of broad public interest within the limits of our capabilities, our facilities and our resources."*

This goal arose from the charter's reference to collecting and distributing information of general public interest. One of the reasons Hobson was particularly attracted to SRI's economics research was that he saw it as a way to work on problems of broad public interest. He was certainly right in this view.

Another policy objective was to advance generally the cause and concept of scientific research:

> *"We further recognize an obligation to stimulate and develop an understanding*
> *of scientific industrial research and research techniques as an important*
> *force in the industrial, economic and sociological activities of the nation."*

The charter speaks about developing and improving research techniques. Hobson often emphasized that this function was as important as research itself and wanted SRI to improve the methods of scientific inquiry, often describing the process as "research on research."

The whole idea as a special endeavor was vague and not really significant even during the mid-1950s. Able people bring effective methods of scientific investigation to any organization.

In the absence of any specific reference in the charter to government, a portion of the paper spelled out a duty with special emphasis:

> *"We accept an important obligation to the government of the United*
> *States to assist with scientific research needed for the national defense and*
> *welfare, and to keep our facilities available for a national emergency."*

Our basic motivation, at that time, was somewhat different. Government contracts had been looked upon as a way to build a capability for industrial research. Hobson also spoke about a patriotic duty. He remembered what had happened to Armour when World War II brought a rapid conversion to military work. We wanted to be prepared in the event of a national emergency, and one was soon to arise with the Korean War.

Our affiliation with Stanford gave rise to another objective.

> *"The Institute will, in every way possible, further the good reputation*
> *and prestige of Stanford University. Our research efforts must have a*
> *scientific status and quality equivalent to that of the University."*

Hobson, McBean, and some other directors knew this statement alone was not enough in meeting the Institute's obligation to Stanford. Some financial support was called for, but we were not in a position to do anything at that time. It would have to come later.

The second part of the policy regarding our affiliation with Stanford turned to money in the other direction.

> *"Although participating in the benefits of affiliation with Stanford, the*
> *Institute will operate without financial assistance from the University."*

This only stated the obvious but, as a matter of policy, removed SRI in the future from any financial dependence on the University. The working capital advances had already been converted into loans. There were no prospects for further help.

Laudable as they were, these two statements did not really satisfy Stanford's president and Trustees. But, they realized the approach was realistic and that more time would have to pass before anything really significant could be done by SRI. In any event, they did not press the matter.

Another one of the Institute's special goals had to do with the American West:

"We have a major responsibility to use our facilities, experience and ability to develop the resources of the western states, to create new industrial opportunities, and to assist in raising the economic level of the region."

This point was based directly on the charter and on what some directors believed was the over-riding reason for the Institute's existence. The international field was not even mentioned although one of the directors urged that we move in this direction. It was simply an oversight and no one else noticed the omission.

One of the last of the special obligations dealt with the local area:

"As an important part of the community in which the Institute is located, we will attempt to be of service to the economic and social betterment of the community."

Hobson felt strongly that such a policy must be included, and he encouraged the staff to be active in school boards, chambers of commerce, and other civic endeavors. He wanted SRI to be a good corporate citizen in its geographical area.

All this was fine, but how was the Institute to go about its work? Three points were spelled out. One involved the idea of scientific teamwork, the very essence of institutional research. Another dealt with research on a confidential basis with results held forever in

APPRECIATION FOR EARLY COUNSEL ON THE AMERICAN WEST AND THE PACIFIC
Right: Laurence W. Lane, Jr. — Publisher, *Sunset Magazine,* and Close Neighbor, with wife Jean.
(Now U.S. Ambassador to Australia - 1986)

confidence at the disposal of the clients. The third was gospel at the time but in retrospect was too restrictive:

'' ... We are a fact-finding organization ... we do not engage in consulting practice ... we do not give advice and opinions supported merely by experience or judgment ... ''

In time, SRI became much more than a fact-finding organization. Among other things it became a consulting group but during its early days insisted that all advice and recommendations be based on research done at SRI.

One reason a change gradually occurred in the 1950s was that the staff soon learned to frame conclusions in a way that, in fact, they became recommendations. However, the policy could not be applied consistently, so it simply faded away. The intent remained to focus attention on the scientific method in all lines of inquiry.

Although this 1950 paper did not stress the Institute's public interest and obligations to Stanford as much as the setting called for, it did serve a useful purpose. The staff gained some sense of unity on the fundamental purposes of the organization. The process was never to be completed and it came to the forefront again a few years later.

A personal note arises. Along with Herbert, Rand and Steffens, I was involved in working on our first search for purpose. All of us went back and forth in the discussions from immediate finances to basic goals; it was not easy to switch from short-term realities to the longer-term future.

The statements in the paper were incomplete. We knew this but hesitated to go further at the time. The directors approved the policies in June of 1950, just as the deficit operation apparently was coming to an end. The whole exercise was timely and McBean was right when he said:

''Now we are starting out again.''

In retrospect, the whole policy endeavor on purposes in 1950 may seem to have been far too late and inadequate. Perhaps, on a few points it dealt only with the obvious. Certainly, it did not come to grips with a few key questions such as the Stanford obligation. But this is hindsight on a young organization that was feeling its way.

Some of the questions might better have been dealt with at the very start of the organization. But this, too, is hindsight. Everyone's attention was centered on getting an Institute into being as quickly as possible. All were content with leaving such things as long-term purposes to the future.

Sterling was quite right in raising his basic questions some 18 months after arriving on the scene. The fact that questions existed within the Stanford faculty was symbolic of some basic thinking on SRI that had not been undertaken. Thus, the new chairman found himself in the position of being unable to answer some of his Stanford questioners.

Within a vacuum of sorts that existed at the time, at least three cross currents were flowing with varying force. Some faculty members were saying that SRI's sole purpose was to help the University. Everyone seemed to have a different idea on what should be done. Some of the directors were stressing service to western industry as the prime pursuit.

McBean was certainly in this group, but at the same time he was saying:

"We are here to help Stanford."

Meanwhile, management was preoccupied with finances and getting some programs under way. Growth was the order of the day in all things. The approach was understandably pragmatic.

In this situation, the faculty was overlooking the problem of developing an institute with an inadequate financial base. Some of the directors felt the growing questions from Stanford were untimely and '' ... none of the faculty's business.'' And, on his part, Hobson was concerned first and foremost with expanding the base.

Despite the rather meager outcome of our first policy exercise, a first move was made to answer Sterling's questions. We knew even before they arose that some thinking was needed on basic purposes. It was clear that something had to be done to help clear the air. One of the real reasons for the outside questioning was the growth emphasis being generated. Had the Institute grown more slowly during the two years following Hobson's arrival in the spring of 1948 and thus moved along without severe financial strains, the questioning on purposes might have come much later.

But, this too is hindsight. The result might well have been a greatly different organization. In any event, Sterling was restrained in his questions and the Institute was energetic in responding even though short of the target in many respects. The chairman did say that a set of public service goals was needed and that more had to be said in due course about Stanford.

Throughout the policy discussions of 1950 McBean was rather impatient. He kept saying "perform first — then talk about the future." During one meeting, he passed around a copy of a well-known adage.

"Nothing will ever be attempted if all possible objections must first be overcome."

There were no objections. But there were plenty of questions and too many new directors to forge a solid consensus.

A personal note at the time mentions the key question — "Our charter is clear — we must assist Stanford — but how? An answer must be found."

The directors most certainly joined in the first search for purpose. Many of the policy matters had to await another day. Much more internal work and discussions were needed to help determine where the Institute should be heading. Meanwhile, 1950 was to be known primarily for breakeven.

An external situation soon put a new focus on our public service obligations. Questions began to be asked in various quarters about the tax status of nonprofit organizations. The regulations stipulated that an institute (such as SRI) should pay income taxes on activities unrelated to its basic purposes. The word "unrelated" was not fully defined and some private firms were saying that the institutes were engaging in unfair competition.

In this setting Hobson and several of his associates began thinking more about our ultimate purposes. Gradually, the idea emerged that two major pursuits (with some overlapping) were involved — contract research and activities in the public interest. The concept called for a surplus on the contract work with a portion to be used in financing various public services. The emphasis was not so much on how income was earned, but on how it was used.

This approach came to the forefront in mid-1953 when a financial forecast to the directors called for $100,000 for various public services and self-sponsored research. The request brought forth many questions on how much money was being spent for these purposes.

The title of a new policy was Services and Obligations. It began with the key purposes in the charter including, for example, Stanford's educational aims, maintaining research facilities, developing a staff of qualified people, creating an information center on scientific and industrial research, and promoting the application of science in commerce, trade and industry. It then turned to research.

> *"These objectives are partly achieved through contract research for industry and government, providing specific assistance where and when it is needed, contributing to the defense of the United States, helping new businesses become established, studying and developing the resources of the Western states, solving the problems of industry to broaden the industrial base, creating new products and processes, improving industrial efficiency, creating employment and expanding or creating markets.*
>
> *"These contract services, for which industry and government are willing to pay ... should be fully self-supporting, although they do contribute to the general welfare, to the regional economy, and to the national defense."*

This part of the policy was intended to make contract research SRI's first and *foremost* objective. A self-supporting concept was emphasized.

The next paragraph in the new policy was central to the concept of public service obligations, as they were viewed at the time (1954).

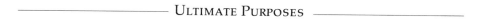 ULTIMATE PURPOSES

> *"Attainment of the Institute's charter objectives, — requires activities beyond the areas of contract research, including public service functions and general scientific and research activities stated in the Articles of Incorporation. ..."*

The message in this paragraph is that SRI was to devote its earnings on contract research to support activities directly and specifically in the public interest. It was never intended, of course, that all net income was to be spent this way.

It had been more or less taken for granted that working capital needs and investments for future operations, including equipment, had first (but not total) call on earnings. Forbes wanted the public service outlays to be an allocation of net income rather than operating costs before the income figure.

EARLY HONOR — RAYMOND H. EWELL OF SRI

(Chemistry and then Economics plus International)
Receiving Armed Services award in 1948 from General Mark Clark and Admiral Donald Beary.
Fellow recipient, Frederick E. Terman of Stanford University (left).

Too little emphasis was given in the 1954 policy to the idea that income-earning activities, or at least a substantial portion of them, also were in the public interest.

In any event, the intent in 1954 was that the Institute's basic reason for existence was to pursue public interest goals, all this made possible by contract research.

The new policy statement was specific that the Institute should earn a surplus on its project activities even though it was a nonprofit organization:

> *"The Institute is entitled to charge a fee in excess of costs on its regular*
> *contract business ... in order to provide the means to fulfill its recognized*
> *public service obligations and it must be run on sound operating principles."*

These words were aimed at a "fixed fee" system beyond partial or full overhead recovery. There were some in SRI and outside who argued that a nonprofit organization should not attempt to make a profit or a surplus. Also, it was not really possible to do so at the time on government projects with no fee.

Although the Institute was to shift within a year to a totally self-sufficient concept, the intention in late 1954 was that we should continue to seek contributions to help on public service activities.

─────────────── CONTRIBUTIONS ───────────────

> *"The regular operations of the Institute should provide for future security,*
> *expansion of activities to meet the service obligations, and fulfillment of the*
> *chartered objectives insofar as that may be possible within sound operating*
> *practice. Additional assistance will have to come from gifts or contributions*
> *since the avenue of investment funds is closed to a nonprofit organization*
> *such as the Institute."*

The 1954 policy also considered ways in which available funds were to be used. Several purposes, in two categories, were spelled out. The first had to do with ways in which SRI could "establish, maintain, and improve its services" — more or less independent of the public service concept. This involved — "meeting all financial obligations, maintaining a sound financial condition, and achieving future security (contingency reserves, equipment and facilities)."

The second category dealt with the heart of the public service idea — the ways in which our funds were to be used:

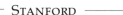

STANFORD

"Assistance to Stanford University in the promotion and extension of knowledge' including: payment to the general funds of Stanford University for services and benefits received, tangible and intangible; participation in the Honors Cooperative Program to give financial support to extending the University's graduate education program; making some of the Institute's staff available for teaching activities; performance of research and services, chargeable to the University, on the basis of 'out of pocket' costs; direct support for certain basic research and perhaps for certain specific educational activities."

This was the first explicit statement by the directors on financial and other assistance to Stanford. Right or wrong, it was long overdue, even though very little or no money could have been given to the University. Had such a policy been adopted in 1946 or 1947, some early misunderstandings with the Stanford faculty probably would not have occurred. In any event, the Institute's first charter purpose was the basis for the policy. Something had to be done to satisfy the Trustees.

In the late 1950s, SRI made some commitments to Stanford both before and during its major five-year fund-raising plan (PACE). The pledge was for $500,000 at $100,000 per year.

Another public service objective had to do with the western states. It, too, came directly from the charter:

THE WEST

"Public service activities directed toward the economic and industrial development of the West such as area development research, water supply and utilization, the supply of power and energy, studies and surveys on natural resources, transportation studies, studies of labor supply and demand, plant location studies, market studies, etc."

It was clear within the Institute that this policy involved both client and SRI-sponsored projects. In fact, the very nature of many client-sponsored area development studies called for reports to be made available to the general public.

The same idea applied to another public service in the 1954 Policy, except that there was no geographical emphasis. A wide range of project activities were included in what was to be known in time as a general public category:

———————————————— PUBLIC INTEREST ————————————————

"Research in the public interest, such as cost-sharing or participation in grant-type studies for which the Institute's staff and facilities are uniquely qualified; studies of air pollution, public health, general agriculture, and waste utilization; the development of new research techniques; new approaches and new ideas; exploratory research in areas of interest or value to industry, etc."

Still another objective was based directly on one of the broad charter purposes. The basic idea was to help make useful scientific, technical, economic and other information available to the general public. It was recognized that many activities of this type might be carried out on a fully-paid basis, but some investment on the Institute's part was contemplated.

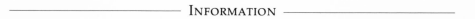

———————————————— INFORMATION ————————————————

"Accumulation and dissemination of information through publication of the Western Resources Handbook, Chemical Economics Handbook, preparation of scientific and technical articles, papers and books, sponsoring scientific and professional meetings and symposia ... etc."

The last of the five ways in which our funds were to be used directly in the public interest included several miscellaneous items. Although by no means fully inclusive, the word training was often used in this category:

———————————————— TRAINING ————————————————

"Developing the techniques and practice of industrial research through the training of research specialists and research administrators for industry, exploring and developing new techniques of research organization and administration, the support of research internships, fellowships for international study; sponsorship of foreign exchange students; the training and development of research talent for the West and for industry; participation on government panels, boards and commissions; activity in professional societies; participation in civil defense activities; advisory services to industry and to public agencies."

It may seem in retrospect that many of the so-called training pursuits, as well as some of the other public service endeavors, were normal operating costs for a research organization.

This was the case. Why then, was so much emphasis placed on putting them in an income allocation category? The reason is simple —to portray the monies as investments rather than operating costs.

The last section of the new policy took up pricing on sponsored projects. There were still some who felt that a non-profit research organization should, in effect, follow a low pricing approach.

PRICING

"The Institute should ... have good people in an environment in which they can be creative. In the present technical market this means good salaries under working conditions that might be considered expensive but will produce economical research, i.e., good research results for the money spent. Good research justifies the necessary investment ... "

This new policy was soon to guide much that the Institute did in its research and related programs. Gradually, however, some began to feel that it dealt largely with "ends" rather than "means" and that something more was needed in basic policy on contract research operations. This idea came to the forefront in 1955 and 1956. (See "The Second Stage.")

On November 30, 1967, during the Institute's twenty-first anniversary, the basic intent of our founders was summarized and reaffirmed in our Newcomen Address on SRI. We were to:

- Promote the broad purposes of Stanford University
- Create our own research facilities
- Develop our own staff
- Engage in research for organizations, public and private
- Build a center of scientific information
- Apply science in commerce, trade and industry . . .
- Improve the general standard of living and peace and prosperity of mankind (including security).

These high goals are the bedrock upon which SRI's plans and actions have been based. Our charter is a remarkable document; it has met the test of time. It has been called "an inspirational vision" of dedicated men.

SRI is moving ahead energetically; a strong base for the future is being created. The pace must be maintained.
— HAROLD VAGTBORG - 1950

SOME PROJECT CRITERIA

——————————— Mid-1950's ———————————

- Extent of research content and susceptibility of the problem to application of the scientific method;
- Ability of the Institute to perform high-quality research;
- Availability of staff, equipment, and other resources;
- Relationships with existing programs;
- Potential usefulness of expected research results;
- Contribution to learning and knowledge;
- Possible conflicting commitments;
- Impact on the stature and reputation of the Institute.

CONTINUING SEARCH

The search for purpose in precise wording within SRI is never-ending. Times and circumstances change. The following statement was adopted in the late 1970s.

———————————————————

- SRI International is a private and independent professional organization. Its purpose is to serve the public interest by providing a broad range of scientific, research, advisory and technical services to both public and private organizations.
- The Institute operates on an international scale, serving governments and businesses throughout the world.
- It is a nonprofit, tax-exempt corporation which generates ... income by performing services under contract to other organizations.
- This income must support all operations and provides the main source of capital funds needed to finance facilities, growth, and internally-sponsored research.
- Although SRI has a tax-exempt status, income taxes are paid on income derived from proprietary work. The Institute is non-endowed, but it can and does accept tax-exempt contributions from donors wishing to advance the organization's purposes.

Also, in the early 1980s, five cornerstones were adopted for the Institute's further development. They appear in the Epilogue. These also are subject to change from time to time (see page 189).

———————————————————

The Institute now assists Stanford University in large part by annual payments based on total revenues. This began in the early 1970s.

An Outside View
THE HOLLAND REPORT

There should be less flying by the seat of the pants and more instrument flying to get safely over the economic mountains.

— MAURICE HOLLAND - 1950

WHEN IN MID-1950 SRI EARNED A SMALL SURPLUS for the second time (the first having been in October a year earlier), an interesting chain of events followed. All may seem trivial from today's vantage point, but this was not the case at the time.

We had thought more red ink was to follow but the directors took a dim view of this prospect. They felt that a slowdown in growth was needed; the Stanford Trustees were outspoken on the point.

McBean was worried about SRI being on a collision course in its expansion, but Hobson had no doubts on what should be done. He wanted more capital and growth. In this setting McBean proposed that some outside advice be sought. He thought that Clyde Williams, Battelle's chief executive and a friend from The Founding Years, should be asked to look over the situation, and he offered to pay the bill.

Hobson realized that some outside support was needed if his views were to prevail. Believing that Williams might be too conservative, he suggested that a new face be brought into the picture. He mentioned Maurice Holland, an old friend and an industrial research consultant in New York. After some discussion with the directors, Hobson agreed on a study by either man. The idea was adopted and the selection left to him but with the stipulation that the report would be made directly to the Board. This was a bit disquieting to Hobson, but he was anxious to get the job under way.

Holland was asked to spend the first three weeks of August at SRI. His visit was not altogether popular among Hobson's associates. Holland was a fast talker, always stirring up things too much and too quickly, or so many felt.

In the meantime, another decision of sorts had been made quietly and tentatively within the Institute — the possibility of a government loan to support more growth was being explored. No stone was to be left unturned.*

Holland's stay at Menlo Park started off like a whirlwind including long meetings with heads of the research groups. He kept referring to them as ''building blocks for SRI in the 1950s and beyond;'' they were asked for all sorts of reports.

Louis Koenig had succeeded Dr. Raymond Ewell (following his move to the economics group in 1949) so he prepared a report on chemistry and chemical engineering. In addition,

---

* See ''The RFC Episode''

the chemistry group included programs in biology, metallurgy, ceramics and air pollution. Koenig reviewed with Holland its principal projects on smog, fluoride contamination, liquid surfaces, rancidity in cereals, ion exchange processes and chlorella algae.

He said that the group was well known with a good reputation, especially in atmospheric pollution, surface and colloid chemistry, micro-biological synthesis and ion exchange work. At the time, very little research was under way on agricultural problems; the group had not sought such projects from other than a few western companies.

Koenig acknowledged that the staff did not include any nationally-known chemists or chemical engineers but pointed to several highly-competent young people. He wanted to see them develop, especially in research on atmospheric pollution, ion exchange and colloid chemistry. In his view, the analytical chemistry staff was of a uniformly high caliber.

The promotional efforts of the group were aimed at research projects on new products and processes. Koenig felt that Hobson's emphasis on "general selling of the Institute" was incidental to creating and merchandising technical ideas. His plans called for about 250 people, some two and a half times the mid-1950 number, with most of the growth in plastics, food technology and radiochemistry.

The economics group had a staff of 31 people and an annual research volume of some $300,000, about two-thirds being for industry. The principal projects included industrial mobilization studies for the Air Force and Navy, operations research for the Army, a training cost study for the Air Force, a techno-economic study on liquefied natural gas for Richfield, an analysis of trans-Pacific shipping, a marketing study on petroleum wax, an economic audit in Cuba, the chemical economics handbook and a new product study for Albers Milling.

Three of these projects provided two-thirds of the work and had been under way for more than 18 months; all the others had started some six months earlier.

ECONOMICS

Economic studies involving technical problems, processes or services, using the Institute's technical knowledge to advantage.

Investigations involving a combination of technical and economic research.

Studies encompassing preliminary economic research and/or distribution analysis as a forerunner to technical research.

Research on fundamental problems in the economy of the West as a public service.

Operations research on systems problems in both industry and government.

Studies on major problems affecting the security of the United States.

Investigations in the international field involving both economic and technical research.

Sixty percent of the economics department's revenue of $660,000 for the previous three years had come from government, the balance being from industry. About half of the industrial revenue came from western companies. We felt that reasonably good progress had been made in diversifying our small but growing industrial work, but Holland wanted to know what unique contribution had been made in building the Institute.

Our response was centered on the techno-economic concept: "There are few, if any, research organizations in the nation engaging in combinations of technical and economic research … no other public service research organization offers a similar service." This approach was indeed a new one for research institutes, and it served SRI well indeed during our formative years.

Holland felt the group's plan for the future was far too conservative and later he was proven right. In essence, we proposed to continue more or less in the same fields with about the same size staff. In fact, the program and staff grew and diversified rapidly during the next five years.

THOMAS C. POULTER (right) and client.

We were right in saying that research on national security problems would increase, but we also wanted to maintain a 50-50 balance between government and industrial research. Holland was greatly pleased with one of our objectives: "To maintain high quality work as one of the hallmarks of the Institute's activities." This was much easier said than done.

Poulter prepared the paper for geophysics and geology. It began with two recent accomplishments, both involving the Poulter Method of Seismic Exploration. It had been applied successfully on the Edwards Plateau in West Texas and in the Tejon Ranch area of California's San Joaquin Valley. Conventional seismic methods had often not been productive in these areas.

The Poulter group was concentrating almost entirely on seismic work in the petroleum industry, although he thought there were other promising applications in reef fields and in finding underground mineral deposits and water. But, in due course, other technologies came to the forefront in these fields.

Poulter had no particular plans for increasing staff but felt that some very high caliber personnel had been added during the previous year when the group had grown from 11 to 22 people. His main motivation was to find support for work in fields of greatest personal interest. This was soon to include shaped-charge applications, solid fuels for rockets, marine biology and voice recording for identification purposes. Poulter retired twelve years later as director of the laboratories bearing his name but continued as a senior scientist until his death on June 14, 1978.

Poulter was well known in scientific circles even before he arrived at SRI in 1948. In the 1930s, he was scientific director and second in command of one of Admiral Byrd's Antarctic Expeditions. He led a four-man expedition on the famous rescue of Byrd who had spent the winter at a camp near the South Pole. For this feat, Poulter received a medal from the U.S. Congress; he later received another Congressional medal for his scientific work.

Following his death, one of his long-time colleagues described him as "a renaissance man of the sciences" who explored for meteorites, designed an Antarctic snow cruiser, invented seismic methods for discovering oil, and studied marine mammal life. He was indeed a source of strength in SRI's development and diversification for more than 20 years. But, in mid-1950, his mind was centered on geophysical work.

Poulter was a man of few words and Holland was unable to extract much from him about the future for his group. There were no dangling participles in his report, but he did have a dangling sentence:

> "As I see the future, there are many new developments, some of them of major importance."

This was less than revealing, but he did go on to mention a few new fields in seismic exploration and geophysics.

An applied biology group had been separated from chemistry and chemical engineering on July 1, 1950. Koenig prepared its report. Having little or no program in place, all he could do was speak of the future. He thought there were good opportunities for industrial-type research in microbiology, enzymology, biochemistry, physiology, plant pathology, entomology, toxicology, agronomy and ecology. This potential was cast as a long-term challenge in SRI's future. The biology group was later to become part of a larger and more diversified Life Sciences Division.

Holland was Hobson's personal friend in addition to being a consultant to SRI. He often visited the Institute and attended its management meetings but never in a silent capacity. In many respects, he was Hobson's personal adviser. They often met in Holland's office on 42nd Street in New York City and Hobson sought his views on organization, promotion, research programs and people. Holland, in turn, showered his "pupil" with ideas on how best to develop SRI. He was impulsive, energetic, never at a loss for phrases and constantly drew examples from a long list of research organizations to illustrate his points.

There is no question about Holland being a forceful individual with a colorful vocabulary. He would speak of our techno-economics work as "pushing industrial research through the economic keyhole" and the main research goal in industry being "to ring up

ENGINEERING AND PHYSICS

Thomas Morrin, head of the electrical engineering department, was away during Holland's visit. However, he and Donald Benedict, associate director, had agreed on what should be presented.

This group had started on September 1, 1948 and had grown to ten people within four months. Its first endeavor was on single-sideband transmitters. Facilities were developed around this program so that it became a nucleus for general electronics work covering television, circuitry, computers, transmitters, receivers and instrumentation. By mid-1949, the staff had grown to 30 engineers, to 40 by year-end, and to 50 professionals and 10 technicians by the time of Holland's review.

Five key research projects had been undertaken in engineering — one on communications for the U.S. Army, one on television systems, one for the Air Force on antennas, one for the Navy on miniaturization of electronic devices and one for RCA and Technicolor on vacuum tubes. Some 55% of all this work was for business and industry. Revenues were running at about $350,000 per year.

Morrin and Benedict felt the group had already made significant contributions. They pointed to such things as radio transmitters, antennas, computers and vacuum tubes — and to a rising research volume — as evidence of the prestige being contributed to SRI. They went on to emphasize diversification and technique development as two features of the engineering effort. The group had not moved in the direction of industrial control electronics to any great extent, and its leaders had decided to stay away from power engineering because of competitive capabilities on the West Coast.

Benedict felt there had been a large element of fortunate timing in recruiting this staff during the immediate post-World War II period. However, he stretched things a bit in saying "it would have been impossible to duplicate it had we started later." He emphasized that the staff was young, able and alert, but did acknowledge there was a shortage of knowledge on industrial problems although there was wide experience in military needs.

Looking to the future, Benedict thought caution, prudence and lack of facilities called for a policy of growing slowly. Then, he turned right around and spoke of having reached the mid-1950 position much sooner than expected and also about plans for more growth.

While this report was being prepared, we were trying to equip one temporary building in Stanford Village for engineering work. Financing was the problem. The plan called for a 75-man laboratory, but at that time we had only $90,000 invested in equipment (including office furniture) and less than $45,000 in leasehold improvements.

This was certainly inadequate for the planned staff even with an extremely spartan operation. The group urgently needed additional investments of at least $50,000 for equipment and $10,000 for building improvements in order to double its research revenues.

Benedict summarized the problem in one sentence: "Any significant growth would involve major expenditures and should be viewed with caution — unless we are prepared to carry the facility burden at a higher level." However, Morrin and Benedict wanted to hurdle the facility barrier with additional military projects and government-furnished equipment.

The applied physics group had been in operation only a short time when Holland made his review. It included only five people with Edward Doll as the director. All were working on a top secret project in the nuclear testing field. Annual revenues were less than $50,000, but Doll had contracts on hand for double this volume. He told Holland that the only problem was finding qualified people.

Although SRI had announced earlier that the physics group would work on problems faced by industry and the military, Doll decided shortly after the outbreak of the Korean War to concentrate on government contracts. The idea was the same as in economics and engineering — to create facilities and a staff that could later be turned to industrial pursuits. He had in mind such fields as shock waves, explosion phenomena, supersonic thermodynamics and many related analytical and experimental areas. He was vague on expansion, saying only that it would be "considerable."

As events unfolded during the next few years, the physics group specialized in nuclear testing and weapons effects studies. It gained a leading position in the field among independent R&D organizations. □

profits on the cash register." He was an idea man, with some good observations, although many were far off the target. Hobson used him as a trial balloon and solicited his views on almost every facet of the Institute's activities.

By August 17, 1950, Holland was all set to give the directors a rundown on SRI. He was working away on a report he predicted would be a "ground mover" in a great new future for SRI. Many of us were relieved by having more time to get on with the main business at hand. But Holland was thinking about the "Building Blocks" in a young institute. These were his words for our research groups.

THE WRITTEN WORD

Even before Holland finished his report, the gist of what he would say was becoming evident. He would call for better planning and tighter controls and, much to Hobson's delight, would include a case for more money and growth. I said at the time.

"He will urge better management of the resources we have but will say we need more capital for growth as soon as possible. Our 'break even' will carry more weight."

During World War I, Holland had been a pilot in the young Army Air Force. He often drew on this experience in coining phrases about some event or movement in industrial research. So it was that his report about SRI included a cryptic note on more instrument flying and less flying by the seat of the pants. He was calling for less expediency, more planning and tighter direction.

Holland wrote a 65-page report covering such things as SRI's position, organization, diversification, staff, international pursuits, facilities, research programs and finances. He made nine recommendations to the directors and six more to management.

His report opened with a brief summary of our history or, as he called it, a "flashback" to the Pacific Coast when the institute idea was emerging. He said the main purpose of the founders was to serve industry with no overriding obligations to Stanford. The latter was certainly not consistent with the charter but Holland wanted to center everything on the industrial thrust. The "flashback" suggested that our Menlo Park location was right because of the affiliation with Stanford and the attractiveness of the area as an ideal place to live.

In reviewing our research programs, Holland emphasized two points. He said engineering was the strongest of its type in any nonprofit research organization in the country and had brought national recognition to the Institute. The group was, in fact, making good progress, but Holland should have said that no other institute even had a similar program at the time.

His second point involved economics and was much too generous: "This department, too, has established a national reputation in service to government and business." This was followed by: "Critical buyers have recognized the unusually high caliber of the ... staff's varied backgrounds and tested experience in ... techno-economics and related fields."

As in the case of engineering, the group was making progress, but it was nowhere near Holland's description. Less than 50 research projects had been undertaken. Many "buyers" had never heard of the group. The staff had far too little experience.

Holland went on to say that techno-economic evaluations by independent organizations would be used by business at an accelerated pace. In this instance, he was too

A WRITTEN REPORT!!!?

conservative. The group grew rapidly in scope and size during the decade ahead and did much in promoting the whole idea of contract research in the social sciences.

A footnote on timing came to light during Holland's brief review of the Institute. He met with Dr. Robert Millikan, chairman of Cal Tech. Millikan made it clear that SRI had his full blessing, endorsement and encouragement and spoke of having earlier recommended "one of his boys" (i.e., Hobson) to be its executive director. Then, he confided that Captain Allan Hancock, a wealthy Southern California industrialist, had offered to help create a research institute at USC but had abandoned the plan upon seeing SRI's strong acceptance by business and industry.

This did indeed happen. Had SRI not been created by Stanford in 1946, a Southern California research institute probably would have been started at USC in 1948 or 1949.

Writing from what he called a 25-year perspective on industrial research, Holland referred to our mid-1950 position as a "pilot plant stage." Then he came to his main point — further growth was necessary and should be expected. He also attempted to explain the cumulative deficit that really did not need much explanation.

"This stage (pilot plant stage) is always expensive. It requires special equipment. It requires high caliber, skilled and experienced personnel, not only to operate the equipment but to make an economic evaluation of the cost of production."

Holland was moving closer to his punch line. "The sequence of operations ... (is) constructed to eliminate all but one variable when the development emerges from the pilot plant stage to full-scale commercial operation. That one variable is volume."

Turning to scientific research in the 1950s, Holland said that SRI was one of the infants in the 1940s group of non-profit research institutes. He acknowledged some obvious growing pains but stressed that the Institute was "testing the market" while "shaking down a team" and reaching out to "new and unknown fields of service" — all this involving a lot of time and money.

Growth for SRI meant more capital. Although some growth was necessary, cap-

ital was urgent even without growth. Holland argued that research markets in the 1950s would be highly competitive and said categorically that with many new institutions in place it would be almost impossible for SRI to earn enough money to build up a $3.0 million inventory in equipment.

The research market did become more competitive in time, and it was certainly true that earnings with such a small capital base could not provide enough equipment when it was most needed. In any event, Holland was laying a base in broad generalizations for a fund-raising program.

Nevertheless, the senior staff agreed with his main point — they wanted to move along with direct action and less committee management. There were eight special committees at the time — policy, finance, project acceptance, self-sponsored research, promotion and development, publications, education and personnel, and an executive group.

He called SRI a well-organized and efficiently-managed operation and said its organization and management were comparable to some of the nation's leading industrial research laboratories. These were strong statements and no one, including Hobson, really believed them. We had some strengths but we also had some obvious weaknesses.

Attention then shifted to our financial struggles. He wrote about severe budget pressures and a few financial crises during the short history of an infant research institute, but went on to emphasize the high morale of an organization that had gone through some trying times. Holland noted that most of the staff were young, ambitious, aggressive and at that stage in their careers when "they took things in stride and rolled with the punches." He was certainly correct about youth and morale. Many were between 30 and 35 years of age, and all were enthusiastic about the Institute and its future.

The next topic to draw Holland's attention was "merchandising, sales promotion and selling effort." He said that on the whole a good job was being done, but he did underline one word, results, as being the final yardstick. Our program on conferences and symposia was commended. Favorable comment was also made on the 'repeat order' percentage with research clients, then running about 60%. Holland said that costs for sales, public relations and promotional travel stood at 7% of revenue, which he considered reasonable. □

Hobson especially welcomed Holland's strong support for promotion — both institutional and for projects. There was no doubt about our consultant's views; he called for a "continuous effort." underlining the first word for emphasis. Then he tried to nail the point down tight: "There must be no relaxation for any reason."

Holland thought the main effort should be on existing rather than new programs and preferably on West Coast project opportunities. He urged Hobson to delegate more to his key associates and spend additional time as "foreign secretary" to business, government and other public organizations. In fact, he was already doing both things.

At the time about 70% of the Institute's industrial revenue was coming from California-based companies, with another 13% from other western states, and the remaining 17% from projects with eastern firms. Almost 40% of SRI's work for industry was in air pollution; geophysics and geology contributed about 20%. The balance was spread over several industries, e.g., petroleum, agricultural, chemical, electrical, transportation, building materials, minerals, forest products, etc.

Holland felt that our commercial revenues were reasonably well distributed even though a few projects accounted for high percentages in several industries. In any event, a good start on diversification had been made.

Holland singled out four "hallmarks" for SRI as being worthy of intensive development. They were techno-economics, seismic exploration, electronics and air pollution. He repeated his previous statement that SRI was well-known nationally in some electronics work and the acknowledged leader in air pollution research. Again, even with some good work under way, he was far too expansive! His suggestion that the techno-economics name be used for the economics group was not followed, simply because it was too much of a "buzz word."

When Holland made his mid-1950 review, more than half of the Institute's revenue was from business with the balance from government sources. He thought the ideal balance would be 50-50 but stressed some benefits that could arise from a growing government percentage. His points included more basic research, staff development, longer projects and less emphasis on immediate results. He was, in effect, justifying what was happening and might happen even more — growing work for government. "The balance ... between industry and government sponsored projects is one of basic policy — combined with expediency."

Some words were included to justify more government work as a public service. Holland was right in this observation. About ten years later, the IRS tightened its rules by calling for a substantial amount of total revenues within research institutes to be directly in the public interest. But the ratio was not defined more specifically. In any case, SRI met the test then and afterwards.

BRAZILIAN'S BABASSU NUT INDUSTRY
– Techno-economic field study –

THE ITALY PROJECT
Holland Explains in English! At left, Prof. Ing. Corbellini.

Holland then gave a boost for international work. An economics study on Cuba was in process and another on Brazil was being negotiated with Southwest Research Institute as a partner. A third was being discussed with the Italian government. Holland noted that foreign projects would give the members of our staff invaluable training — ''there being no substitute for actual experience ...''

Armour, Southwest and SRI had worked out a scheme for pooling their talents on international projects. Holland endorsed the idea and applauded the retention of James Drumm, an SRI director, and his New York partner, John Abbink, as consultants. ''We are in good hands with these gentlemen, both of whom are nationally known and highly respected.'' Both were quite helpful in developing our economics project in Italy; Abbink headed the SRI team for some nine months.

Holland then reviewed the building and equipment picture. He thought — as did others — that the temporary structures in Stanford Village would suffice for near-term needs but did mention future permanent buildings. The idea was that, once the ''proving period'' ended and with some financial solutions, an Industrial Sciences and Technology Building might be erected on or near the Stanford Campus.*

This acknowledged a basic fact; no decision had been made to remain at Stanford Village. Holland recognized that a new building was a question for the future. This was

*See ''A Village Home''

obvious to everyone. But he mentioned a possible Stanford location as one way to develop closer relationships with the University's Engineering and Business Schools. He was on weak footing in this respect; short distance between SRI and Stanford was not a barrier in the relationship.

The equipment problem was dealt with briefly. Holland's idea was that the meager investment of some $1,700 per research worker should be raised several times over — perhaps to the $15–$18,000 range for electronics. No one questioned his statement; our investment was insignificant by any reasonable measure even in 1950.

Business and financial affairs in the Holland Report were covered in bold brush strokes based on the idea that it would be difficult, if not impossible, for SRI to earn money at a rate sufficient to keep pace with its early growth. Some $100,000 for electronic equipment and $200,000 for working capital were mentioned.

Holland felt that a surplus operation could be maintained with more sales effort, higher prices on commercial projects, and additional government contracts with higher recovery rates. Thus, his view was quite clear; a surplus operation depended on growth, and this called for more capital. Holland felt no single plan or procedure would provide a solution and urged the directors to form a task force to raise capital.

Taking everything into account, Holland submitted two sets of recommendations, the first for the directors and the second for management. The word growth was not mentioned but was inherent in many of his points. The first call was for capital.

Having brought Holland into the picture in the first place, Hobson now found himself in an awkward position. He felt the report went way overboard in flattering him personally, in praising SRI to the skies, and in telling the directors in staccato language what they should do. Also, the flippant language was too much even for Hobson.

Much of the paper sounded like a whitewash. No one would ever believe SRI was so great. Even Hobson didn't think so, and neither did his associates. In fact, the senior group was embarrassed. The report was too breezy and gave a "once-over-lightly" impression.

However, the plan had called for a report to the directors — not to Hobson — and it was Hobson in particular who liked the gist of Holland's growth concepts. He was concerned, however, with the directors' reactions upon receiving such a report.

Hobson knew before mid-August what Holland would say and was at work on a diversion. He shared his feelings with McBean and Sterling and soft pedaled the whole exercise. At the same time, he sought general agreement among several directors on the idea of SRI coming up with a new development plan taking some of the points from Holland's report. He promised a more realistic and definite plan than the one he knew his friend would submit, and dropped a hint that maybe the directors "might not want to wade through the whole report."

Hobson let Holland know the directors would need time to study his paper, and that the best course was a very short presentation. He said the meeting would be short and the agenda tight. Gradually, Holland got the message; by August 17 — report day — he was rather quiet and subdued; it was the first time we had ever seen him so out-of-character.

Holland's paper also had several recommendations for management. None of them was controversial and as time went by all were acted upon in whole or in part.

RECOMMENDATIONS TO THE DIRECTORS

1. Provide means to supply $200,000 to $300,000 additional operating or working capital.

2. Provide laboratory equipment, or funds for its purchase, of approximately $400,000.

3. Executive committee of the board to appoint sub-committees as 'task forces' to deal specifically with capital funds, financial review and policy, university relations, promotion and development, and new departments.

4. Provide for review of plans for a department of food technology.

5. Review plans and stimulate top level executives' interest in national conferences sponsored by SRI.

6. Undertake with the assistance of outside experts a salary range study of top level staff members.

7. Increase the Technical Advisory Committee to include more industry representatives with at least one member from each major industry in California.

8. Suggest ways and means to procure support, both financial and operational, for public services.

9. Carefully select and invite more directors to the board from the southern part of California.

RECOMMENDATIONS TO MANAGEMENT

1. Employ Daniel Voorhees of Standard Oil to conduct a Post-Graduate Course in Research Organization and Management on fifteen Saturday mornings.

2. The Director to organize his office and personal staff in order to more effectively serve as 'Foreign Secretary' of SRI.

3. Continue a more intensive study with the business manager's office on all features to be included in SRI's price structure.

4. Improve procedures in recruiting, hiring and terminating personnel.

5. Devise means for better market analysis — industry by industry.

6. Develop and periodically revise a three-to five-year overall policy plan for Institute growth and development.

In ending his report with a call for more instrument flying, Holland sounded a warning. Business was good, but, he said, the management had never been through a major depression. He could have added that few were old enough to have been in professional life during the 1930s.

Very little happened at the August 17 meeting with the directors. The report was presented and promptly tabled for later discussion. This never took place because attention soon shifted to a new SRI plan which was in the works. Very few directors, if any, read the report, and this was just as well. In any event, it was soon put on the shelf as SRI and the directors began considering a possible loan from the U.S. Government.

One might well ask if the Holland review had any useful result, particularly since it was never really considered by the directors. It did serve one useful purpose with a lasting impact. Although their articulation left much to be desired, the Institute's program leaders were forced to think about their situations and make more plans for the future.

THE FOUR HORSEMEN

"A football foursome from Notre Dame lives on in memory. So, too, should a quartet in industrial research be remembered in other circles."

— CHARLES N. KIMBALL - 1979

Aunique and in some ways fascinating feature in relationships among some of the independents during SRI's Take-Off Days was a group some of us in a light vein called "The Four Horsemen." They were Harold Vagtborg, Jesse Hobson, Maurice Holland and Harold Leedy.

In various ways, Vagtborg and Hobson alternated as playmakers. Holland was a player-coach, being at times a consultant to Southwest, SRI and Armour. Kimball at Midwest was very much on the scene, but more as a general manager and coach of a new franchise in the league.

Having been the chief executive at Armour and Midwest before taking up the same poisition at Southwest, Vagtborg thought of himself as the leader of the post-World War II institute movement. He and Hobson were alike in many respects, both believing in vigorous promotion of their young organizations. Both admired Weidlein and Williams at Mellon and Battelle, but looked upon them as leaders in an older fashion.

The "praise" Vagtborg and Hobson independently and together would give their counterparts in the two older eastern institutes were, in reality, expressions of envy. They wanted very much to enjoy the kind of high respect the research world showed for their two friends.

Aside from the positions they held, there was little in common between Weidlein and Williams on the one hand and the leaders of Southwest and SRI on the other. They altogether different personalities, the former being more reserved than their western disciples.

In some respects a unique relationship existed between Vagtborg and Hobson. They were very good friends and always turned to each other in times of need when one thought the other could be helpful. However, they often irritated each other, sometimes for trivial reasons. They were competitors in a personal rather than an institutuional sense.

There was, in fact, very little competition between Southwest and SRI or among the nine institutes for particular projects. Much to their credit, the two men spoke over and over about cooperative possibilities. Even so, specific opportunities were hard to find.

Vagtborg had an inner drive to be a leader and statesman for the "independents." Deep down, Hobson wanted to develop SRI as rapidly as possible thus quietly showing his earlier mentor that both he and SRI were #1.

A chain situation prevailed among three of the Horsemen. Vagtborg thought he had already proven himself by developing Armour, starting Midwest and carrying on at Southwest. Hobson thought he had taken Armour to new heights after Vagtborg's tenure and wanted to overtake Southwest and Vagtborg quickly in an SRI upsurge.

Both of them tended to think of Leedy as a high draft choice looking for a head position. They liked him but, without saying so, wanted to be asked for coaching help.

Leedy was striving to make Armour stronger than it had been under Hobson. He seemed to feel that a new style of quiet and more-organized leadership, particularly on business affairs, was needed. He liked Vagtborg and Hobson but, quite understandably, wanted to do things his own way.

Holland was in an entirely different position. He was a catalyst — some said a gadfly — in the foursome. At times, each of the trio would share innermost thoughts about his

THE FOUR HORSEMEN
L to R: Harold Vagtborg, Maurice Holland,
Harold Leedy, and Jesse Hobson — 1948.

institute with ''Maury;'' at other times, each would distance himself from the energetic adviser in Pelham, New York.

Some of us thought ''erratic'' a better word than ''energetic.'' One had to be a ''speed listener'' to know what he was talking about. His handwriting defied even the most skilled ''codebreakers.''

Holland was well informed on many aspects of R&D management, but times were changing. The truth is that Vagtborg, Hobson and Leedy each felt he could not afford to sever the Holland tie, but each found the relationship exasperating at times. Each benefited from Holland but had to work at the task.

Almost to a man their separate associates did not wish to be involved. The author came into the picture often in view of his economics and international post at SRI. Both Vagtborg and Hobson, as well as Holland, were intensely interested in these fields.

With Holland urging them on, the group would talk about showing Mellon and Battelle how the job should be done. With Vagtborg and Hobson, Holland would wonder if Leedy could keep up the pace at Armour. Then, Holland and Hobson would lay out a course to keep SRI moving faster than Armour and Southwest. Also, Holland would combine with Vagtborg and Leedy as they questioned Hobson's overdrive at SRI.

The combinations continued. Holland would urge Vagtborg to do things aimed at propelling Southwest and its leader more and more onto the national stage. He would counsel the trio one at a time to lend a hand to Kimball on Midwest's strong regional course, whether or not he was asking for anything.

Hobson and Leedy were not on close terms. However, all the Horsemen liked Kimball very much and highly regarded his leadership at Midwest. He, in turn, had a high respect

for all of them and especially for what Hobson was doing at SRI.

It was amusing to hear Holland say time after time that he had taken one of the Horsemen ''behind the woodshed for a spanking'' or to give him a ''pep talk.'' To some of us, the whole situation was humorous at times and distracting at others. But, now and then, kernels came forth from the chaff. The problem was to find them.

Hobson had a tendency to get Holland involved in some way on almost everything new that might arise whether in administrative or research pursuits. Time after time he would ask Holland to join management meetings, meet individually with his associates and attend their own staff sessions. Furthermore, he brought Vagtborg's and Holland's views to our directors' attention any time he felt ''outside'' counsel might be helpful.

On a couple of occasions, Hobson arranged for Holland to attend board meetings but stopped the practice simply because even Hobson could not be sure what his unpredictable adviser would say. Time after time, however, he would refer to ''successful experiences'' at Southwest and Midwest but interestingly enough, never about Armour.

In retrospect, Hobson found the Four Horsemen to be helpful primarily because Vagtborg and Holland shared his views on rapid development through vigorous promotion. Some days with the group and especially with Holland were more productive than others, but they were never dull.

No one can say with certainty how much impact the individual Horsemen had on SRI during the early days. Nevertheless, those who were involved in one way or another knew that it was considerable. ☐

A personal note may add perspective on the Holland exercise. We knew him very well indeed. He could be exasperating at times, going way off the deep end. Although exuding confidence and strong convictions, he was nevertheless insecure in many ways, often feeling that the industrial research profession was passing him by. But amidst all the talking, he had some excellent ideas and thus often did make a contribution. Hobson, as well as several of his associates, recognized the situation. One had to sift the wheat from the chaff and go from there.

The Holland-Hobson relationship was amusing at times. They would become terribly upset with each other and then go to the other extreme in being confidants. The rest of us were sometimes tossed around in the process. Hobson often urged us to talk things over with Holland and then would question such talks when he was in a different mood about our ''advisor.''

SPEAKER!

Holland was much interested in our economics program and often talked about serving in some sort of a consulting capacity. We invited him to join an SRI group on a study of research institutes. Our interpreters were hopelessly lost in trying to deal with his cryptic language. Once before a major gathering of Italian business executives he spoke rapidly and critically about the U.S. Bureau of Standards. We wrote ''Slow'' on a piece of paper and passed it to him. This touched off an indictment of the Bureau as being ''slow'' in all its endeavors!

There were other lighter moments. As a member of a project team in 1953, Holland joined in an audience with His Holiness Pope Pius XII at the Vatican. Being a devout Catholic, this was the highlight of his life. He memorized a lofty message. We warned him to speak briefly and identify English as his tongue since the Pope spoke several languages. However, Holland had his mind on a speech. After explaining our mission in Italy and receiving the Pope's blessing, we turned towards Holland who began with the words: ''Holland is my name ...'' He got no further. Thinking the man before him was from The Netherlands, his Holiness spoke in Dutch and moved on without hearing Holland's words. It was the only time we ever found Holland speechless!

Holland often said later that he was an architect for our take-off days. He over-stated the case, but he certainly played a role in 1950 and beyond. ∎

STRENGTH IN DIVERSIFICATION Program Areas — Revenues		
Area	1950 Percent	1955 Percent
Engineering	23	38
Sciences	55	34
Economics/Management	22	28
TOTAL (Percent)	100%	100%
Dollars (Millions)	$ 2.0	$ 10.0

The RFC Episode

The Government needs SRI and should help finance its further development.

— (SENATOR) RICHARD M. NIXON - 1950

URING SRI's CREATION, no particular thought was given to possible government financing. In fact, very little attention was given to projects for the federal government. The founders had service to industry in mind. They wanted to avoid any restrictions that might flow from government capital in whatever form.

Even during our first three and a half years or so before moving to black ink, there was no talk about seeking capital from Uncle Sam. The rising deficit was financed largely by loans from Stanford and a group of California banks. Receivables mounted as staff and revenues increased. The debt for working capital and equipment had passed through the million dollar point by mid-1950.

Perhaps some such investment should have been planned when SRI was launched. This was not done. Nevertheless, the institute grew rapidly. A "ratchet" effect was at work — growth, red ink, more growth to build up earnings but more losses with higher volume.

A drive was on during early 1950 to reach a "breakeven" point. Both cost reductions and revenue growth were involved. For the second time, a real surplus appeared at mid-year. However, the prospect was for more red ink for several months to come. It was clear that something had to be done. More "equity" capital or the equivalent or more borrowing was urgently needed. Neither Stanford nor the banks wanted to increase their loans.

Hobson wanted to continue and even accelerate the growth pattern believing it was essential to our long-term development. He and his associates were worried; the directors were greatly concerned; the Stanford Trustees were alarmed. The so-called Holland study was under way.* No one knew what the future might hold. There was talk in many circles that SRI might have to fold.

Hobson was hoping the Holland review might lead to some sort of fundraising plan to provide more working capital However, it was obvious that any action along this line would take time and there was none to lose. A sharp cutback had ominous implications; the momentum would be lost. A "Safety Plan" was needed.

An initiative was taken even while "break even" was bringing new enthusiasm around the Institute. The possibility of help from government (particularly the Reconstruction Finance Corporation) came into the picture.

Even prior to talking with the board's executive committee, two meetings were held with RFC officials in Washington.

---

* See chapter "An Outside View"

It soon appeared that something might be worked out. In any event, more meetings were scheduled even though several directors doubted that anything acceptable would arise.

Along with Hobson and James Drumm (an SRI director in New York), Herbert and others were involved. It soon came to light that the RFC was prohibited by law from making loans to nonprofit corporations. Hobson's reaction was simple enough — get the law changed. Most of the directors thought this was an impractical hope. However, encouragement came from an unlikely source — the RFC itself — a possible amendment to the Defense Production Act of 1950. It had been passed by the House of Representatives and was before the Senate Banking and Finance Committee.

Meanwhile, Hobson was telling the directors that the initiative with government was based on getting SRI in a position where it could respond to project requests by the Department of Defense. Although concerned about growth implications for the Institute, no one wanted to champion a stance of "turning down government work." Management was well aware of this new feeling, the first time it had emerged among the directors. There was a quick follow-through with one and all of them. The task was made easier by newspaper stories about military setbacks in the Korean War.

There were indeed several approaches to SRI by the military services immediately following the invasion of South Korea. One of these in the electronics field was by the Office of Naval Research (ONR). The project involved some $750,000 per year — a very large amount at the time. ONR readily agreed to provide needed equipment and finance building improvements. The main problem was working capital. Four possibilities were suggested to the directors — advance payments by the government, additional bank loans, some form of assistance by western companies, and an RFC loan.

This possible "new course" in financing was discussed by the directors on August 17, 1950. Never before had there been such an agenda involving government.

McBean and several other directors felt that some way should be found to finance a larger operation. This attitude quickly led to a request by the board for a new plan covering the next stage of the Institute's development. There was little interest in the idea of company financing associated with government projects. No one wanted to approach the banks for such a loan. A request to Stanford was out of the question. The advance payment route was filled with unattractive conditions. Thus, attention soon centered on the RFC.

Drumm and Herbert contacted several members of the Congress including the Senators from California and in due course, were brought in touch with the Senate Committee. At our urging, a phrase was inserted in the proposed legislation to cover certain nonprofit organizations. Immediately following a reference to "private enterprises," the words "including research corporations not organized for profit" were added. All this was done quickly and without fanfare. Very few people were involved. The insert attracted little attention.

The amending words remained in the Act as finally passed by the Congress and signed by President Truman. The RFC was to be the lending agency. Thus, the way was cleared for SRI to apply for a loan. By mid-September, 1950, a plan was being discussed with the RFC and our directors. These talks continued in rapid succession for about a month.

The whole idea of RFC financing involved five objectives. One was to increase our government-sponsored research by about $1.0 million per year, from the existing $800,000 rate (40% of total revenue). The second called for a $1.0 million increase in industrial projects to some $2.2 million per year. Thus, in effect, our annual revenues would be doubled — from some $2.0 million to $4.0 million with only a modest increase in the government percentage. This was certainly in line with the director's views.

The other three goals were to provide more scientific and technical equipment, create a cash reserve for contingencies and retire half of our long-term debts ($500,000 to Stanford and $600,000 with the banks).

The plan was aimed at getting a ten-year loan with 3% interest. The principal would be repaid from a reserve fund in which one half of our earnings would be deposited. We thought such a loan would enable the Institute ''to reach a volume between $3.0 and $4.0 million during 1951, and to operate with a surplus between $150,000 and $250,000.''

Hobson and the Institute's finance group felt these earnings were possible (especially in light of recent cost reductions) by broadening the base for charges to sponsors (clients) and from earlier increases in overhead recovery rates.

The RFC loan was to be for $1,892,000. Quite rightly, the first emphasis was on accounts receivable that had accrued from earlier growth.

First Idea

$ 250,000	Accounts receivable financing
550,000	50% reduction of long-term debt
250,000	Additional working capital
200,000	Deposits in a cash reserve
642,000	Institute expansion (equipment, staff, etc.)
$1,892,000	TOTAL

The last item for expansion was included to finance a staff increase from 275 to about 400 and to cover equipment needs, building improvements, some new offices, inventories, service facilities and the beginnings of a staff retirement plan.

Everyone had in mind that an RFC loan would greatly alter the Institute's financial position giving some breathing room for the operation. The numbers were large at that stage in SRI's development. The possible balance sheet changes were considerable.

Items	Mid-1950	Mid-1951 (Est.)
Accounts Receivable	$ 453,000	$ 925,000
Cash on hand	99,000	300,000
Inventories	39,000	85,000
Equipment (net)	285,000	700,000
Debts	1,100,000	550,000
RFC Debt	—	1,182,000

These projections did not include possible new Associate funds nor any surplus that might be generated from operations. However, Hobson emphasized to the directors and others that, aside from building construction, the plan covered everything needed to double annual revenues within two years or so.

The directors considered all these details as well as policy implications associated with an RFC loan. They sought assurance that the new financing would not bring the Institute under too much government control. Several wanted to be sure the loan would not be "permanent" or even "semi-permanent."

With an understanding that the loan would strengthen our capacity for service to industry, the executive committee agreed on further negotiations with the RFC. This decision was made on September 11, 1950. We lost no time in moving ahead; a prospectus had already been prepared and was given to the RFC the next day in Washington. Strategy was worked out on an overnight flight.

During the following month, more discussions were held with RFC officials on the proposed loan application. Considerable progress was made by mid-October. The RFC looked favorably on the idea of a ten-year, 3% loan of $650,000 to cover equipment and facility needs plus a $700,000 line of credit for working capital. However, it did not like the idea of loan funds being used to reduce the Stanford and bank loans. Still further, it was asking within government for a clear ruling on authority to make loans to nonprofit organizations.

TRUMANESE

In connection with an Aviation Commission session in the autumn of 1950 (in which the author was involved), President Truman had heard about our RFC loan idea. As an aside, he made a typical blunt but humorous remark: "They are experts in delay; by the time you get it you may not want it. A country bank is faster."

Discussions with the RFC and other governmental agencies continued through the balance of October and November. Several directors including Paul Davies of Food Machinery (now FMC) joined the meetings at various times. In late November, the Department of Commerce was designated as the "certifying agency" for loan applications involving nonprofit research organizations.

This was fine with SRI since the arrangement had more or less been steered in that direction. We had a good friend and supporter in the Department's upper echelon. Meanwhile, more information was delivered to the RFC's San Francisco office.

These negotiations finally led to a loan application for $1,630,000. In transmitting the papers, Hobson pointed out that $800,000 was needed immediately — $400,000 for working capital and $400,000 for equipment. The RFC was asked for an additional $830,000 before the end of 1951 — $300,000 for added working capital, $230,000 for more equipment, and $300,000 to retire long-term debts.

We wanted the loan in two parts, a line of credit for $700,000 and a ten-year instrument for $930,000. The credit withdrawals were to be repaid from internal cash generation. The loan repayment was to be over eight years beginning two years after receipt of the money.

Our loan application was, of course, cast in terms of services to government rather than to industry. The purpose was "to enable the Institute to expand its facilities and staff to accept additional research and development programs vital to the present national defense effort … "

The application did go on to include "assistance to prime contractors of the government for military equipment ... '' This was as much as could be said about private industry. We knew that government would not openly help finance our industrial thrust.

This language must be viewed in light of Congressional interest in passing the Defense Production Act. The Korean War had begun during the summer; the Cold War was expanding elsewhere; the nation was in an emergency. The application went on to say that the loan would enable SRI to increase its staff of some 280 people to about 475 and that annual revenues should rise to $4.0 million or more by the end of 1951.

The RFC was told that adquate temporary space in Menlo Park was available leaving additional laboratory equipment and working capital as urgent needs. A reworked application showed how the loan funds would be used.

SECOND TRY

$ 200,000	Increase in working capital
500,000	Investment in accounts receivable
460,000	Additional equipment and fixed assets
60,000	Building improvements
50,000	Acquisition of new staff
300,000	Debt retirement
$1,570,000	TOTAL

Late in December of 1950, the RFC office in San Francisco sent a favorable report to Washington. At year end, the matter was in the hands of the RFC and Department of Commerce. Prospects looked good for early action. Meanwhile, Hobson was telling the directors that the loan could help bring in earnings of $20,000 to $25,000 per month by the end of 1951. He was, in fact, even more optimistic; maybe the line of credit would not have to be used. This was, in effect, handwriting on the wall.

Events were not, however, to move rapidly in the government bureaucracy. Many more discussions with the RFC and at Commerce were held during the first quarter of 1951; many more papers had to be submitted. To hasten matters along, a Washington attorney, Harvey Gunderson, was retained.

By April 1951, almost eight months had gone by since loan discussions with the RFC had started. In the meantime, our financial situation had improved and other money possibilities had arisen. Everyone, especially Hobson, was growing impatient with the drawn-out delays.

Prospects were still favorable, but the question was when something would happen. The new financial situation soon made it appear that no more than $200,000 of the equipment loan might be needed. Nevertheless, negotiations continued.

Just prior to an SRI executive committee meeting in early June 1951, the RFC decided that the loan would not be made. Both the RFC and the National Production Administration (NPA) were afraid a precedent might be created for all sorts of loan requests from nonprofit research organizations. The decision was timid in light of the new legislative authority.

Drumm thought the whole matter should be taken to higher authority. Hobson and others at SRI were inclined to do nothing more. We were becoming more convinced that the money was not really necessary and were fearful about future dealings with the RFC. The directors agreed, but the door was left open should Drumm or others receive any information that suggested further negotiations.

This opened the way for an interesting turn of events. We had become disenchanted with the whole exercise. But the RFC decision aroused a new motivation. Being reasonably confident that another solution on finances could be developed, Hobson had a deep-seated desire to get the loan approved if only on the grounds that a matter of principle was involved. He knew that, even so, an approved loan might not be utilized.

Thus, for an entirely different set of reasons, we moved into high gear on the application. The RFC decision was discussed with Richard Nixon, then a senator from California. He was upset by the story, feeling that the government needed SRI and should do something to help finance its development. Going directly to the counsel of the Senate Committee that had handled the Defense Production Act, he found that indeed the legislative intent was being thwarted.

This forceful intervention quickly led to a reversal on the loan decision. The application was approved by NPA for $520,000 at 5% interest with SRI to set aside 2.5% of its revenue for repayments. But this was only an NPA action; the RFC was yet to be heard from. But Hobson's urge to pursue an unwanted loan was heightened. The situation was almost unreal, but he was not alone in the pursuit. It boiled down to who was the more influential — the RFC or SRI.

By late June, 1951, word was reaching the Institute that the RFC was approving a loan for equipment and facilities only with the new assets to be collateral. Our response was simply to wait for something in writing. This did not come until August 2, 1951 — a year after things had been set in motion. The amount was only $300,000 for equipment and building improvements.

Everyone — including the directors — felt that the terms were unacceptable. However, discussions with the RFC indicated that most of the objectionable provisions could be adjusted satisfactorily.

The RFC? It may need a loan more than we do.
— DONALD J. RUSSELL - 1950

Feeling that his motivations had been fulfilled at least in principle, Hobson promptly recommended a turn-down decision to the directors. Our financial position was improving, more working capital from Stanford was in prospect, and difficulties of working with the RFC were evident. Furthermore, the loan was only a token in comparison with the first application.

GEORGE R. HERBERT
Organizing the case.

It was with some satisfaction, then, that the RFC was told that nothing more would be done about the matter "for the time being." The application had been in process for ten months. So, in late September, 1951, the matter was brought to an end. Hobson was satisfied while being critical of the government decision process.

In the meantime, however, SRI was not standing still. Revenues almost doubled in one year from around $170,000 per month to approximately $325,000. Earnings grew from less than $1,000 in September 1950, to about $15,000 a year later. More importantly, other solutions on financing — to be unfolded later — were found.

The RFC plan, nor anything of a similar nature, was ever to be reconsidered by either SRI or its directors. It is fortunate that the loan never materialized; it could have greatly changed the Institute's basic thrust. The entire RFC episode is interesting in several respects. It was launched with high expectations and enthusiasm. Hobson was motivated in some respects by the concept of proving to the government, to himself and to our directors that the nation needed SRI, that the Institute had an obligation to increase its government-sponsored research, and that Washington should demonstrate its interest by participating in a financing plan. Hobson felt, with some justification, that we had, in effect, written the law to make this possible.

Herbert was "point guard" on the RFC front. I was involved in the Washington meetings and in "drafting" an addition to the Defense Production Act. We knew that the government officials directly concerned were extremely reluctant to include nonprofit corporations within their orbit. They envisioned a flood of loan requests from all sorts of underfinanced nonprofit groups. They were probably right.

Nixon was most helpful when we wanted to reverse RFC's first turndown of the loan application. Two meetings with him on other matters were to follow several years later. Also, he was the key speaker at one of SRI's international conferences. On one of these occasions, he showed a good memory — "How did that RFC loan work out?"

In perspective, the episode was useful. We sensed at the time but did not fully appreciate the implications. It marked the real beginning of an attitude by the directors that the Institute should actively seek to serve government (including the military) as well as business. It was part of a Search for Purpose.

This shift was much more fundamental than it may appear today. Some of it was subtle; some was substance. In any event, the Institute was the beneficiary. In many respects, the words "government" and "military" as clients entered the mainstream. The day was to come when projects from these sources would be sought energetically as a matter of policy and obligation, rather than being accepted with some hesitation.

This gradual change in attitude helped generate a protocol of sorts to our Charter and an annex to our founder's intentions. All this was part of some rethinking about SRI's role. From a policy viewpoint, the Institute was taking a great step forward. In the eyes of some directors the pendulum was to shift too much, but the basic change was right.

In any case, those on the firing line with the RFC in 1950 were greatly relieved that it was not to be a part of our financial future. Thus, the RFC played its part without the loan.

A personal note at the time still applies. ''We are lucky that nothing happened. Now we can go ahead as planned.'' ∎

QUAYULE FIELD STATION IN SALINAS, CALIFORNIA

FURTHER WORD ABOUT PROJECT NUMBER 1

SRI's first project began in mid-1946 before the Institute was incorporated. It was aimed at developing rubber from the guayule plant.

Work was transferred to the U.S. Department of Agriculture on August 1, 1947. On January 17, 1986, the National Science Foundation announced a claim by a University of California (Irvine) scientist that he had succeeded in cloning the rubber plant.

Nothing was said about what may transpire in *another* 40 years.!!

Some Equity Capital

You gentlemen on the West Coast have an unexcelled opportunity ... (for) public service.

— David Sarnoff - 1951

ONE OF THE REASONS SRI WAS ABLE TO RESPOND at a rapid rate during its early years, was help from an Associates Plan. It was, in effect, an all-important source of "equity" capital. The money enabled the Institute to increase its staff fourfold and its revenues fivefold in little more than four years during the first half of the 1950's.

The idea of raising capital through contributions by companies arose prior to SRI's formation in late 1946. Several attempts were made off and on during 1947 and 1948, to get some sort of a fundraising program under way. However, on each occasion the directors set plans aside while waiting for the Institute to demonstrate that it could earn a surplus.

By mid-1949, it was generally agreed that a fundraising plan should call for company memberships at $15,000 per unit. On this basis, an Associates brochure was issued in the form of an invitation that could be placed before selected companies. In fact, the plan was never adopted formally by the directors. It was a case of McBean deciding that something should be done and Hobson's readiness to go into action. Even so, not much happened before 1951; the other directors were not enthusiastic about raising money for a "red ink" operation.

The 1949 brochure outlined in concise terms the purpose, organization and operations of the Institute. It emphasized that money was needed for buildings, equipment, additional people, public service research and working capital. The plan called for lump sum payments or annual contributions over a three-year period. Associates were to receive certain "tangible" as well as intangible benefits. Among these were consultations, technical information, recognition and satisfaction in helping develop the West.

The Associate invitation indicated that SRI was organized for the specific purpose, among others, of translating science into products and processes of commercial value, particularly for the benefit of the West. No special mention was made of Stanford University except in referring to an affiliation between the two institutions.

Although invitations were presented here and there to various companies during part of 1949 and through 1951, the results were meager. Only a few came into the Plan and most were brought in by McBean and SRI itself. Only $35,000 was received in 1950. However, cumulative contributions by July of that year had reached $152,000 plus $45,000 more in pledges. Two-thirds of the money on hand had come from McBean and two companies with which we had close ties — his family firm, Newhall, and Standard Oil Company of California (SoCal). By May 1950, the directors were convinced that the Institute would soon be operating with a monthly surplus and, therefore, agreed to support an intensive campaign aimed at getting Associate memberships. Hobson arranged for a man by the name of George Keller to join SRI and take charge of the exercise.*

Three things then happened that once again brought the infant Associates program to a virtual standstill. First of all, Keller was hardly the man for the job. The basic idea at the time was to sign up 120 or more companies in the western states. Keller was pessimistic. He doubted that there were anywhere near 120 companies on the West Coast that might be prospective Associates. Also, he said it would not be possible to attract eastern companies to the Plan. Several of us thought he was wrong on the last point and told him so, but with little effect.

This pessimism worried McBean, Hobson and several other directors. In July, the Institute began operating without an "approved" financial plan while negotiations were under way on a possible loan from the Reconstruction Finance Corporation (RFC). Under the circumstances, the directors thought it best to leave the Associates Plan on dead center. Keller soon resigned.

The third reason why nothing much happened during 1950 involves the so-called Holland Report taken up in an earlier chapter. Keller's ideas on the Associates Plan were included in Holland's proposals on the Institute's future development. As mentioned earlier, the directors paid little attention to Holland and, in fact, Hobson was less than enthusiastic about his report. Thus, by mid-August 1950, it was clear that nothing more would be done on the Associates Plan for some time to come.

In the spring of 1951, Hobson and others decided to make still another move on the fundraising program. We had operated for ten months with a surplus and the RFC negotiations had come to a virtual end. Hobson arranged for Hugh Buhrman, a professional fundraiser in New York, to meet with some of the directors. This took place on June 6, 1951. By this time the need for more capital was urgent; only $45,000 in Associate funds had been received since July 1950.

Buhrman spent several days at the Institute before meeting with the board's executive committee. The main thrust of his plan was that while he could help organize the effort, solicitations would have to be handled by board members. His approach was to lay out the program, see that it moved on schedule and follow up as necessary. Neither Buhrman nor any of the senior staff and directors felt that debt retirement was a good basis for soliciting funds. On the other hand, he was highly enthusiastic about featuring SRI as a regional asset in the West. He believed that a broad base of industrial support could be developed in the order of $200,000–250,000 per year. No one thought much of his idea of a dollar quota for each potential Associate, but in the interests of getting on with the project no particular objection was raised.

Buhrman felt strongly that if he was to work on the fundraising program his prime tie should be with the board, rather than with management. He was wrong about this, but it did not matter too much in the end. He was retained for 13 weeks at a $6,500 fee. The cost was to be charged to capital rather than operations. In those days, even $500 a month in costs had a noticeable effect on the bottom line.

There was an immediate result of the decision to retain Buhrman. McBean saw it as a

---

* Not George Keller, currently an SRI director.

signal that the fundraising program could finally get out of the starting blocks. This pleased him greatly — so much so that he immediately wrote out a check for $10,000 bringing his total to $40,000.

At the meeting with Buhrman, one of the directors raised a question about possible conflict or competition with Stanford in fundraising. This was not the first time the question would arise. Sterling, our chairman and the University's president, was in the middle. Some of his Stanford colleagues were concerned about competition while at the same time Sterling did not want to create further problems having to do with our urgent capital needs. The question was set aside with general agreement that some competition might develop but not of a severe nature.

As the situation unfolded during the next few years, there was some competition in the eyes of a few University administrators. But it was not serious or basic simply because Stanford had not yet geared up for a major development program involving companies. Furthermore, we took care on many occasions to tell prospective Associates that SRI did not wish to drain away any potential gifts to the University.

Another financial question involving Stanford was raised by Sterling with the directors in early June 1951. He wanted to know when SRI might be in a position to assist the University financially as had been expected at the beginning. Again, the question was moved to the future. Everyone agreed that some payments or gifts should be made in due course. But the consensus was clear — '' ... the University could not expect to receive any financial income from the Institute for some time.'' The matter was not pursued at the time even though some of the Trustees and a few Stanford people felt that the situation could be different if the Institute would restrain its growth to a far greater extent.

The first outline for a fundraising campaign was presented by Buhrman to the directors at the end of June 1951. Several of us worked with him in developing the plan. We were most anxious to see something happen and certainly wanted to make sure another "Stop" sign did not appear. Buhrman finally proposed that the goal be $1.5 million over three years with $500,000 to be raised during the last four months of 1951. Many of us knew that the immediate goal was unrealistic, but Buhrman was being urged by Hobson to give the board a sense of urgency on capital needs.

> *There are many ways to grow; the best of all is in quality.*
> — DAVID PACKARD

To some extent, a bit of play-acting was being carried out. McBean was working behind the scenes with Hobson who, in turn, was doing the same with Buhrman — all this while Buhrman was supposed to be working directly for the board. The directors went along with the act, knowing that McBean was the leading man while Hobson was the stage manager.

Hobson was a master in making a rapid run sound like a slow walk, being well aware some of the directors felt that he always wanted to move too fast. So, he urged Buhrman to describe his program as a small, conservative and quiet effort. Buhrman did just that, but went on to suggest two $150,000 pledges as a good campaign starter. He also proposed a series of luncheons and dinners in the San Francisco Bay Area, Southern California and the Pacific Northwest.

Less than a month after the directors decided to go ahead on an expanded Associates program, the SRI-Stanford situation came up again. A few Stanford Trustees, who were also our directors, began to worry about competition. Their concern was not allayed by suggestions that the Institute campaign might open up new sources of support for the University. In any event, Sterling emphasized that our search for support should be in harmony with Stanford's development program.

The directors heard from Buhrman in late September, his appointment having been extended for a further 13 weeks. By this time, Follis of SoCal had agreed to head a special development committee of the board; with behind-the-scenes urging by McBean, he was recommending an initial goal of $500,000 for equipment plus $250,000 for working capital.

Buhrman told the directors about McBean's idea to invite General David Sarnoff, chairman of the RCA board, to speak at a San Francisco dinner that would formally open our fundraising program. Sarnoff was familiar with the Institute's work on color television for RCA; McBean thought a kickoff event with Sarnoff as the speaker would give great impetus to the whole development effort.

MILLION DOLLAR LUNCHEON — SAN FRANCISCO
L to R: ATHOLL MCBEAN, DAVID SARNOFF AND GWIN FOLLIS, after the luncheon on November 14, 1951.

Sterling wanted to see something done to relieve the Institute's capital problem, but he was still worried about the implications for Stanford. He outlined his concerns point by point to the directors, saying emphatically that all fundraising contacts must be cleared with the University. This was fine with SRI, and we did exactly what he said. Never once was there anything other than a "Go Ahead" response.

When ''sticky cases'' arose, they were usually settled quickly with Kenneth Cuthbertson, Stanford's vice president, or during a late afternoon ''caucus'' with the chairman at his Campus home. Some 30 years later, Sterling spoke about the coordination — ''everything was handled quite easily.''

Nevertheless, McBean was restive about the matter and often spoke privately about the ''attitude'' at Stanford. Sterling's position was certainly right and fair in every respect. The problem was simply that McBean was not accustomed to doing anything under wraps. In the final result he made all sorts of contacts while merely saying to us now and then, ''Do whatever you need to do to inform the University, while I get on with the job.''

No time was lost in arranging for Sarnoff to be in San Francisco. The directors hosted a luncheon on November 14, 1951 for a large group of West Coast business executives, civic leaders and editors. Follis presided as chairman of the board's development committee. The event, later to be called ''The Million Dollar Luncheon'' marked the beginning of a long-delayed, energetic drive for some equity capital.

Sarnoff spoke about and emphasized the importance of scientific research in economic and industrial development:

PARTNERSHIP

As we face the challenge of these times, we can be sure that the way we are going to live — the kind of economy and government we are going to have — will be determined largely by the things industry produces and the uses that will be made of them. These things are the end-products of research.

The pattern of our industrial progress is clear. It lies in a partnership between those who create good things and those who produce, distribute, and service them. It lies in teamwork between research and industry.

Sarnoff then turned to a perspective on SRI's role in the partnership between business and research. He was unstinting in a salute to the Institute, taking special note of our pioneering work under way in applied economics.

AN OUTSTANDING EXAMPLE

(SRI) is important not just because it has fine laboratories and able researchers, which it certainly has, but because it is an outstanding example of the natural partnership between research and industry.

We can all appreciate how important it is to know the facts about a problem before we undertake to solve it. That is why the facts developed by the Industrial Economics Department of this Institute will play an increasing role in the solution of industry's problems.

All this was well and good but the whole purpose of the luncheon was to lay the base for a stepped-up Associates campaign. Thus, Sarnoff called upon industry to support such institutions as SRI. It was crystal clear to everyone present that his plan was centered on the Institute.

AN OPPORTUNITY

Business can and should bring to this partnership with science their money, their encouragement, their advice, their ability to make available to the public the things that researchers develop, and, above all, faith in the sincerity and ability of scientists to produce results. They are truly our partners in the enterprises on which we are embarked, and they deserve the treatment due a trusted partner. You gentlemen on the West Coast have an unexcelled opportunity to advance on this front and, in doing so, to render public service to the entire nation.

As might be expected, everyone connected with SRI was greatly pleased with Sarnoff's presentation. He had set the stage for an energetic campaign on capital contributions. A wave of enthusiasm swept through all of the Institute, and well it should have. It was immediately apparent that Sarnoff had made a considerable impression on the luncheon guests. Many of us felt that his fifth anniversary present — delivered at San Francisco's Fairmont Hotel — was to be a benchmark in our history. We agreed on a few words.

We can now move on — it will be a jet-assisted take-off.

The board's executive committee met immediately following the Sarnoff luncheon. Ten directors were asked to serve with Follis and McBean on the development committee. The group included Bechtel, Blyth, Crafts, Davies, Lyon, McKee, Pigott, Roach, Stewart and Zellerbach. A campaign goal of $1.5 million was immediately set up.

Sterling, the board chairman, turned once again to the touchy question of SRI-Stanford relationships. He emphasized that the development committee had an opportunity to do an educational job with industry on the role companies could and should play in supporting research, both basic and applied, and higher education as well. He was, of course, well aware that the upcoming campaign would involve SRI almost exclusively, but wanted to do everything possible in smoothing the path with University fundraisers.

The new committee lost no time in getting some action under way. Carl Titus, one of Hobson's colleagues from Armour Research Foundation days, was put in charge of the program. Many of us worked with Hobson, Titus and Buhrman in the planning exercise. The days were feverish with activity, one reason being to have everything in place

FAIRMONT HOTEL — SAN FRANCISCO
Home of the IIC and other frequent meetings.

EQUITY CAPITAL MAN
L to R: Carl L. Titus and E. Finley Carter, (SRI's first president).

before the Christmas holidays. This is just what happened. All was in readiness for the board by mid-December. The centerpiece was a pamphlet describing the development program. Taking a cue from Sarnoff, the title was "Research and Industry."

The committee's program, as outlined in the new brochure, opened with a reference to Sarnoff's earlier remarks:

THE CASE FOR RESEARCH

Technology is the strength of our free enterprise system, and only research, both fundamental and applied, can supply the technology to keep our industry free. General Sarnoff very ably emphasized the necessity for private industry to support research in universities and public research institutes to avoid government domination of the country's research effort; and, through domination of research, the eventual domination and control of industry. Only strong and continuing financial support by industry of the privately-endowed universities and research institutes will keep them free.

The brochure continued with reasons why business and industry should provide some financial support to SRI. The spotlight was put on equipment and facility needs (the so-called capital items) while making it clear that the Institute was not seeking funds for day-to-day operations.

As is evident from the opening passages, the Associates booklet referred specifically to privately-endowed universities and to Stanford in particular. This was in keeping with Sterling's strong urging that every opportunity be taken to advance the cause of the University while centering attention on our capital needs.

The booklet was specific on the Institute's development program. Pointing out that an annual research volume of $4 million with only $500,000 of equipment was neither sound nor adequate, the first objective was to provide funds for new scientific and technical devices. In terms of optimum size, our goal was said to be annual research revenues of up to $5 million, a staff of 500 people, and some 125,000 sq. ft. of floor space.

These were modest goals, even at the end of 1951, but by no means did they tell the full story. Hobson, for one, was already thinking in much bigger terms. Nevertheless, he was persuaded by several of us, including Follis, to set conservative targets in the publication.

Several other objectives followed the outline of growth plans. They touched on SRI's independence, debt retirement from earnings, public services and assistance to Stanford.

GENERAL OBJECTIVES

a. Make the Institute independent of any need to accept government research.
b. Assure SRI's ability to retire its own indebtedness on schedule from earned surplus.
c. Provide support for public service research needed by Western industry.
d. Broaden the base of support for the Institute's research activities.
e. Enable the Institute to increase the scale of its basic research.
f. Place SRI in a position to contribute to and further the basic research program of Stanford University.

The first of these objectives reflected the directors' concern about rising government work in the wake of the Korean War. One might read into the statement that somehow SRI was striving to work only for industry. This was certainly not the case. The wording was subtle, meaning, in effect, that government projects should not be sought and accepted merely because of a fundamental financial need. As time went on, many questions were to be asked as our government volume continued to increase.

Most of the directors never did accept Hobson's concept that government work should be undertaken for patriotic reasons. Even he knew that this reasoning was on weak ground.

The last of the general objectives is simply further evidence that SRI recognized an obligation in time to make gifts in undetermined amounts to Stanford. It was quite clear to everyone that this was the intent of the first broad purpose in our charter.

The development plan also was specific on what could be accomplished with $1.5 million in new capital. This money was to generate financial security and, except for permanent buildings, no further capital contributions were to be sought. In the words of the committee document " ... with this support the Institute can make its own way."

The new Associates drive was aimed at getting pledges for one-third of the $1.5 million before the end of 1951. This goal was unrealistic even though discussions were already under way with several companies. In any event, the $1.5 million was to be used for three purposes: $1 million for laboratory equipment; $250,000 for fundamental research; and $250,000 for working capital. Even the additional equipment would have brought our per capita investment to only $3,500, a meager figure even in 1951.

It was intended at the time that Associate funds used to support basic research would be supplemented by appropriations from earnings. Furthermore, a direct tie with Stanford was very much in the picture:

> *A major part of the Institute's fundamental research program will be undertaken at Stanford University, financed by the Institute, to take advantage of the staff available there, to augment the basic research program of the University and to bring a closer working relationship between the academic staff and the Institute.*

The basic idea was that something on the order of $250,000 from SRI's annual earnings and contributions would be given to Stanford for general support of basic research programs pertinent in one way or another to SRI's interest. In addition, the Institute would have its own program.

This policy was, in fact, initiated later in the 1950s and worked quite well. It was replaced by an annual gift plan under Stanford's first major fund-raising program, known by the acronym PACE. A somewhat higher annual amount was contemplated. Unfortunately, this commitment was cancelled by SRI in the mid-1960s. Stanford officials were understandably upset, but they did not press the issue at the time.

The episode was both unpleasant and unnecessary. I was present when the University was notified through its Provost, Frederick Terman. Much of what Sterling and others had tried to do in cementing the Stanford-SRI affiliation was brought to a standstill. Later on, during the Stanford-SRI separation days, when some faculty members were advocating such a move along with even higher payments by SRI, Terman took a glance backward.

Had the Institute continued along the path laid out in the 1950s the separation issue would not exist.

Terman was partly right; other factors were involved in the separation. All was worked out in the early 1970s; but this is part of another stage in our history.

Several operating matters were made clear to prospective Associates. The new brochure took up the key points one by one.

OPERATIONS

None of the contributed funds will be used to retire the existing indebtedness of the Institute ... The current operating surplus can and will be maintained ... Government contract research will be limited to not more than 50% of total activity during the present emergency and in normal times to not more than 25% of annual volume ... The optimum operating level for the Institute is an annual volume of about $4.5 to $5 million under present circumstances ... Expansion beyond an annual volume of $5 million is not desired, and will not be permitted in the foreseeable future ... The future operating surplus will be used for: (a) debit retirement; (b) replacement and additions of equipment; (c) support of public service research in the broad interests of the West; (d) support of fundamental research at Stanford University and in the Institute laboratories, and (e) expansion of the Institute's services as and where needed. Contributions will not be sought where such contributions would diminish financial support to Stanford University.

We were certainly not happy about setting such a strict limit on expansion of the Institute beyond $5 million in annual revenue. However, this was the price we had to pay to offset the directors' and Stanford Trustees' concerns about raising money to finance an expanded operation.

It was well known how strongly some of the directors and Trustees felt about Hobson's growth philosophy. None of us wanted to make the stricture on expansion so tight, but it had to be done to get the Associates plan in high gear. As things worked out, we soon moved from one growth plan to another with board approval in each case and thus left the earlier limit in limbo. All this was the right course in our long-term interests and certainly was the only approach that could have held Hobson's attention.

Just before moving the Associates program to center stage at the end of 1951, the directors again discussed at some length its relationship to Stanford's long-term plans. The consensus was the same as before — there was little conflict between the two programs. Some of the directors felt that an initial contribution to SRI would make it easier for a company to give to Stanford. McBean spoke forcefully about the idea from the beginning, asserting that SRI's existence would tie the University closer to industry.

The affairs of the Institute in late 1951 were dominated in many ways by the growing fundraising effort. Many of us were involved with the development committee in preparing company lists, schedules and supporting materials. By year-end, total capital contributions under the Associates Plan had reached $370,500, there having been an increase of $198,500 during the year. Along with earnings, this capital gave SRI a net worth of $73,472 as 1952 began; one year earlier there had been a negative worth of $274,486.

Early in 1952 Hobson proposed that some of the Associate funds be released for equipment purchases. Follis took the occasion to emphasize a conservative policy in using this money. He felt that SRI should strive for real solvency so it could withstand any severe economic jolt. Follis went on to stress that the main goal in using Associate funds should be to make the Institute strong financially with some reserves. He did not want to see any of the money used to cover current costs, including working capital.

The Associates campaign moved along very well indeed during 1952. Some $169,000 was received in the first quarter along with $311,000 in pledges. About $412,000 came in during the first eleven months, bringing the cumulative total to almost $783,000. Moreover, pledges on hand amounted to some $375,000. The campaign was already a success, and no one saw any problem in reaching the $1.5 million goal. More importantly, the severe capital problem had been eased.

The importance of the first $783,000 of Associates support cannot be over-emphasized. It literally made the difference between a financially strapped organization and one with some financial security. Although ostensibly not for the purpose of supporting further growth in size, staff and revenues, the equity money did just that and left SRI with about $111,000 of capital in the bank. Here is how the money was used:

USE OF ASSOCIATE FUNDS AS OF NOVEMBER 30, 1952

Amounts	Uses
$ 75,884.83	Institute-sponsored research
34,491.70	Fundraising expenses
115,000.00	Working capital transfers (prior 3/49)
153,000.00	Working capital transfers (after 3/49)
3,807.56	Associate Days
280,000.00	Equipment — facility improvements
$662,184.09	
10,000.00	Equipment gifts
91.23	Miscellaneous
111,000.00	Reserves
$783,275.32	TOTAL USES

The Institute continued for some time to benefit greatly from the Associates program. Total receipts passed the $1 million point in April 1952. The figure reached $1,235,000 by the end of 1953. By mid-1954, total receipts had risen to $1.4 million, with more than enough pledges to exceed the $1.5 million target.

The goal set in 1951 was reached in January 1955 when the Associates account stood at $1,442,958.54 (not counting pledges). This figure included $223,000 received prior to mid-1951. If this amount is taken out, the $1.5 million point was not reached until September

1955, with total contributions of $1,750,458.54. In the meantime, the post-1952 campaign operated more or less on a routine basis.

Although the Associates Plan was obviously of great value as a source of equity capital, it also led to a variety of research relationships. General Electric became the 100th Associate member in mid-1955 and soon thereafter moved into the number one position on our revenues from industrial firms. Only 27 of the first 100 Associates were not or had not been clients as of the end of 1955.

During the early 1950s, it was made clear to prospective Associates that the funds being sought would be used for equipment, basic research and working capital. The possibility of seeking Associate funds for buildings did not come up until January 1954. Plans were afoot at the time to construct buildings on the Stanford Campus at a cost of about $2 million. The directors thought it might be possible to raise half of this amount by a special campaign with both current and prospective Associate companies.

McBean took a special interest in this idea and often urged it on during the spring of 1954. As was his usual practice, these sessions were often one person at a time with McBean taking the initiative. Years later upon hearing about this style practiced by a director, an Institute executive (not familiar with McBean) suggested that the Institute's chief executive should have put a stop to such approaches. This overlooks McBean as an individual and his

WE NEED SOME CAPITAL!
L to R: J. E. Wallace Sterling, Louis B. Lundborg, Jesse E. Hobson.

conviction that SRI was his creation. One who did not accommodate himself to McBean's "overseeing" system would, sooner or later, be on the outside figuratively and literally. The directors did not want to tangle with McBean. After all, he was the "founder."

So it was that McBean talked with Titus on April 9, 1954 about extending the Associates campaign to a permanent building program. He told Titus that the minimum goal should be 50 companies and $750,000 for the first structure. Then, he instructed Titus to do nothing about such a campaign until a firm decision had been made on our permanent location. McBean was confident that once such a decision was made the building funds could be raised in sixty days with help from all the directors. This was an unrealistic view, but it was characteristic of the man; he was always in a hurry to get things done.

The reason McBean wanted to hold up on the new Associates campaign in this instance was to find out if SRI might indeed be staying on the Stanford Village site. Anyhow, Hobson was not too happy about McBean's unilateral action, but, as usual he did not stir up the waters with our friend at 225 Bush Street in San Francisco.

Nothing much happened regarding this matter until after SRI acquired rights to the Stanford Village property in the summer of 1955. Then, on August 30, more or less on his own, McBean wrote to the chief executives of nineteen western companies, most of them located in the San Francisco Bay Area. In writing these letters McBean had Follis' approval in his capacity as head of the directors' development committee. But, in the process there was little discussion with Stanford.

The letters put Sterling, our board chairman, in a somewhat embarrassing position. McBean simply said he had written to present Associates and saw no reason for what he called an "unnecessary delay." The step could easily have been handled in much better fashion, by telephone or otherwise. In any event, McBean's appeal was direct and to the point:

A NEW ASSOCIATES OBJECTIVE

"After nearly nine years of operations in the converted, temporary building in Stanford Village, Stanford Research Institute has acquired title to the land from the federal government and is now able to plan and begin the construction of permanent buildings. The Institute has negotiated a two million dollar loan with ten banks.

"It will require between $2.75 and $3 million to build the initial units of the permanent buildings and laboratories, and the total cost of construction, extending over a number of years, will be approximately $5 million.

"In order to raise the additional money above the bank loan, it has been suggested by several of our Associates that a number of present Associate Members would be glad to take an additional membership. I hope you will look upon this request with favor and that your reply will indicate your desire to assist in these plans."

This letter produced some results, but less than McBean had anticipated. Within four months a total of $290,000 in new Associate units had been pledged. Seven of the $15,000 units were from new companies contacted by McBean, Titus, and others during the summer of 1955. Some of the money came from the nineteen existing Associates and the balance from others approached by McBean.

This special Associates drive was more or less suspended early in 1956 following Hobson's departure from SRI. It appeared at the time that two or three years might have to pass before the Institute would be ready to start construction of its first permanent building. Nevertheless, we continued during the 1955-1960 period to seek Associate funds on a quiet and restrained basis, including complete coordination with Stanford. The new funds ranged between $100,000 and $200,000 per year. Cumulative receipts, less direct expenses, reached $3.6 million by the end of the decade.

During the summer of 1961 the finance committee of the SRI board discussed the possibility of organizing a new Associates campaign to provide money for a stepped-up basic research program and equipment purchases. In the meantime, however, Stanford had launched its PACE campaign aimed at raising at least $100 million over five years. Sterling and most of the directors, other than McBean, felt that the Institute should not increase its fund-raising during the PACE period. Consequently, a new policy was adopted by the directors on December 4, 1961. It more or less confirmed what had been the practice since 1956:

COORDINATION WITH STANFORD

Invitations to be issued from time to time on a selective basis to a few U.S. companies having some close relationship with the Institute.

Each proposed invitation to be coordinated with the University and issued upon mutual agreement.

Each prospective Associate to be clearly advised by the Institute concerning the SRI-University affiliation followed by a statement that an Associate membership does not constitute a gift of support of the educational and research programs of Stanford University.

Once agreement on issuing an Associate invitation has been reached between the Institute and the University, interested Board members may be invited to assist in the discussions if this seems advisable.

This understanding with Stanford was most certainly appropriate at the time. The management of the Institute and most of the directors fully agreed that nothing should be done by SRI that might complicate the University's capital campaign. Only McBean felt strongly that the policy was unnecessary and indeed far too restrictive.

We knew at the time that, in effect, the new policy signalled the end of the Associates Plan. The momentum was winding down. The 1962 receipts were only $107,000. A mere $45,000 was received in 1964. This brought total contributions to the $3 million point. The search for equity capital from business and industry was at an end.

As before, it fell to me to draft the new Associates policy in 1961 and along with Titus to coordinate it with Stanford. In retrospect, it appears highly restrictive. In fact it was not.

Except for a few companies tied closely to the University, which SRI never approached, our detailed plans were always acceptable to Stanford. This was the case right from the beginning and during the early 1960s.

In the mid-1960s, SRI's senior executive wanted very much to seek new Associate funds to support a basic research program at the Institute. McBean wanted to go ahead on some basis but none of the other directors was enthusiastic and neither was Stanford. The initiative simply faded away. The main result was McBean's growing unhappiness with Stanford and several of its Trustees and officers, and even with some of his fellow directors. This was unfortunate to say the least.

On growth — let it first be in quality.

— J.E. WALLACE STERLING

The circumstances were quite different in the late 1960s when we proposed to finance an International Building through an International Associates Plan. All the directors, as well as Stanford and the Trustees, energetically supported the effort.

The University gave the Institute blanket approval on the whole exercise. The program was completed in a couple of years to the full satisfaction of everyone concerned. Having been responsible for the program, I well remember the coordination with Stanford. The only steps needed were a short meeting and one letter.

SRI must be greatly indebted to its directors of the early 1950s and especially to their development committee for all they did in helping raise some "equity" money for an organization with no capital. The amounts, the first $1.5 million as well as the later $3 million, seem small today. But they were significant and they helped enormously in moving SRI along the way. We must always be grateful to our early Associate companies for their support at just the right time.

About 85% of the first $1.5 million in contributions came from companies in the American West. One way to measure the value of their support is simply to look at the impact on our net worth. By 1955 this figure had reached $2.6 million. Had it not been for the Associates program and its $1.8 million, the net worth (from earnings alone) would have been less than $800,000.

Follis and his colleagues on the development committee thought in late 1951 that three years would be needed to raise $1.5 million in Associate funds. The actual time was three and a half years, not counting the money received earlier.

The committee promised the Associate companies that none of their contributions would be used for debt retirement. This commitment was strictly observed. The plan called for no more than 50% of research revenues to be from government during the then-present emergency and no more than 25% in normal times. The emergency was the Korean War. New work for the U.S. military caused our government percentage to go beyond 50% and to remain there throughout the next three decades.

The development committee also said that $1.5 million in capital would enable SRI to increase its annual research volume to $5 million. The plan was even more specific, further growth would not be permitted. What actually happened is another story indeed. Our revenue in 1955, the year the fund-raising goal was reached, went over the $10 million mark and it continued to grow year by year on to some $200 million three decades later.

Obviously, the strict $5 million limit was unrealistic. Keeping the lid on so tightly would not have been in the best interests of SRI, Stanford or anyone else. The directors were, in effect, asking Hobson once again to slow things down. As before, he took the initiative in setting a ceiling or in agreeing to one — finding it easier to explain later how growth had been pushed along by demands of the market place rather than trying to convince the directors in advance that the Institute should expand rapidly as a matter of policy. What happened under the Associates campaign in this respect was par for the course during the early 1950's.

One more thing must be said about the Associates program. Many played a role in getting new companies in the plan and in cementing relationships with the group. But it was Carl Titus who saw to it that all went along in an orderly fashion. He made it his job to know the top executives of the companies and worked hard on the ''family'' concept.

Titus was well liked by our Associates and did an excellent job in a quiet way. He joined SRI on March 1, 1949 and retired on February 3, 1971. More credit is due him than has ever been recognized in a lasting way. He was our equity capital man. ■

WELCOME TO STANFORD RESEARCH INSTITUTE
Lobby of Building 100

--- THE FIRST FOUR DECADES ---

Chairmen	Presidents – CEOs
Donald B. Tresidder	William F. Talbot ‡
Alvin C. Eurich	J. E. Hobson ‡
J. E. Wallace Sterling	E. Finley Carter
David Packard*	Karl Folkers
Ernest C. Arbuckle †	Charles A. Anderson
E. Hornsby Wasson	William F. Miller
Edgar F. Kaiser	
E. W. Littlefield	
H. J. Haynes	
Myron Du Bain	

*Executive Committee
†Also CEO for a period

‡Executive Director

A Village Home

Stanford Village and SRI were made for each other.

— WILLIAM STOCKWELL - 1953

SRI HAS ITS MAIN OFFICE AND LABORATORIES in Menlo Park, California. The site was named "Stanford Village" shortly after World War II, when its barrack-type buildings were being used by Stanford University for student housing. During the war, the area was known as "Dibble Hospital," and earlier was part of the Hopkins Estate.

Timothy Hopkins was one of the great names of California business during the second half of the 19th century. He was one of Stanford's original Trustees and his name is closely linked with the early history of the University. Hopkins once owned the land on which much of Menlo Park and Palo Alto (California) now stand. As his estate passed into the hands of others, each lot carried a proviso that no alcoholic drinks ever be sold on it.

Our headquarters site was largely vacant until World War II. Construction of the hospital began on June 15, 1943. Sixty-two temporary buildings were ready for occupancy two months later and the complex was then given the Dibble name. Colonel John Dibble of the Army Medical Corps was aboard an airplane that vanished in the South Pacific in 1942.

The first combat wounded arrived on February 22, 1944, the second group at the end of March. Others came frequently thereafter mostly from the South Pacific. The peak load was reached on June 10, 1944, when 458 patients were admitted.

By the time the hospital was closed in mid-1946 more than 16,000 patients had received care in its eye, dental, plastic, orthopedic, physical therapy, neuro-psychiatric, and physical reconditioning sections. Spur tracks made the area a terminus and storage center for hospital trains; the operation was aptly called the General Dibble Railroad.

At one time more than 800 people were employed at Dibble, and when it was closed the 72 temporary buildings had more than 700,000 square feet of floor space. Until September 1945, when Congress passed legislation permitting annexation of the hospital land by Menlo Park, the $8 million facility was a "city within a city."

The Palo Alto and Menlo Park communities had been pleased when the War Depart-

GATEHOUSE — HOPKINS ESTATE, 1950
Now part of Menlo Park Civic Center

COL. JOHN DIBBLE
U.S. Army Medical Corps —
Early World War II Casualty

PRE-STANFORD VILLAGE
Menlo Park — Mid-1940s

62 BUILDINGS AND CORRIDORS BY THE MILE

ment decided to build the hospital between the two cities. When it became evident in late 1945 that the hospital would soon be closed, a wave of concern arose as to what might be done with the area and the buildings. It was located in a growing Menlo Park community and the City wanted to see the land on the tax rolls, preferably in the hands of an organization that would develop it with local interests in mind.

Stanford University was confronted in 1946 with a heavy influx of students, many of them veterans of World War II. The Dibble buildings, located a short distance away offered a temporary solution to the housing problem. However, acquisition of the property was not an easy matter. Negotiations continued off and on during the latter part of 1945 and early 1946 until it appeared that the complex would not be declared surplus and, therefore, could not be leased or obtained by Stanford in any way.

It so happened that Dudley Swim, a Stanford alumnus involved in SRI's origin, was vice commander of the American Legion at that time. In March 1946 he arrived at Stanford to talk about the proposed Institute and learned that the University had lost the Dibble site because, of all things, a Legion recommendation that it not be declared surplus.

This was the first Swim had ever heard of Stanford's interest. He promised to look into the situation and did so immediately. Events moved rapidly. The University leased the land, acquired title to the buildings in August 1946, and quickly began preparing the site, primarily for married students.

This was the same month that William Talbot, SRI's first executive, arrived at Stanford. I had the good fortune to join the prospective Institute shortly thereafter.

The story about our headquarters site appears here in some detail. The move from three offices at Stanford University to Menlo Park greatly affected our future. Although the main events were to come later, they were set in motion during our Take-Off Days.

In May 1947 the Institute moved into the Village and occupied the main hospital building. As time went on we rented one building after another from the University, as soon

FIRST HEADQUARTERS – 1948

as they could be released from housing use. There were only a few Institute people at the beginning and they occupied the first floor of what is still known as Building 100.

A solution to a space problem in late 1947 was not too difficult to find — part of the growing staff simply moved upstairs. The practice was to fix up one office at a time, as the need arose.

The Institute was surrounded on three sides by student quarters. Many of the families had young children; consequently, the office environment was often interrupted by young-sters at play and by mothers looking for their offspring. For a while our main building was also an entrance to the student family quarters!

By the late 1940s it appeared that the government would soon find Dibble Hospital sur-plus to its long-term needs. Although the University was planning more student housing on the Campus, it was very interested in buying the Dibble complex as it seemed certain that the land and buildings would be needed for several more years. There was also the possi-bility, although somewhat remote at the time, that eventually the complex might be acquired by SRI for our permanent location.

In April 1950 Stanford asked the Public Housing Administration (PHA) to sell the Vil-lage to the University under the Lanham Act passed by Congress in 1940. However, shortly thereafter, all actions on surplus property were stopped by an Executive freeze order as a result of the Korean War.

During 1950 through 1953, discussions continued between the University and the gov-ernment, but no progress was made. It was learned that Washington was considering var-ious possible uses for the site. Menlo Park wanted some of it for a civic center; a school dis-trict and a church were also interested.

A question arose as to whether the Institute qualified under the Lanham Act to pur-chase the property once Stanford's housing needs were met. This was finally settled in the affirmative, but it took more time for definite action by the federal agencies. Finally, at the Institute's urging, the Housing and Home Finance Agency (HHFA) called a meeting in May 1953.

University and Institute representatives (including two from SRI) attended and helped convince the Department of Defense that the land should indeed be released under the Lanham Act. HHFA officials then called a second meeting of interested parties.

In addition to the Institute, Stanford, Menlo Park, two churches, a second school district, the U.S. Geological Survey, and a local board of realtors were involved. At this meeting, Stanford made a proposal:

THE STANFORD PLAN

''The University would take title to the land and use the temporary buildings for housing and for SRI needs for a period of five to ten years.

''When the land became surplus to University needs, it would be sold at cost to such nonprofit organizations and agencies (e.g., SRI, school districts and churches) as were approved by Menlo Park.

''The City of Menlo Park would be given an option to buy any remaining land at cost.''

Menlo Park's Mayor said the city favored the transfer to Stanford and would buy any available land at cost, but would oppose sale to any organization (except churches and school districts) that did not pay property taxes. We said SRI wanted to locate permanently in the Village on a tax-paying basis. Soon thereafter the San Francisco office of the HHFA recommended to Washington that the land be transferred to Stanford.

Hobson told our directors in midsummer of 1953 that prospects looked good for the University to acquire the Village. The plan was that the Institute would eventually have 26 acres for its headquarters but would have to affirm its intention to replace the temporary buildings with permanent structures. By this time we had occupied about 100,000 square feet of Village space. Thus, the place was, in fact, becoming home.

The government had bought the Hopkins land early in the 1940s for about $1,000 per acre. Both the Institute and the University hoped it could be bought from the government at the same price or, at the most, for a modest markup. However, this appeared to be out of the question. Uncle Sam was taking the position that the land should be sold at market value — perhaps for $15,000–$20,000 per acre.

This news was most disappointing, particularly since the law did not require ''market value'' and in fact specified ''sale at cost.'' However, Washington was timid about selling land at a price that would give the buyer an immediate book profit. Consequently, a move was made by Stanford and SRI to amend the law.

The West — Our country's future is here.
Think big thoughts about the West.
— ATHOLL McBEAN - 1953

ALTERNATIVES

Hobson and others among us soon became greatly concerned about the long delay in a decision on the Stanford Village. By November 1953 we had invested about $430,000 in leasehold improvements and another $1 million in plant and equipment. Moving to another site was becoming most unattractive from a financial viewpoint.

Nevertheless, our directors decided that alternative sites must be considered. One possibility was to move to some University land being developed for light industrial use. A study of the situation was initiated with help from John Forbes (financial adviser) and Alf Brandin, the University's business manager. Within a month this initiative resulted in a possible lease by the Institute of a 25-acre site between Palo Alto and Stanford.

The site was attractive and was near the center of the University. However, we had to consider several problems, including relations with Menlo Park, the time factor, and financing. Furthermore, Menlo Park officials were most anxious that the Institute remain at Stanford Village.

In early 1954, the outlook for eventual acquisiton of the Village became dim. The University was told that a new bill would soon be introduced in Congress relieving the government of any obligation to sell surplus land at cost. There were signs that an early settlement might be possible, but it seemed unlikely that purchase of the property could be on financially attractive terms to the Institute. Consequently, the Stanford site for our main office and laboratories was recommended by management to the directors. The die seemed cast for a move away from the Village.

The directors began considering a proposal to construct a diversified facility rather than beginning with a single office-type unit. One possibility was that an 80,000 square foot building might be constructed for $12 per square foot, plus 100,000 square feet of laboratory space for $20 per square foot, for a total investment of $3 million. (The space estimate was based on the Institute's needs in moving from the Village and the nearby leased buildings.) The directors favored the full construction program, but no formal action was taken at the time.

Menlo Park officials were greatly perturbed when they heard about the Institute's decision to move to a University site. The Mayor and members of the City Council made strong pleas to the government, and asked for help from their Congressmen. These efforts, together with some uncertainty regarding government policy on land disposal, caused the directors to pull back on their decision to move to the University.

In the meantime, a construction firm had submitted preliminary plans for a 222,000 square foot building. The construction cost was set at about $2.5 million, with an additional $364,000 for site preparation. The plans involved a two-story office building, six single-story laboratory structures, and separate units for maintenance, machine shops and a cafeteria.

The decision to move to University land was by no means viewed with enthusiasm by everyone involved. Hobson for one felt that the Institute and the University would be better served in the long run by separate locations. He might have been guided by his earlier experiences at Armour, where a building was jointly occupied by both the

Foundation and the Illinois Institute of Technology.

McBean at first favored the University site. Later he came to feel that the Institute should not move into an area where it would be, in his words, "merely another factory." Also, he thought we should be located in a community where SRI could be a significant factor in the eyes of the public, and not just one of several firms.

In any event, the move was not really feasible because of our investments in the Village buildings. They had little, if any, resale value. In time, enthusiasm for the University site began to wane in spite of the fact that the Trustees were indicating that Stanford might erect a building for the Institute on a lease basis.

An entirely new possibility was then introduced by Hobson. Angel Island in the San Francisco Bay was no longer needed by the Department of Defense; Hobson thought the island, with its many barrack-type buildings, warehouses, and shop areas, might be a good place for the Institute.

He pursued this idea vigorously for several months, developing, in his mind, a plan for special boat service for staff and visitors, and stressing its proximity to San Francisco and the uniqueness of the site as important features for the Institute's future.

Not all shared his enthusiasm for Angel Island. Most of Hobson's associates viewed the idea with dismay and considered it a very poor choice for the Institute's main operations. I, for one, disliked the whole idea. Eventually, as the Village alternative came closer to reality, Hobson lost interest in Angel Island, and everyone breathed a sigh of relief. □

Uncertainty surrounding the Village is illustrated by comments made by both Hobson and Forbes in the spring of 1954. Hobson told the directors — " ... there is now sufficient confusion on the subject to prevent an intelligent estimate of the final outcome." Forbes said, "We do not yet know what our problem is." Hobson went on to say that if the Village land should later be offered to the Institute a few points would be quite important in arriving at a decision:

TILTING TO THE VILLAGE

"It would be difficult to reject high-value land having a very low price in relation to value.

"Holding title to the land would permit its use as equity in financing construction of new buildings. (Stanford-owned land cannot be leveraged in the same way.)

"The Institute has invested about $450,000 in leasehold improvements on the Village of which about $300,000 has been amortized.

"If, after considerable effort, Menlo Park should succeed in obtaining the property for the Institute, it would not be diplomatic to reject the offer and move to the University land."

In the light of these points, the directors decided to table their previous decision favoring the University land.

Late in the spring of 1954, the PHA indicated that negotiations could proceed on the Village property. Its plan did not include the Institute.

The University was studying the housing portion of Village property and this was to be the basis for a market appraisal by the government. Later, it would be the basis for further negotiations on land disposition.

We had decided that the government was not fully aware of complications created by our operations in the Village. Our use of the temporary buildings was clearly not within the housing framework adopted by the government to guide the land transfer. We thought it entirely possible that the Stanford Trustees might decide to buy about half of the Village and continue student housing for a number of years.

Another possibility was that the Trustees might not acquire any of the property and close out the Village by the summer of 1956. In any event, the Institute had the problem of purchasing enough acreage in the Village at a higher cost than originally anticipated or constructing new buildings on University land.

STANFORD VILLAGE – EARLY 1950

Up to this point our thinking on University-versus-Village property had been based on land cost. However, by 1954 the situation had changed. Our research programs had been expanding rapidly and space needs were becoming urgent. It was in this environment that a new plan surfaced — Herbert and I put pen on paper:

THE SRI PLAN

"In the interests of ending this indecision, permitting intelligent programming, and for the long-range good of the Institute, we recommend the following:

a. "The Institute to decide in the near future that the permanent location be on the Stanford Village property, no matter what the ultimate price per acre may be. The range is between a bargain price of $4,000 per acre, which we once hoped for, and the appraised market value which may be as high as $15,000 per acre.

b. "To consummate agreements with Menlo Park and the University to resell to the Institute those parcels of land which we desire in the Village at the City's or the University's cost.

c. "To work out an agreement with the City to provide a proper zoning ordinance to cover our anticipated operations.

d. "To conclude an additional agreement with the City authorizing our use of temporary buildings for a period of up to seven years.

"The Institute would then prepare a building program that would extend over a seven-year period, and provide for the construction of permanent buildings and transfer of operations thereto, as contributions and earnings create funds for this purpose with a minimum of outside financing."

We were confronted with some stark facts. It was estimated that in addition to construction outlays the move to another location would cost at least $600,000. Furthermore, immediate construction at a new location would have involved the Institute in a financing plan it could not afford. On the other hand, remaining in Stanford Village would make it possible to spread a building program over several years.

This plan was supported by all of the Institute's senior staff and, while awaiting moves by the government, the University, Menlo Park and the directors, a lot of time was spent making sure it had everybody's backing. We decided to keep on investing.

The government finally appointed appraisers for the Village in late summer of 1954. Although there had been a possibility earlier that the land would be sold to Menlo Park rather than Stanford, it appeared that a decision had been made toward a sale to the University. A final decision was expected by early October 1954.

In the meantime, while the directors awaited the outcome of the University/government negotiations, we retained Skidmore, Owings and Merrill to study our building and laboratory needs. The consensus within the Institute was that the Village would eventually be obtained on acceptable terms.

A PERMANENT HOME

By December 1954 the situation had reached a much more hopeful stage. The PHA said that an announcement on the sale price would be forthcoming soon. The land had been appraised conservatively at about $16,000 per acre and Stanford was to sell it to SRI at cost. Menlo Park agreed to zone the property (so as to cover our requirements) and also to approve use of the temporary buildings for seven years.

In early 1955 HHFA offered to sell 79 acres to Stanford at about $16,000 per acre. The arrangement called upon Menlo Park to certify that any structures retained on the land were satisfactory for long-term housing or non-housing use. From the University's viewpoint this was a significant change since under terms of the existing land lease Stanford was obligated to remove its temporary buildings at the end of the rental arrangement. The Institute was planning to purchase 35 acres from the University as soon as Stanford acquired the site.

The HHFA issued a notice of transfer to Stanford University covering the 79 acres of the Village site. Our directors immediately approved the purchase of 35 of these acres. Menlo Park certified that the temporary structures were suitable for long-term housing or non-housing use and its Council approved an agreement between the City and Stanford on further disposition of the land. It called for the sale of the entire 79-acre site by the University when it was no longer needed. A right of first refusal was given to SRI, followed by any non-profit or public body acceptable to Menlo Park, and then by the City itself.

The concept of this agreement (with SRI as the forceful partner) was that Village land would be sold to the Institute as rapidly as parcels were no longer needed for student housing. The University Trustees had agreed that Stanford would not dispose of the land in such a way as to create an appreciation profit. In the eyes of the government, the temporary buildings had a value of only $1.00. We agreed that SRI would relieve Stanford of any obligation to remove these buildings. This was done because we needed additional space and did not want the buildings razed.

The basic arrangement under which Stanford and the Institute acquired the Village called for these temporary buildings to be razed or brought up to code by June 1965. A formal resolution along this line was adopted by Menlo Park in 1957. The due date was to be extended as time passed.

Although the Institute was to receive the Village land free and clear of all resale restrictions, our intent was that the site would be our permanent home. Local land values were rising rapidly. Had we decided in the late 1950s to sell our portion of the land and move to another location, using the resale profit to finance the move, faith would have been broken with Menlo Park.

This possibility was never seriously considered. For one thing, it would have put in jeopardy some 50 acres of Village land that we did not acquire at the time of the first purchase by the University from the government.

Just before the Institute made a financing commitment in 1957 on its first new building, one last policy review was made on our permanent location. The group included Sterling, David Packard, Finley Carter (then head of the Institute), and the author. Potential value to SRI in acquiring the balance of the Village land from Stanford was a key factor in confirming a "Go Ahead" on the new building. Also, it was doubtful that financing could be arranged to move to another location. No one wanted a split operation.

STANFORD VILLAGE BECOMES SRI HOME
FIRST LAND PURCHASE — JULY 29, 1955

From U.S. Government: Lee Mitchell, left, and Arthur Chladek, second from right.

From SRI: Matthew Stafford, second from left.

From Stanford: Hazel Flagler and Dwight Adams (business manager).

At the end of June 1955 the only remaining steps were formal transfer of title to the University and purchase by the Institute of the first increment of the Village site. It had been finally agreed that we would buy about 30 acres as a first step.

On July 29, 1955 the long drawn-out transaction was completed including payment of about $480,000 to the University from funds obtained under a new bank loan. A deed for 30.165 acres was delivered to SRI the same day — about five years after purchase of the Village site had been proposed and two years after active negotiations began with the government. A personal note written at the time adds some perspective.

Our check and the deed today should long be remembered in our annals. The trials and tribulations are over. The Village is our home. It is the best possible course. Now we can get on with the main business at hand.

This was not, however, the last purchase of Village land by the Institute. Another five acres were bought directly from the government in 1958. During the same year, 16 additional acres were acquired from Stanford; and a further 3½ acres were purchased in 1961.

Two land dedications involving almost two acres were made for street improvements. Another two acres were purchased from Stanford in 1964. One small parcel, isolated by a street, had been sold earlier to Menlo Park. Some of the Stanford-owned land also was dedicated to street use. About 30 acres were purchased from the University in the 1960s as housing on the property was no longer needed.

Buying the 5-acre parcel in 1958 involved an interesting chain of events. The land was originally transferred to a school district with the proviso that it be used for school purposes within five years. This was not done. Hence, the General Services Administration (GSA) attempted to sell the land by auction. The GSA expected bids on the order of $40,000 per acre; instead, the high bid was only a fraction of this amount and the property was put up for sale on sealed bids.

We had decided in the meantime that the 5-plus acre plot had a value of at least $150,000 to the Institute. The bids were due in San Francisco in mid-August of 1958. Sterling, as well as several other directors (including Carter) were away from the area. A personal note, written some years later, tells what happened:

QUIET STRATEGY

A call to McBean seemed in order. He was at his summer home in Woodside and within the hour was at SRI. He suggested that we offer about $160,000 for the property and said he would be responsible for the purchase price if, for any reason, the directors did not concur. Not having formal authority to make an offer, we decided to submit a 'blind bid' through a title company.

A bid for $160,201 was given to the GSA on August 19, 1958. The extra $200 and an odd dollar were added in case someone else should make a round number bid.!! Our blind bid was the highest of the eleven submitted. Within a few days we received word from the GSA (through the title company) that all bids were below the appraised value. Bidders were invited to appear in San Francisco on September 10, 1958 with higher bids.

Upon reviewing the list of bidders we felt that most of the individuals and companies were interested in the property only for speculative purposes and would not wish to compete with the Institute. We knew most of the persons involved. Within a few days they learned through careful 'plants' about our interest in the property as a part of our permanent site.

As we had thought, word soon reached us through various channels that several of the bidders were dropping out. We were quite certain by September 10 that only one "bidder" would show up at the San Francisco session.

This proved to be the case. The meeting lasted about two minutes. Along with counsel, we represented the title company and indicated no desire to submit a higher bid, but reaffirmed the earlier one.

We already knew what would happen ... the bid was promptly accepted and the meeting was over.''

Madison Avenue Entrance
– Pay phone inside –

A SUCCESSFUL VISIT IN 1956 ON FINANCING OF SRI'S HEADQUARTERS BUILDING

Metropolitan Life — No. 1 Madison Avenue, New York City

(A ''NO'' answer in the executive suite — A 25¢ phone call on a rainy day to another company — A ''YES'' response — Take an application to our Menlo Park office next door to Stanford Village — No problem.)

Headquarters Building — Stanford Village Site. Planning started - 1955, Occupied - 1958.

The balance of this transaction was completed within two months. Our directors soon approved the purchase and a deed was issued on October 3, 1958. At long last, a valuable corner portion of the original Village had come into our hands.

In the meantime, one additional transaction took place. When we decided to build our first permanent building it seemed highly desirable to move a church in front of the building site to some other portion of the Village. This was agreeable to the church

A church close by!

leaders because they wanted a new building. We gave the church an acre in a corner of our property in exchange for the same amount of land in front of our building site. As an inducement, permanent parking privileges for the church were included.

A church building was soon erected on the new site. Following the Institute's earlier purchase of the five acres of land, the church was no longer in the corner of Village property. Instead, it was surrounded on three sides by Institute land.

On several occasions attempts were made to purchase the church land and building so that we might have an unbroken property line. However, the negotiations came to naught when we could not agree on price. We later offered to trade lands a second time, but the church was not interested in the site offered.

At one point the difference between the offered and the asking price narrowed to about $50,000. We were willing to pay $325,000, the church wanted $375,000. There was no basis to justify the higher figure on economic grounds; the only reason for a purchase at $375,000 was a long-term view. Moreover, there were other priority needs for our available cash.

There is no question that the Stanford Village site contributed greatly to the Institute's development in its early days. With ample available space SRI was able to grow and develop with only minimum investment in brick and mortar. The Institute invested its limited funds in people and equipment and, of course, in the operating deficit which, at its maximum, stood at about $450,000.

Without the available temporary structures the Institute would have had a heavy investment in buildings. This surely would have restricted its growth.

Another advantage of the Village was that the temporary units could easily be modified to meet special laboratory needs. Our Menlo Park location soon became one of the City's largest enterprises. Local pride developed in the Institute as the center of a far-flung international operation.

The low book value of our land was a key factor in attracting mortgage money for construction of our first two permanent buildings. By 1957 the land had a market value of at least $70,000 per acre. Although not reflected in our net worth, this meant that the Institute had a book profit of more than $4 million on 79 acres of land.

In time, however, the Menlo site brought some disadvantages to our operations. As the surrounding area developed, SRI was under increasing pressure to make reasonable progress on its permanent building program and to get on with demolition of the temporary structures. As the ten-year grace period came to an end, it was

SECRET WORK INSIDE!

obvious that a request for an extension on the use of the temporary buildings would have to be arranged.

Meanwhile, zoning and building regulations became more and more important. This meant that the Institute could no longer have the same freedom in altering and modifying the temporary units. Finally, there was the problem of planning and constructing new buildings in an area already covered with temporary structures fully occupied by people working on scores of research projects.

Even when our first new building was constructed in the late 1950s, the thought was still about that some day we might find it advisable to move away from a high-value, center-of-town location. Accordingly, the building was designed in such a way that it might have maximum resale value.

However, for all practical purposes we had long passed the point of no return on a world headquarters site. The day may come when the Institute has a second principal site, but the Menlo location will be its main home for many, many years to come — if not indefinitely.

The Institute did indeed make some plans in the late 1950s for a second home area since we believed that, sooner or later, a certain amount of open land would be needed for research programs. With this, as well as other possible needs in mind, discussions were held with Stanford about lands in the hill area near the Campus. In early 1960, the University was told that SRI was interested in acquiring — at some future date — 100 or more acres under long-term lease. However, nothing more was ever done about the matter.

By 1958, the City of Menlo Park had bought 28 acres (of the original 127-acre Dibble site) to be used for a park and a civic center but still wanted the Institute to maintain its headquarters on Stanford Village land. The Mayor often said that persuading SRI to make Menlo Park its home was one of his and the City's major achievements and remarked in 1957 that (not counting the utilities), the Institute was its biggest taxpayer.

Although the Stanford Village name was used well into the 1950s, it gradually gave way to simply ''SRI,'' particularly as student housing came to an end. The ''Hopkins Estate'' and ''Dibble Hospital'' names also eventually passed into history.

MENLO PARK WELCOMES SRI
Mayor Charles Burgess and J. E. Hobson.

The Institute has never wanted to move in any way against Hopkins' proviso on selling alcoholic beverages. Also, he had treasured the area and probably would be well pleased to see the use to which his acres are now devoted.

Even though there were some lingering thoughts, (even as late as 1960), about location of our permanent home, the Rubicon was, in fact, crossed in 1957 when excavation began on our first building.

There were mixed feelings by some on the decision to stay in Menlo Park. Perhaps, wishful thinking on a Stanford site is a more accurate description. However, as time passed, it was clear that the Village was the *only* feasible solution. It was soon to become ''world headquarters'' for an international institute.

And, now, to another personal note. During a ceremony at the start of the new building, We used the phrase ''A Village Transformed'' in referring to the course of events still in motion. The words have meaning today with more than 1.3 million square feet of space on the Menlo Park site. Building 100, our first home in Stanford Village, remains in full use.

In looking over the site in 1953 after speaking about the Village and SRI being ''made for each other,'' William Stockwell made a promise:

> '' ... Perish the thought about any other home for the Institute ...
> Timothy Hopkins surely would want his oak trees kept in place; we'll do just that.''

As the Institute's first architect, he made good on his promise. □

Some Colleagues

—————— A FEW AMONG MANY ——————

ENGINEERING

Donald L. Benedict	John V. N. Granger
John T. Bolljahn	Ray L. Leadabrand*
Archibald S. Brown	Ernest J. Moore*
Hewitt D. Crane	Thomas H. Morrin
Kenneth R. Eldredge	Jerry D. Noe

Donald R. Scheuch*

LIFE SCIENCES

Harris M. Benedict	Gordon W. Newell
Bruce Graham	William A. Skinner*

THE PHYSICAL SCIENCES

George R. Abrahamson*	George E. Duvall
Donald L. Benedict	Robert D. Englert
Robert M. Burns	Nevin K. Hiester
Charles J. Cook*	Thomas C. Poulter
Edward B. Doll	Lawrence M. Richards

Oliver F. Senn

ECONOMICS – MANAGEMENT – INTERNATIONAL

A. K. Beggs*	D. B. Meyers, Sr.
Bonnar Brown	William J. Platt
Raymond H. Ewell	H. E. Robison*
Charles L. Hamman	Robert O. Shreve
Paul J. Lovewell	Robert W. Smith

STAFF AND SERVICES

Emery F. Bator	Charles F. Hilly*
William A. Casler	Merritt L. Kastens
Lucien G. Clarke	Charles A. Scarlott
William C. Estler	Carl L. Titus
Jane Goelet	John E. Wagner

Robert L. Woodcock

———————

*Later vice president

RICHFIELD PILOT PLANT
— phthalic acid process
developed at SRI

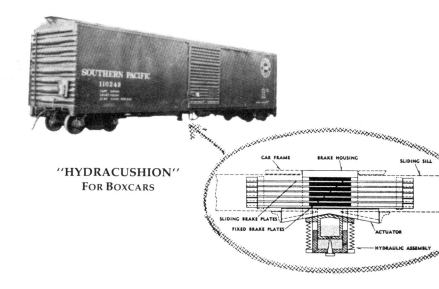

"HYDRACUSHION"
FOR BOXCARS

FEASIBILITY PROJECT

**APPARATUS FOR FLUIDIZED
PYROLYSIS OF SAWDUST.**

THOMAS C. POULTER
→

100 TON AMPHIBIOUS BARGE
Showing Giant Tires (BARC)

A Typical Account Item

Under the ERMA system each check carries account information in coded bars on the back of the check as shown in insert

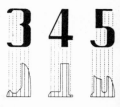

THE CHECK SCANNER "READS" MAGNETICALLY

A magnetic pickup head somewhat similar to that of an ordinary tape recorder enables the traveler's check scanner to identify Arabic numerals by the specific wave forms produced by each numeral.

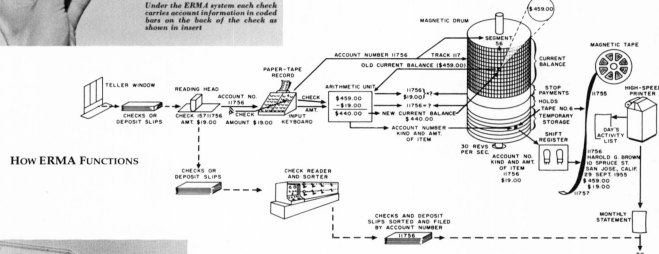

HOW ERMA FUNCTIONS

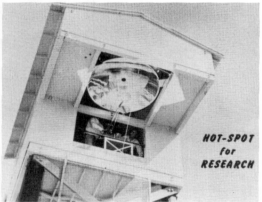

HOT-SPOT for RESEARCH

SOLAR COLLECTOR

Improved, lightweight, kenaf harvester-ribboner prototype now being prepared for commercial production

INCREASING ANTENNA SIGNAL POWER

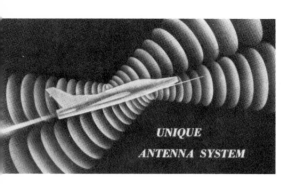

UNIQUE
ANTENNA SYSTEM

Some examples of SRI's "R for I" News Bulletin.

Weather Radar
"Seeing Eye" for Aircraft

Dotted lines on radar scope in cockpit show possible corridors pilot can follow for smooth flight through storm which appears solid to unaided eye

BETWEEN 1938 and 1953 some 236 persons died in 28 commercial airline accidents attributed to storms. In a like number of instances, aircraft were badly damaged by hail.

These Civil Aeronautics Board figures do not indicate the discomfort of countless passengers during many other storms, nor the loss of money and time often made necessary by uncertain weather conditions and subsequent delays or circuitous routings.

Most of the major airlines are vigorously conducting research and development programs aimed at doing something

about this situation. Radar—born of the World War II emergency—is apparently one answer. Several types of radar especially adapted for weather data are being tested, and at least one major airline has an accelerated program to install weather radar units on its entire fleet before the spring thunderstorm season.

In co-operation with the Radio Corporation of America, SRI's Radio Systems Laboratories have developed the antenna and special housing equipment for a C-band weather radar installation already being set up in the nose of United Air Lines Convairs and DC-6's. The research was carried out at the Mount Lee field

station of the Southern California Laboratories.

Operating on 5,400 megacycles with a 22-inch parabolic reflector, the Institute-designed antenna combines low cost, simplicity of manufacture, minimum maintenance, and optimum electrical characteristics with maximum reliability.

Reduced Side Lobes

The antenna feed and reflector are designed in such a way as to reduce the effect of side lobes (off-target interference), thereby increasing the "readability" of patterns on the radar screen.

The entire antenna unit weighs 25

Centerspread from Research for Industry

**DAVID ROCKEFELLER AND
VICE PRESIDENT NIXON.**
– SRI Conference Speakers –

*Industrial
Economics
Conference*

LOS ANGELES · CALIFORNIA
JANUARY 30-31, 1956

For World Economic Progress —
INTERNATIONAL INDUSTRIAL
DEVELOPMENT CENTER

MENLO PARK   ZURICH

SRI Around the World–1950 to Present

WORLD'S LONGEST PIPELINE
– SRI Study –

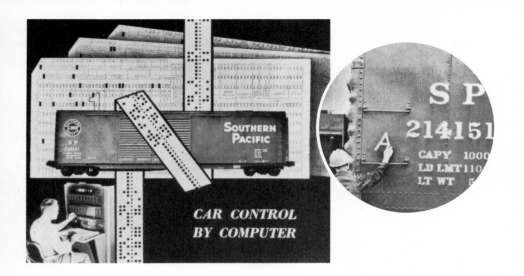

CAR CONTROL
BY COMPUTER

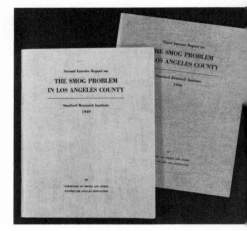

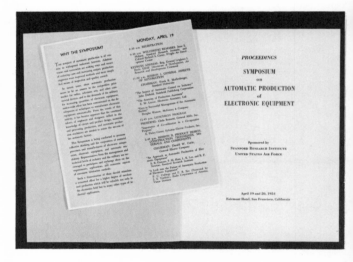

NEW HOMING SYSTEM
Helps Pilots Find Their Way

PILOT REDWOOD BARK BRIQUETING EQUIPMENT

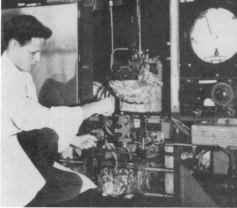

The Area Outposts

The Institute should not be in Menlo Park alone.

— WILLIAM L. STEWART, JR. - 1949

O NE OF THE FEATURES OF SRI's TAKE-OFF DAYS AND LATER UPWARD SURGE was a movement involving branch offices and in some cases research operations away from Menlo Park headquarters. It began in Southern California, but soon spread to other parts of the American West and then to the East Coast. Other parts of the world were to follow in later years.

Motives were different for the western outposts from those in Washington, D.C., New York City, Europe, and elsewhere. The idea was, first, to create small but growing research groups in key metropolitan areas of the West. Quite naturally, the first steps were taken in Southern California. One of the founding directors, William Stewart (Union Oil), was a moving force and urged that a strong presence be maintained in the area.

Even in the earliest days there were several temporary offices and field sites in the Institute's operations. Their purpose was to serve the needs of particular projects. This was the case in 1947 in Salinas, (California), on a synthetic rubber project, and in 1948 in Southern California in connection with a smog project. Later on, field stations were set up in Alaska, Utah, Greenland, Nevada and elsewhere.

There is no question about Hobson's early enthusiasm for western offices. He thought the approach was most appropriate — and indeed necessary - if the Institute was to pursue energetically a key economic development purpose in its charter. (As director of our economics group, I was equally enthusiastic about the concept.) Aside from project-financed field stations, this sort of decentralization was much more practical for economics programs than for those in the sciences and engineering.

The first operation in Southern California was started on September 1, 1948. It was a small air research laboratory. For several months the Pasadena station was the center for an embryonic Los Angeles Division of the Institute. With Stewart's encouragement Hobson later appointed A.M. "Abe" Zarem (an electrical engineer and friend from Cal Tech student days) as our representative in the area.

A.M. ZAREM
The L.A. Man

On May 17, 1949, Zarem opened a downtown Los Angeles office where he was soon joined by a small group working on economics projects. Thus, the first of several branch offices came into being. They were to play a considerable role in the Institute's development during the 1950s and in some cases to the present day.

EARLY SCL CREW
L to R: Fred Ortman, Carleton Green, James R. Lee, and Robert D. Englert.

Even during the financial crisis at the end of 1948 and as part of a Search for Purpose in 1950, the idea of offices or branches in the West was being discussed. One reason for such a move was to help offset a growing external image that SRI was a ''California Institute'' and not fully ''western'' in scope.

Hobson was, in fact, looking further afield — ''one or more branches in the industrial Midwest and East ... we must move quickly on the national scene ... we will need an office in New York ere too long.'' This seemed like wishful thinking but it was affirmative.

The L.A. Division was created to meet several immediate and long-term needs including such things as economics projects, public relations, laboratory operations, and relationships with universities and other research organizations. Los Angeles was a convenient contact point for project clients in the area and a base for promotional and research activities. Also, we wanted to ''throw off balance'' any Southern Californian attempts to create a separate research institute. The move did just that; local initiatives were soon set aside. Also, seeing what we were doing, Battelle decided to drop a similar move and ''leave California to SRI'' - a phrase used in a light vein by Clyde Williams, Battelle's CEO and a good friend of the Institute.

By mid-1950, the new group included four industrial economists along with Zarem. The economics unit — an extension of the Menlo Park operation — was working on a study for the military on machine tool requirements for the aircraft industry, especially in Los Angeles. Zarem was enthusiastic about other potentials in Southern California and was thinking about an even larger geographical area:

> ''The West possesses tremendous untapped resources of minerals
> necessary to industrialization. To be on the alert and ensure that the
> Institute shares in this potential is the future function of the Los Angeles
> Division. Within the next few years we will be continually faced with
> challenges which may make it necessary to expand the facilities and
> laboratories of the Institute in the Los Angeles area.''

Zarem was our senior man in Southern California from 1948 until his departure from SRI at the end of November, 1955. Much of his time and attention was devoted to the air pollution field. He and Stewart were close friends and together they were always urging Menlo Park to build up the Los Angeles activity. With great energy and in a forceful way, Stewart and Zarem spread the word in Southern California about SRI and its capabilities. Even as early as mid-1950 both were calling for a sizeable local operation on the basis that the long-range future for the Institute was highly promising.

Our first office in Los Angeles was essentially a one-man operation. As the staff began to grow the group moved twice to larger quarters where some thirty economists were to be assembled.

SOUTHERN CALIFORNIA LABORATORIES

PASADENA AIR RESEARCH LABORATORY

By mid-1955, it was evident that the Institute could operate more efficiently in Southern California by consolidating its activities at one location. In addition to the Pasadena laboratory and the economics group in Los Angeles, we had an antenna station atop Mt. Lee in North Hollywood.

An opportunity then arose to obtain a 40,000 sq. ft. building in South Pasadena from Beckman Instruments. Total lease costs by the Institute at the time were running at some $36,000 per year, and with added space needs a $49,000 figure was in the offing. The Beckman offer was for a five-year lease at $33,000 per year, with a purchase option (later exercised) of $325,000 (some $8.00 per sq. ft.).

This was indeed a good proposition, and our directors quickly approved the plan. The building was renovated in time to accommodate SRI groups in the area and other staff due to arrive from Menlo Park by early spring of the following year.

Hobson had announced the Southern California consolidation during the Tenth Meeting of our Associate Companies held in early November 1955. He spoke in expansive terms:

> *"When remodeling is completed, this new facility will provide office and working space for a staff which may grow to 200 or 250. More importantly, however, this consolidation goes a long way toward realizing our ambitions for an increase in the scope and convenience of our service to the industrial complex that has spread over Southern California."*

Less than a month after this announcement Zarem left SRI to form his own development company and within two months Hobson had resigned. Then, within six months and prior to the SCL opening, George Herbert resigned from his position as executive associate director.* Finley Carter, the new executive director, and the author were on hand for the June 1956 ceremonies at the Pasadena site.

The story of SCL's subsequent development, including a move to "The Irvine Ranch," south of Los Angeles, construction of a building, and finally its closing in 1971, must await a later book. But, one facet of the move is pertinent here. Even before Fred Ortman took up his post as Zarem's successor, he had spoken with Charles Thomas, the Irvine CEO about the possibility of SRI acquiring a parcel of land for which some major development plans were afoot. In due course, a combined gift-purchase plan was worked out with an assist from Edward Carter of Broadway Hale (now Carter-Hawley-Hale) in Los Angeles. Carter was one of our directors. In any event, as the Take-Off within SRI came to a close in the mid-1950s, the Southern California operation was entering a new stage.

NITROGEN OXIDE SAMPLINGS
– Pasadena Laboratory –

The SCL idea was much more than a consolidation of existing units. The intent was to build up a sizeable independent operation. This was part of a general expansion movement away from Menlo Park, where by mid-1956 the staff stood at around 1,250 with some 375 projects in progress. It seemed quite appropriate that some growth away from headquarters should be set in motion not only for research reasons but also on financial grounds. Capital for new buildings at Menlo Park was severely limited; leasing or buying good space elsewhere at lower cost was, therefore, attractive.

The first emphasis for the new SCL was, of course, on research opportunities in Southern California. This was made clear in a widely distributed brochure released in mid-1956. The centralization and planned expansion of economics, the sciences and engineering were described as enhancing our ability to serve the applied research needs of Southern California.

---

*To accept a post at American & Foreign Power in New York.

A COMMUNITY PROBLEM
Pasadena at 9 A.M.—November 1949

Research for Industry
A News Bulletin from
STANFORD RESEARCH INSTITUTE
STANFORD, CALIFORNIA

VOL. II, No. 2 • NOVEMBER 1949

A NATIONAL SYMPOSIUM ON AIR POLLUTION INVESTIGATION

NATIONWIDE scientific activity in all phases of air pollution investigation will be covered in the four general sessions and two luncheon meetings of the first National Air Pollution Symposium to be held November 10 and 11 at the Huntington Hotel, Pasadena, California.

Sponsored by Stanford Research Institute with the co-operation of California Institute of Technology, the University of California, and the University of Southern California, the conference is expected to attract approximately 500 scientists, industrial representatives, and civic and national government leaders throughout the country.

The program is planned at a scientific level and will include twenty-two objective papers covering the principal aspects of the growing smog problem in many American cities.

The objectives in organizing a first national symposium on the nature and causes of air pollution, its effects and correction, have been outlined as follows: (1) to present scientific and technical papers by authorities in the field; (2) to promote the interchange of thought and comparison of ideas and methods through a meeting of workers; and (3) to stimulate increased interest in the important and complex problems of air pollution by revealing the magni-

tude of the scientific effort being directed toward its solution.

"Sampling and Analysis"

The first session, which will occupy the morning and early afternoon of the opening day, has as its subject, "Techniques of Sampling and Analysis." Dr. A. O. Beckman, president of the National Technical Laboratories at Pasadena, will be chairman.

Following are the papers and speakers for the opening session:

"The Collection and Measurement of Aerosols," Dr. V. K. LaMer, professor of chemistry, Columbia University.

"Determination of the Concentration and Size of Particulate Matter by Light Scattering and Sonic Techniques," Dr. F. T. Gucker Jr., chairman of the Department of Chemistry, Indiana University.

"The Concentration of Sublimation Nuclei in Atmosphere," Dr. V. J. Schaefer, research chemist, General Electric Company Research Laboratories, Schenectady, New York.

"A Continuous Recording Condensation Nuclei Meter," Dr. Bernard Vonnegut, meteorologist, General Electric Company Research Laboratories, Schenectady.

Applied Research Center for the West

EARLY NEWS BULLETIN

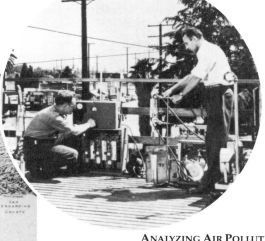

ANALYZING AIR POLLUTION

POSITION of the AREA of EYE IRRITATION
8 A.M. to 3 P.M.
County of Los Angeles
LEGEND
——— 8 AM —o—o—12 N
——— 9 AM —△—△—1 PM
——— 10 AM —+—+—2 PM
········· 11 AM —·——·—3 PM

Courtesy of McCabe et al — American Chemical Society Annual Meeting, March 1949

AIR CURRENTS —
LOS ANGELES AREA

DISNEYLAND

The economics program in the area was given new purpose and energy in early June 1950 when a man by the name of C.V. Wood joined the group. One early project was for the Disney brothers who were planning a small playland site in Burbank, California. The project included studies on such things as location, attendance patterns and economic feasibility. Wood and his associates, including Harrison Price, selected a much larger Anaheim site for the amusement park and prepared reports on many facets of its operation.

Later on, during the days immediately preceding the opening of Disneyland, several SRI people (including the author) were pressed into service on various administrative and get-ready tasks. Some even helped direct traffic at an uncompleted site when Disneyland opened its doors on July 19, 1955. A personal note at the time illustrates our involvement:

> *"Helping lay out the parking lot and giving a hand here and there to Art Linkletter, the Master of Ceremonies, is hardly research, but is helpful !!!"*

Announcements of the Institute's role in bringing Disneyland into being led to countless newspaper and magazine articles. By this time, four SRI staff members had joined the new Disney organization. Wood was its first president and general manager beginning in late 1954.

Price followed Wood as manager of the L.A. economics group and continued the Disney work for some time as the park expanded. A long list of other recreational studies was to be carried out under Price's leadership and later by others after he left SRI in early 1955 to start his own firm.

SUN SYMBOL FOR AASE
Zolita Robinson (SRI) demonstrates use of the 3-dimensional motif.
– Association for Applied Solar Energy

JOHN I. YELLOTT
Solar Energy Enthusiast

In retrospect, this approach was right under existing circumstances. The operation did grow in many ways and definitely advanced our interests in Southern California. More could — and should — have been done. There was, however, an internal problem from the very beginning. The approach called for decentralization of program responsibility from the Menlo Park divisions. There was a natural — and perhaps understandable — reluctance within the headquarters' groups to delegate to a separate branch or division. This problem was to arise many more times over the years as the ''outpost'' movement continued. Neither the first Los Angeles operation nor the others that followed elsewhere were real divisions — nor were they ever to be fully independent.

Some in Menlo Park had a perceived conflict of interest. One division director summarized the situation:

> *''The idea is right for SRI as a whole but cutting across program lines from the center will not work. Somehow, someway, we must find noncompetitive programs or some other formula. What and how are the big questions.''*

The questions remained for years to come. The only workable solution is close cooperation all around. Companies have the same problem in geographical responsibilities. The tide often goes back and forth between ''product line'' and ''separate'' divisions.

In any event, SCL was closed in the early 1970s on economic grounds plus, in part, to solve the ''turf problem.''

PATRICK M. DOWLING
First in Portland and
then New York.

Although for awhile the Institute had a one-man Associates Plan center in San Francisco, its second office was started in Washington, D.C. in 1952. Many had been spending considerable time in the capital. Far too much time was being spent merely on arrangements and on following up later on whatever had been set in motion. Hotel rooms looked more and more like offices. We came to feel that a small staff in the city could be of great help to everyone involved in government work. Hobson quickly agreed, George Hayes took up the post and served until early 1957 when he returned to Menlo Park and was succeeded by Ralph Clark, an expert in communication systems. To say that the Washington Office was a great help during and after our Take-Off Days and Upsurge Years would be a vast understatement. It was abundantly clear from the very beginning that the office was much needed in connection with our growing relationships with government.

The next three operations away from home were quite different from the Southern California and Washington, D.C. outposts. Their activities were centered on area development with an emphasis on one of our charter purposes — further industrialization of the West.

The three initiatives were in Phoenix, Portland and Honolulu. The Mountain States Office was opened in Phoenix on October 1, 1953 with Beardsley Graham in charge. The Pacific Northwest Office, under Patrick Dowling's and later Royce's leadership, was started on April 1, 1954 in Portland. The Hawaii Office, with William Hosken at the helm, got under way on September 20, 1954.

ROBERT M. BURNS
First in Zürich

GEORGE T. HAYES
First in Washington

WILLIAM E. HOSKEN
First Aloha Man

Although the Phoenix, Portland and Hawaii initiatives were not taken until the mid-1950s, they grew directly out of the search for purpose during the Take-Off Days. Thus, they are really a part of that Institute stage with its emphasis on the West and on public services beyond contract research.

Many discussions were held in 1950 on "branch offices" in the West as one means for SRI to become more fully involved in area development work. This emphasis was to fade in time, but it was certainly uppermost as the SRI "spring was wound" from 1948 through 1950.

For financial and other reasons, there was little we could do at the time to advance the whole idea. We simply had faith that opportunities would arise in due course. Our main thoughts were on Seattle and Phoenix because of their perceived growth potential. No one mentioned Honolulu in a serious tone. McBean and several other directors thought everything should be concentrated on doing more in Southern California.

The later follow-throughs in Phoenix, Portland and Honolulu were in response to urgings or requests from business in the three places. In retrospect, the Institute moved quickly — perhaps too much so. But, all this was part of a "get things moving" philosophy at the time. Both short-term successes and some longer-term problems were to arise.

The rationale for these regional outposts including Los Angeles was outlined in late 1954 in a report to our Associate companies:

> *"The objective — to provide research services over a broad geographical area at the least possible cost to clients, and ... to attain an intimate familiarity with the technical and economical problems of various industrial centers."*

Hobson always looked upon the four bases in Southern California, Phoenix, Portland and Honolulu as being a direct follow-through on our function as a public service organization. He said many times that the Institute's charter called for development assistance in the

---

PHOENIX

By early 1954, the Mountain States Office, (with headquarters in the Mayer-Heard Building in Phoenix), was operating quite successfully; Beardsley Graham was in charge. Both Arizona Public Service and the Valley National Bank had become Associates, primarily as a result of our move to the area. Several projects were under way, including one on economic opportunities for the Apache Indians of the San Carlos Reservation jointly financed by the Institute and the Apache Tribal Council.

Also, the governor of Arizona and several of the state's business leaders (including Henry Sargent, president of Arizona Public Service) were encouraging SRI to create a Laboratory of the Sun in the area to investigate possible useful applications of solar energy. In addition, we had undertaken on our own account a study of the tourist industry of Northern Arizona.

The Apache Indian project is an interesting one in the Institute's early history. The San Carlos Reservation included about 2,600 sq. miles of desert, mountain and forest land. Some 4,000 Indians with no federal subsidy were living on the land in the early 1950s. In November 1953, the superintendent of the Reservation urged SRI to become interested in economic problems of the tribe. We were encouraged along the same lines by several Arizona business and civic leaders.

We felt at the time that the study could lead to similar fully-paid projects in other parts of the West. This proved to be the case as word about the endeavor spread throughout the western states. The SRI report presented a development program to the Apaches, and for some time the Institute continued to assist the Tribal Council.

In a report in the spring of 1954 the directors were told that the Mountain States Office was proceeding satisfactorily, and that plans were complete for an International Symposium on Applied Solar Energy to be held under our auspices in Phoenix in early 1955. An Association of Applied Solar Energy (AASE) formed in Arizona under our leadership had allocated $25,000 for planning and preparing the Symposium.

West and that branches — especially in economics — were created with this objective in mind.

The Institute's interest in solar energy grew out of Hobson's strong belief that too little research on new sources of energy was being undertaken particularly by the electric power industry. During many SRI meetings, he advanced his views on the subject with force and enthusiasm. Also, he used every opportunity to present his thinking on energy problems to national groups.

In many respects, SRI was ahead of the times regarding the nation's energy situation. Hobson seized every opportunity that came his way to sound warnings about future energy shortages and argued forcefully for more research on sources. His views were often brought into question especially by the utility companies. Nevertheless, he continued a one-man crusade for some time.

He thought the nation's energy producers and equipment companies were far too complacent and conservative. One of his many speeches on energy was, in fact, given to this very group at an American Power Conference in Chicago on March 24, 1954. McBean cautioned Hobson about his heavy emphasis on energy, but this did not deter him in any way. Sargent also was concerned about the nation's energy situation in light of the rapidly rising demands.

When Hobson left SRI at the end of 1955, our solar energy pursuits came more or less to an end. The project market was miniscule, and the professional staff soon turned their attentions elsewhere. Both SRI and the Arizona group had done all they could do.

The Mountain States group was soon expanded to include several economists who devoted their time to various area development projects in Arizona and neighboring states. Green was transferred to our Southern California Laboratories as administrative director in mid-1957. The office was closed in August 1960. The workload was far too sporadic to justify its continuance.

MINERALS STUDY ON SAN CARLOS APACHE INDIAN RESERVATION
H.E. Robison (left).

SOLAR ENERGY

Dr. Farrington Daniels, a solar energy specialist and a professor at the University of Wisconsin, had interested Sargent in solar energy. Sargent and Hobson had many discussions during late 1953 on solar energy potentials. One result was creation of the AASE, a nonprofit corporation dedicated to advancing research on solar energy. For this endeavor, some forty Arizona businessmen, civic leaders and educators joined in support.

Sargent was the first chairman of AASE. Other members were Lewis Douglas, Walter Bimson (Valley National Bank), R.J. Harvill (president of the University of Arizona), Grady Gamage (president of Arizona State College), Frank Snell (a Phoenix attorney), and Graham of SRI. Merritt Kastens, an assistant director at SRI, was appointed to work with AASE. Graham devoted a lot of time during 1954 and 1955 to the proposed solar energy program. He and Kastens were particularly active in planning the Solar Energy Symposium. By mid-1954, the worldwide meeting had been scheduled for November 2-5, 1955.

Hobson was highly enthusiastic about this event. He told our directors that public announcement of plans for the Symposium had elicited widespread response in the press and American industry. About 200 leaders in solar energy working with industrial executives with similar interests had been contacted in preparation for the program. Several government agencies, including the National Science Foundation, had promised support. Contacts also were being made with scientists and industrialists in many foreign countries in an attempt to insure truly worldwide participation. I, for example, visited solar energy installations in Asia and Europe during the summer of 1954.

Graham and Kastens also were making contacts with both American and foreign groups. The Mountain States Office was heavily involved with the upcoming symposium. A unique event, it was attended by about 1000 delegates from the United States and 34 other countries.

MERRITT L. KASTENS
Solar Energy Man

In the meantime, the Institute was stepping up its research in solar energy. An experimental solar stove was constructed, and plans were completed for development of a new and powerful solar furnace. Several reports were prepared on solar energy and its applications in various parts of the world. A comprehensive directory (including a bibliography) was released by the Mountain States Office in the spring of 1955. The catchword around SRI at the time was ''Look to the Sun.''

Although several attempts were made (in cooperation with AASE) to establish a Laboratory of the Sun or its equivalent in Arizona, the efforts were not successful; the necessary money could not be found. When Graham left SRI in late 1955, John Yellott became manager of the Mountain States Office. He was on a split-time basis with an appointment as executive director of AASE. He subsequently became full-time director of the Association following which Carlton Green of our economics group became manager of our office in Phoenix.

During the latter part of 1953 while the Mountain States Office was being started, The Institute was moving ahead on several economics projects in the Pacific Northwest. A study

PORTLAND

Edgar Smith, a leading citizen of Oregon and Washington who later was to become an SRI director, hosted the Portland inaugural. Some seventy business executives were on hand. McKee represented the directors. Hobson told the group that we hoped SRI could make a substantial contribution to the Northwest. He also said we looked forward to harnessing SRI capabilities with the mineral, timber, agriculture, fish, metal, and ceramic resources in the area. The timing was right; we were off to a good start.

The office opening was soon followed by another SRI event in the area. Thirty executives of our Associate companies participated in a Research Management Tour from April 28 to May 1. The group visited several companies in Oregon and Washington including Tektronix, Crown Zellerbach, General Electric (Hanford) and Boeing. Fred Olson, vice president for research and development at Olin Industries, keynoted the final session in Seattle.

The Portland Office was quite successful during the first three or so years of its six. The early staff included several economists working on area development studies. In

WILLIAM S. ROYCE
Portland and Washington

March of 1957, Dowling was transferred to Washington, D.C., and then moved on to New York where an SRI office was opened in August. Royce was Dowling's successor in Portland; the operation was closed in 1960. The reason was the same as for Phoenix — uneven workload.

There was another behind-the-scenes motive in setting up the Pacific Northwest Office. It appeared there was good potential for an SRI laboratory in the area centered on forest products. This idea was pursued energetically during the autumn of 1955 but faded away after Hobson left the Institute. There was little support for the plan among the timber companies. □

HAWAII

The story of our office in Hawaii is an interesting episode from the mid-1950s. Our first key association with The Islands came in the summer of 1953 when an economics study was carried out for Matson Navigation Company on possible expansion of its operations. Then, in September, William Estler, director of public relations, went to Hono-

WILLIAM C. ESTLER

lulu with a Chamber of Commerce group. Robert Woodcock of our economics group made a similar trip in October with a trade delegation from San Francisco. Both met and talked with many business and civic leaders. They returned with an optimistic view of opportunities.

In early 1954, Neil Houston, also of our economics group, visited Honolulu in connection with a project for the Island Trading Company of Micronesia. He and others, who traveled to Hawaii soon thereafter on work for the Hawaiian Sugar Planters Association and on a study for the Matson Company on the tourist trade, found that local business leaders were hoping SRI would take a special interest in Hawaii and its economic problems.

One result of these visits was an invitation to Hobson to spend several days in Hawaii. He made this trip in April 1954, during which he spoke before the Rotary Club of Honolulu on the importance of research in economic and industrial development. Also, he was guest speaker at a luncheon arranged by Leslie Hicks, president of the Hawaiian Electric Company. His luncheon remarks gave strong emphasis to economic and area development work in stimulating the growth of a region.

NEIL HOUSTON
Project Work in Hawaii

The guest list for this luncheon included chief executives of the principal economic and business organizations in the Islands. It was there that we first met Robert Craig of the Hawaiian Economic Service and Henry White, president of the Hawaiian Pineapple Company, who were to figure prominently (along with Hicks) in our later entry into the Islands.

Craig and also Thomas Hitch of the Hawaiian Employers' Council were invited to visit the Institute. They spent the first four days of June 1954 at SRI in discussions about research needs and opportunities in Hawaii. And they also met with several directors in San Francisco.

On June 28, Charles Blyth (a director and Stanford Trustee) hosted a luncheon in San Francisco in Hicks' honor. Hicks urged the Institute to become interested in Hawaii and, if possible, to open an office in Honolulu. Hicks visited SRI that afternoon and met McBean. Again, he urged the Institute to extend its operations to the Islands.

Upon returning to Honolulu, Craig and Hitch went into action. At their urging, White wrote in July urging SRI to set up an operating base in the Islands. Then, on August 5, the House of Representatives of the Territory did the same thing by resolution. Shortly thereafter McBean received a letter from the Chamber of Commerce:

A FORMAL INVITATION

At its last meeting, the Board of Directors of the Honolulu Chamber of Commerce approved a recommendation from the Economic Development Committee that an unconditional letter of invitation be written to SRI. We hope that you might take this matter up with your Board of Directors with a view to considering the establishment of a field office in Honolulu.''

McBean liked ventures of this sort and sent Craig's letter including the business-sponsored invitation to SRI along with a cryptic note — ''Let's do something.''

Things moved rapidly during the next two months. At a luncheon on September 29 the opening of an SRI office in the Honolulu Gas Company Building was announced with William Hosken in charge. Several area development projects were received during

ALOHA TOWER
Fourth Western Outpost

the following few weeks. By year's end it appeared that annual revenues would be at least $100,000 for 1955. The staff soon included seven people.

This forecast soon proved to be far too optimistic. By early 1956, the hand-writing was on the wall. Something had to be done to bring costs and net income into balance. It became clear that the office should be closed. As matters developed Hosken returned to Menlo Park in mid-1956. The last person, Paul Magill, came home in February 1957.

PAUL MAGILL
A Mainstay in Hawaii

An amusing situation surrounded the decision to close the Honolulu Office. The announcement spoke first about our continuing interest in the Islands, and the way in which they would be served from Menlo Park. Only at the end was Magill's return to the mainland mentioned. The press then took over with an interesting twist about SRI's ''expansion in Hawaii.'' One of our directors remarked, ''first I ever heard that closing and expansion are synonymous.'' □

was under way for the State of Oregon on highway taxes for motor carriers. A major project was being sponsored by Weyerhaeuser on the outlook for forest products.

Alcoa had asked SRI to analyze the impact of the aluminum industry on the economy of the area. The Pacific Power and Light Company (PPL) was interested in several technical projects. Furthermore, Paul McKee, president of the company and a former SRI director, wanted the Institute to study long-range power developments and needs in the area. A research program was under discussion with the Oregon Development Commission.

During the early part of 1954, we met several times with McKee and others in Portland and also with the governor and several business and civic leaders in the state. We were urged to set up an Institute office in Portland. We told McKee that the Institute would respond if PPL became an Associate Company and if he returned to its board. Also, it was understood that he would help broaden our contacts throughout the Pacific Northwest. McKee agreed. The office was announced on March 31, 1954 and the very next day it was opened in the Equitable Building. Patrick Dowling was in charge.

The Institute's regional office network in the West was at its peak during 1954 and 1955, the last two years of Hobson's time at SRI. Offices were opened later in several eastern and midwestern cities, but they were essentially one-man efforts for development purposes. By the beginning of the 1960s the three-area development initiatives in the West (except for Southern California) had come to an end.

Two questions in retrospect are obvious: Was the whole exercise justified and why were the outposts closed? The answer to the first is "Yes." They helped make SRI a "western institution." They brought our economists and other specialists in touch with local development problems. They attracted support for the Institute from local industrial and government groups. They signalled our early interest in and dedication to all the western states.

The answer to the second questions is simply "economics." The offices in Phoenix, Portland and Honolulu were financially viable in the short run. In each case, projects were received one after another in quick succession. The resident staff was increased accordingly; at one time the Phoenix staff included 25 people. It was not long, however, before immediate research needs in each of the areas had been met. It was increasingly difficult to maintain a proper balance between projects and staff skills. It soon became necessary for each group to broaden its fields of interest. This called for more and more professional help from Menlo Park. This, in turn, meant more travel. In time, the economics of each operation became even more unfavorable. All this led to consolidating operations at Menlo Park.

In a backward glance, one must keep in mind that our objectives were to extend SRI's activities to the three areas and, simultaneously, to render a public service. These goals were attained in ample measure. Under the circumstances, both the openings and the closings were right.

One might wonder why the initial decisions were not made on a simple return-on-investment analysis or on a straightforward allocation of money for public services. Had the first route been taken, the offices probably would not have been opened. This would not have been in the Institute's best interests. Had the second approach been used, sufficient incentives for the staff would not have been present. At the time, we did not have a good system for such investments.

MISCELLANEOUS PUBLICATIONS FROM SRI

The facts are that the offices were set up, played their role in our early development and then were closed. There were other justifications in the Phoenix and Portland initiatives — a possible solar energy laboratory in the former and a forest products laboratory in the latter. They did not materialize, but neither have many other projected programs in our history. The important point lies in the overall thrust of the organization; the regional offices made a definite early contribution.

Another regional emphasis had its beginnings during the 1950s. It had to do with Europe and Japan. Our objectives then were quite different from those for the regional outposts at home. Public service and area development goals were not uppermost in the later decisions; the driving force was simply program development and research operations.

There were times during the ''outpost days'' when some of our senior people and directors wanted to close down the peripheral operations. At the same time others were calling for more investment to help make SRI a truly western institute. We were, in effect, experimenting with rather vague policies, plans and criteria. We knew the handwriting was on the wall by early 1956. Hobson was gone; many questions were being raised internally; the directors were lukewarm. Our thoughts were ''how and when'' rather than ''whether or not'' for Phoenix, Portland and Honolulu.

> On economic grounds, our regional offices are in the wrong places;
> better they should be in several eastern industrial centers, in Europe and
> in Japan, for different reasons; the public service goal is fading away.
>
> The day will come when our "offices away" can again include professional
> staff, especially in economics and management sciences. Until then, they
> must be small outposts. Meanwhile, the Washington Office will become
> more and more important to SRI. And we must find ways to make our
> offices far more useful in the sciences and engineering.

With some adroit maneuvering, the western offices idea, started enthusiastically during our Take-Off Days, came to a gradual and quiet end. ∎

INTERNATIONAL FELLOWS (AT SRI)*

*... to promote the general interests of International exchange
... in research ... and research techniques ...*

Kenneth M. Alexander — **AUSTRALIA**

Another from **JAPAN**

David Tabor — **ENGLAND**

Armando Lopez Maglaque — **PHILIPPINES**
Jean-Pierre Cornaz — **SWITZERLAND**
Hiroshi Nagano — **JAPAN**

Two more in Physical Sciences

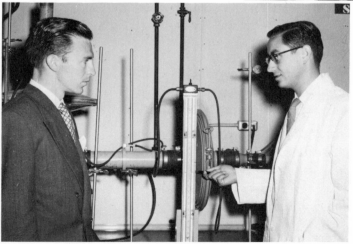

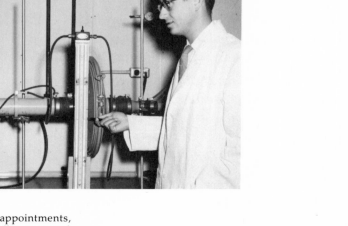

*Some early appointments,
each externally sponsored

Alice Okada — **JAPAN**

The Second Stage*

Now Begins the Onward Course.

— ROBERT E. WOOD - 1950

THE CHAIRMAN OF SEARS ROEBUCK DURING THE MID-1900s was much interested in SRI and its prospects for the future. General Wood, as he was widely known, was one of the nation's most optimistic and forceful executives.

He was predicting a boom in the American economy and then for world business. Although not involved in SRI's creation, he knew some of our founders and strongly endorsed what they had done.

Wood's interest was even higher as he saw the Institute grow to almost 300 people and about $2 million in annual revenue. He was aware of some of our research programs including one on color television; word about the latter came from a mutual friend, David Sarnoff, chairman of RCA.

In this setting, in late 1950, our Chicago friend's enthusiasm for SRI centered on the future. This was when he spoke about an "Onward Course." As for the nation as a whole, he sensed what might happen during the next five years or so.

ROBERT E. WOOD
An enthusiastic observer.

COURTESY-SEARS ROEBUCK AND CO.

A LONG DELAYED PLAN

The Stanford Trustees applaud the decision to limit the size of the Institute.
— W. P. FULLER, JR. - 1951.

DURING THE NINE MONTHS following the first surplus in July, 1950, the Institute's finances steadily improved. However, everything was on a month-to-month basis. There was no development plan.

This hiatus was the result of a chain of circumstances and not an oversight or lack of diligence. The directors had asked for a plan. However, the approach was derailed by the RFC negotiations.

Accounts receivable rose sharply and put a severe strain on cash. Once again, growth was a problem.

Revenue for 1950 was about $2 million, some 19% higher than for 1949. More importantly, the year's deficit was only $58,000, about a third of the red figure for the previous year. The cumulative deficit was $451,000, the highest point.it was ever to reach. A negative net worth after contributions of $274,000 was also at its highest point.

One of the most important developments of the year was the beginning of a self-sponsored research program. The main purpose was to demonstrate commercial possibilities of promising ideas before seeking sponsors for continuing work. Seventeen projects were started. Five involved new products and pro-

---

*1950–1955 — A Digest. See also some Equity Capital, A Village Home, and Area Outposts.

cesses; four were fundamental scientific studies; one was a public service study on civil defense. Six dealt with technical publications; one was in chemical economics.

The staff count rose only slightly during 1950. Thus, most of the year's growth in revenue came from a more efficient operation. The whole belt-tightening exercise was beneficial and put the organization in a stronger position. By year-end the growing electronics group had 43 engineers; physical sciences led with 56 professionals. Economics was in third place with 27.

It is not easy to portray the staff environment and feeling that pervaded the Institute in 1950. Everyone felt, especially during the second half of the year, that SRI was finally on its way. A drive was on to get new projects and carry them out successfully. Pride in the Institute and in its output was definitely rising. A stimulating environment was evident all around.

Our first international project began in 1950. It involved a World Bank study in Cuba. Then, after long negotiations with the Italian Government and the U.S. Mutual Security Agency, a contract with Italy was signed late in the year. It dealt with recovery of the nation's heavy mechanical industries and marked the beginning of our continuing involvement in Europe.

MULTIDISCIPLINARY TEAM

Standing L to R: Donald B. Benedict, Physical Sciences, and Gordon Newell, Biological Sciences.
Seated L to R: Sylvan Reuben, Physical Sciences, and Clinton Kelly, Engineering.

Other project work was growing apace. At year-end, a public report on the Los Angeles smog problem was being prepared. It was to be controversial, with a spotlight on combustion in automobiles, trucks, incinerators and industry as smog contributors.

The aircraft antenna program continued to grow. Sinclair Oil Company started a project on the Poulter Method of Seismic Exploration. The Chemical Economics Handbook went into high gear with about 100 clients including most of the nation's largest chemical and related-process companies.

In light of the nation's rearmament much of the Institute's attention in the winter of 1950-51 was on national security. The annual report took up this theme. ''Scientific skills and knowledge are rapidly becoming (the nation's) most important national resource. We must use them with utmost effectiveness and zeal to defend our way of life, our freedoms and our very existence while we strive at the same time to preserve the world's highest standard of living.''

It appeared that the U.N. forces in Korea might be driven off the peninsula. Men were being called to arms; the U.S. was mobilizing once again. Prospects for World War III were ominous. Thus, the Institute's report referred to a ''gigantic effort'' in marshalling the country's research facilities.

> ''Even now the united research endeavors of industry, government, private individuals, and research organizations present an imposing bulwark for the safety of the nation. But this is not enough. All of us must labor to extend and intensify our system of 'organized' research ...''

Growth seemed certain from existing and promised contracts. The biggest problem would be to hold revenues within a $5 million rate. Hobson then said something that would later plague him in many ways. His words stuck with the directors and Stanford Trustees. He said that SRI would level off at between $4.5 and $5.0 million in revenue. No such thing ever happened, even briefly, and questions were to be asked along the way.

We had a staff of 338 at the time. The predicted count for a year later was 450 at a ''leveling off'' point. This was the real key — 30% growth for an organization already expanded to the hilt.

Knowing that SRI might ask for additional funds from Stanford, its Trustees discussed the possibility even before a request was made. The result was a reluctant decision to advance an additional $250,000 if urgently needed.

This showed some new confidence on the part of the Trustees, but at the same time they called upon the SRI board to move as soon as possible on long-term financing. They felt that enough had been done by the University.

One Trustee said that the decision to level off carried considerable weight, particularly since the group felt that limits had to be placed on the amount of money to be "invested" in SRI. Additional bank loans were out of the question.

We knew that the Stanford Trustees and some of the directors wanted a check on expansion. Nevertheless, the Institute was in a position where it had to grow fairly rapidly or turn downward financially. A 25% growth rate was finally accepted by all in light of the "decision" to level off in size.

All were greatly relieved the afternoon of April 26, 1951 when a long-delayed plan was adopted. At the very least, a few months of breathing time were at hand. We certainly did not realize that a new gate to the future had been opened.

John Forbes, to whom the Stanford Trustees and directors looked for the final word on business plans, was a conservative and cautious man. Nevertheless, he gave a "go ahead" on the early 1951 plan. He later wondered why he had done so under the circumstances. But, he did and everyone rallied around. SRI did not let him down in the years to come. □

FROM RED TO BLACK

I am pleased with the fashion in which SRI is handling its ... affairs.

— JOHN F. FORBES - 1951

ALMOST IMMEDIATELY FOLLOWING adoption of the April 1951 plan, continued growth produced a problem. Accounts payable began to pile up. A withdrawal from Stanford helped ease the situation. Tight expense control became even more important.

In mid-summer, a major breakthrough was made with the federal government on cost reimbursement contracts. Negotiations by several nonprofit institutes, including SRI, resulted in a 6% fixed fee based on total costs.

The fee principle was significant because it overcame the government view that nonprofit organizations were not entitled to a surplus on government contracts in view of their basic exemption from federal income taxes. Charles "Chuck" Hilly at SRI was a key negotiator.

Our urgent equipment needs in mid-1951 were very great indeed. The hope was that several critically-needed items — an emission spectrograph, a mass spectrograph and a chemical library — could be obtained as gifts. No such help was to be found.

Our study in Italy got under way in the spring of 1951. We were welcomed in effusive words by Dr. Eng. Senator Professor Corbellini at a large public reception in Rome before going to the Vatican for an audience with Pope Pius XII. Corbellini was head of a "Hoover-type" commission.

His welcoming remarks lasting some thirty minutes were elaborate and involved. At the end, the interpreter merely said, "Professor Corbellini bids you welcome!!." But we had a copy of his text which included:

"I do not know ... what advice Stanford will give us. But even if their advice is nothing but what we already know, and even if we disagree with it ... their coming here is well worthwhile. ... we have now met a group from North America upon whom we can rely and whose word we can trust."

Although our host knew that an SRI rather than a University group was present, his reference to Stanford was more or less commonplace at the time. There is no question that before being widely known around the world the Institute benefited greatly from the Stanford name.

Our equipment problem simply would not go away no matter how well current operations were moving. Among the seven leading institutes, SRI had the highest annual revenue per person with next to the lowest equipment investment. At a minimum, our needs were upwards of $1 million.

Several field laboratories and stations were in operation at the end of 1951. They were at Detroit Lakes (Minnesota), Dugway Proving Ground (Utah), Portland (Oregon), Frenchman's Flat (Nevada), Fairbanks (Alaska), Provo (Utah), and Midland (Texas).

A Few From Engineering

Standing L to R: Milton B. Adams, Byron J. Bennett, Clinton M. Kelly, William M. Lynch, Oliver W. Whitby, Philip J. Rice, Jr., A. Robert Tobey, Howard M. Zeidler, and Fred J. Kamphoefner.

Seated L to R: Jerre D. Noe, William E. Evans, Jr., William D. McGuigan, Kenneth R. Eldredge, and Low K. Lee.

The Dugway installation was set up in connection with U.S. Army tests involving an underground explosion of 320,000 tons of TNT. The Portland and Provo laboratories were being used for air pollution projects. The other sites were for geophysical work, particularly in connection with the Poulter Method for Seismic Exploration.

Air pollution research continued to be an important activity. A major report was issued on the Los Angeles situation. It identified more than fifty chemicals as smog contributors. Sixty percent of the area's combustion and other products being put in the atmosphere was associated with automobiles, homes, stores, office buildings and other public activities.

The other forty percent was said to be from industry. By this time, the Institute was heavily involved in other air pollution work having to do with the effects of plant emissions on vegetation and buildings. Alcoa and U.S. Steel were the main sponsors.

The tight cash situation did not hold back other research programs. A major report for the AEC on industrial uses for radioactive fission products attracted worldwide attention. A size-

able project on single side-band radio transmitters and receivers continued during the year. It had grown out of concepts that originated in Stanford's Engineering School.

Also, Engineering was busily engaged in developing its electronic computer program that was soon to be involved in our largest and most important industrial project of the 1950s — an electronic accounting system for Bank of America.

The first Italian project was largely completed by the end of 1951. The whole exercise ended with another audience with Pope Pius XII, this time at the Vatican's initiative.

During 1951 several meetings were held with Vittorio Valletta, head of Fiat. He and several other Italian industrialists proposed that SRI create a branch or subsidiary in the country. They offered to "guarantee" a substantial sum.

Discussions continued off and on for almost a year. It later became clear that Valletta had in mind guaranteeing a bank loan SRI would arrange in Italy. The idea was quickly dropped; we were in no position to borrow either lira or more dollars.

During the latter half of 1951 and early

37 airshot blast showing Poulter Seismic Method in West Texas, early 1950.

THE ITALY PROJECTS

– Early 1950s –

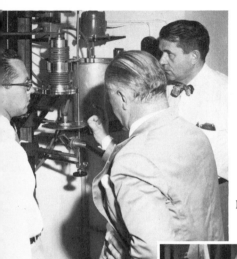

POPE PIUS XII receives SRI GROUP and guests at the Vatican, 1953

FRED C. LINDVALL (right).

L to R: LORENZO FRANCESCHINI, the Author, SIGMA ARDITI, RALPH LAMBERSON, and PROF. FERRITI.

DISCUSSION GROUPS

1952, new emphasis was given to our internally-sponsored research. The Institute had started its fifth year with ten projects carried over from 1950. Twenty new projects were added and five were completed, leaving twenty-five active at year-end. Thirteen were in basic sciences, dealing for the most part with chemical and physical phenomena. One was a feasibility study on a western resources handbook. Others ranged from work on pesticides to effects of shock waves on steel.

A few changes were made in the Institute's operations in mid-1951. The chemistry division, as it was called at the time, included four departments — physical and analytical chemistry, organic chemistry, food chemistry and a combined group in chemical and metallurgical engineering. There were also two specialized laboratories — air research and applied biology.

The physics division included a department for geology and geophysics and one for applied physics. A special laboratory for radiation engineering, based on a radioactive-cobalt energy source, was being planned.

The engineering division, devoted almost entirely to electronics, included groups for materials, television, computers, communications, advanced techniques, mechanical engi-

PAUL MAGILL
Physical Sciences

**A TRANSISTOR
VIDEO AMPLIFIER**

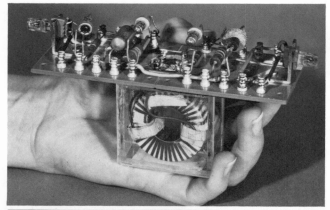

neering and maintenance minimization. Specialized laboratories had been set up on aircraft radiation systems and electron tubes.

Business and Economics continued with programs in operations research, area development, management systems and economic studies of various types at home and abroad.

As the Institute approached the end of its "delayed plan" in the spring of 1952, more and more attantion was being given to the role of scientific research in the quest for greater industrial productivity on the national scene. An earlier report emphasized the theme.

"In the years ahead, productivity will remain one of the decisive factors controlling the strength and success of the free world. Management capital and labor have an equal stake, and the international statesman cannot overlook its significance ..."

EARLY TV LABORATORY
WILLIAM E. EVANS (right).

One of Hobson's associates inserted "international statesman" in the 1951 statement and prepared a further note:

"... it is not enough to strengthen our own economy alone. Greater productivity in friendly areas outside our boundaries must play its part in meeting increasing domination by unfriendly interests. The issue of the world conflict of ideas, goals and freedoms may well turn on production attainments ..."

This theme was becoming increasingly appropriate for the Institute. Projects were under way in Italy, Brazil and Korea; more were being sought around the world.

The "long-delayed" plan was completed by the end of February 1952. The results were reasonably well on target.

Item	Plan	Actual
Revenue (monthly)	$345,000	$320,000
Surplus	231,760	186,000
Building Improvements	63,750	62,000
Equipment Purchases	424,000	404,000
Accounts Receivable	854,0001	896,000
Bank Repayments	112,500	225,000

These figures show a characteristic pattern in one respect. Although only $125,000 of outside capital was available, instead of the $450,000 or so requested, the Institute moved right ahead on its expansion path.

On the other hand, withdrawals from Stanford were sharply curtailed and greater payments than planned were made to the banks.

ECONOMICS PROJECT IN ISRAEL
Second from far right, Harry Robinson and J. Knight Allen.

Once again, the cash situation was severely tightened. Something had to be done, and it had to be internal.

Meanwhile, the Institute passed two milestones in its longer-term development. The 1951 plan began with a capital deficiency (negative worth); it ended with a positive net worth. We had finally become "solvent;" capital contributions had put the balance sheet in the black.

The second milestone had to do with international. In thinking and action the organization had become world-oriented to a considerable extent. This is illustrated by presentations to executives of the Institute's Associates at a meeting on December 12, 1951. One had to do with developments on the German research scene growing out of an SRI project; another was on the industrial situation in Italy. □

A PAUSE FOR CASH

We seem to pausing and expanding simultaneously.

— WILLIAM L. STEWART - 1952

By SPRING OF 1952, a new one-year program for the Institute's further development was in place.

The main problem — as so often before — was lack of cash. With less than $9,000 in the checking account and only about $29,000 in all, accounts payable were in poor shape. Our credit reputation was in question. Even though some capital from the Associates Plan was expected, the timing for a new growth plan was certainly not propitious.

Hobson, nevertheless, was determined to "keep the ball rolling." This led to be doing two things simultaneously even though they were conflicting to some extent. One was to pause for cash and thus proceed with some care. The other was to have a flexible plan within a ceiling of four to five million dollars per year. A 25% expansion was involved. The first order of business was to improve the cash position.

A new milestone was soon reached. The $10 million point in cumulative revenue was at hand. Contract backlog was at an all time high. Moreover, the total number of research projects since the Institute's formation had gone above the 550 mark.

In May, 1952, the Institute hosted a group of European research executives who spent several weeks visiting scientific and technical organizations throughout the country. The leader of the so-called OEEC Mission 82 was George Heberlein, a Swiss industrialist. A member from the United Kingdom, Frank Kearton, later became chief executive of Courtaulds, a chemical company. The visit led to a long friendship with both men; they halped SRI in various ways over the years.

One of the reasons the OEEC group came to SRI was to see at first hand the operations of a university-affiliated research institute. Many more missions from abroad were to visit Menlo Park for the same purpose. The whole idea was attracting attention around the world.

In any event, the European group apparently was impressed with what they heard and saw at SRI. Kearton later spoke to the point at a meeting in New York. "In all our trip through the United States and Canada, I was especially impressed with ... (SRI)." He then went on to say it was "an outstanding example of research institute operation."

Although the British are not inclined to overstatements, he probably did so on this occasion. But there was some merit in his view, and in any case all at SRI were immensely pleased.

In the spring and summer of 1952, two events of some significance were sponsored by SRI. The Second National Air Pollution Symposium was held in Pasadena on May 5-6 in partnership with Cal Tech, UCLA and USC. The audience included some 420 people The event attracted national and international attention

EARLY SRI PROCEEDINGS

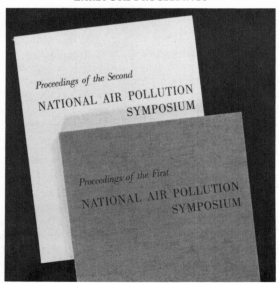

and helped project an image of our air pollution research program.

On June 17, the sixth SRI Associate's Day took place in Palo Alto, near the Institute's headquarters. Several technical papers were presented by SRI people, one of them involving new uses for television in industry.

The Associates Plan was already a key factor in our growth. Hobson emphasized this fact at the 1952 session.

> *"One of the most significant developments in the history of the Institute has been the Associates Plan. This has provided us with an opportunity for working closely with industry in its role of developing the West ..."*

> *"... each Associate contributes money or equipment to the Institute without strings attached. These funds are not used for operating expenses, but to provide essential laboratory equipment and working capital, and to carry on Institute-sponsored research ..."*

He might well have gone further by saying that without the Associates Plan SRI probably would have gone out of existence or at least its development would have been severely restricted. The Plan was our only source of external capital aside from loans. The alternative would have been a pure "bootstrap" operation.

A second public service program,* the Western Resources Handbook, was started in July, 1952. The basic idea was to publish comparative data on a wide range of western resources. Both Handbooks originated in the Institute's economics group; the purpose was to help in fulfilling one of our charter objectives — the dissemination of economic and technical information.

These initiatives were quite important, especially because of our strong emphasis at the time on special public service activities. The announcement went directly to the point. "This is one of our major forward steps. We hope that ... this Handbook will become the most valuable single source of work available on the economy of the West."

The Handbook was indeed a useful publication. It was issued for several years, and then discontinued with most of its contents shifted to the Chemical Economics Handbook and to a new Industrial Economics Handbook.

Our total contract volume had just passed the $14 million point, divided about equally

---

*The first: Chemical Economics Handbook.

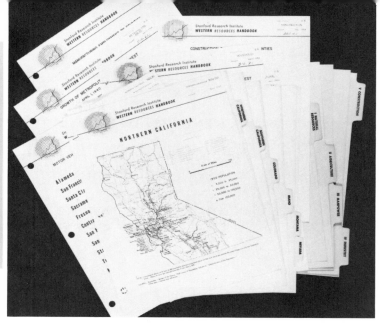

BINDER WITH DIVIDERS AND DATA SHEETS — 1954

between government and business. Some 836 projects were involved, more than 40% being for business and industry.

Almost two-thirds of the $7.0 million in commercial revenue had come from "big business," the balance being from associations, individuals and "small business." The $7.0 million in government work was divided fairly evenly among the Army, Navy and Air Force.

Although the Institute in many ways had become a national and international institution, California still provided a major portion of the commercial projects. Around 60% of total commercial revenue had come from the state, 35% being from the Los Angeles area alone.

There was no question about our activities being brought to the attention of an ever-widening national audience. During the preceding year, articles appeared in newspapers across the nation with combined circulations of more than 100 million.

Institute periodicals were being sent to some 74,000 people; more than 3,400 reports had been sold to the general public; clients had distributed another 18,000 SRI reports. The Chemical Economics Handbook had almost 300 subscribers, and the Western Resources Handbook another 120, including the Associates.

Our staff at the end of August stood at 504 of which about two-thirds were in technical and professional categories. Almost 450 lived in the immediate Menlo Park area. The Institute had become one of the leading entities in its community.

Our operations were far-flung as well. We had offices — some temporary, some permanent — in Washington, D.C., Provo (Utah), Los Angeles, and Rome (Italy). In addition, project groups were at work — or had been recently — in Hawaii, Alaska, Mexico, Brazil, Venezuela, Cuba, Japan, Korea, Germany, and France. Mobile laboratories were stationed in Alaska, Utah, Nevada, Texas and Minnesota. An air pollution laboratory was operating in Pasadena.

As September, 1952, got under way, contract backlog was the highest ever. Prospects for the future in almost all respects seemed to be very good indeed. In this environment, the time had come for a new plan. No one doubted the organization's growth record, but some had a different interpretation. Their image — quite correctly — was an organization that seemed always to expand beyond any "predetermined" size.

Nevertheless, the Institute was set on moving rapidly to a new and higher level. Hobson had solid support from the senior staff on our ability to acquire and maintain a higher research volume — assuming more capital could be found. Perhaps, under the circumstances, this support was to be expected. Almost all programs had good potential and were growing.

In any event, a new 15-month plan was laid before the directors in mid-September. It called for an increase in revenues to an annual rate of $6.0 million by the end of 1953. Earnings were set at 5% of revenue. The plan also called for 70% of the growth to be on work for industry.

One feature of the plan is interesting in retrospect. There was talk about a "gradual expansion" but the surplus estimate for 1953 ($300,000 at 5% of revenue) shows that it really contemplated about $6.0 million for the year — not a buildup to that rate by year end. In any event, the point was not made clear and it would lead to some questions.

Some of the directors were skittish about the extent and timing of the expansion. The chairman pointed out that it was a change from the earlier decision to hold the Institute's size to $4.8 million in annual revenue. The plan began with a ceiling of $2.5 million per year on government work. We were, in fact, already at this level. ☐

THE BOTTOM LINE

Wonders can be done when there is no red ink.
— J. D. ZELLERBACH - 1952

MUCH OF A SENIOR STAFF MEETING on September 16, 1952, had to do with a new resolve within SRI. Another development plan adopted earlier in the day was most welcome news. But, discussions soon turned to the bottom line on the income statement.

Net worth stood at just over $500,000. We had no red ink on the balance sheet but the final figure on the income statement was conspicuously red. Another $115,000 in earnings would take care of the situation.

So it was that the senior staff laid down a self-imposed goal — remove the red figure by the next annual board meeting in March 1953. In many ways, this was the development plan; everything else except research was secondary.

Right in the middle of preparing the 1952–53 program, an important insurance problem had to be handled. Our brokers were unable to find workman's compensation and general liability coverage because of SRI's pending installation of a radioactive cobalt energy source.

Finally, with time literally down to the last day, another broker (Johnson and Higgins) got the coverage. The result was a change in brokers and the beginning of a long and beneficial relationship.

Shortly after the 1952–53 plan was adopted, the Institute was approached by the West Coast Electronic Manufacturer's Association (WEMA) on a possible government project. The idea was that SRI would operate an environmental test facility in Los Angeles. Government facilities were available in the East but the electronics industry wanted one in the West.

It was a good project from SRI's viewpoint. The financing was satisfactory, including possible advances for working capital. But it could not be handled without pushing the Institute well beyond the board limit of $2.5 million in annual revenues from government.

In any case, the project was taken to the board. No one wanted to turn down the opportunity. The limit was raised by whatever might come from the endeavor. But some conditions were added — no SRI capital or operating funds were to be used and the work was to be for government only so as to avoid competing with commercial laboratories in services to industry.

Discussions continued for some time on the laboratory but nothing happened due to changing interest by the government. However, a policy point had been brought to the forefront.

The government ceiling came up again soon in early 1953. A far larger project was involved — upwards of $10 million a year for a decade.

Basing the case on the nation's precarious position in R&D, Hobson said that needs for new weapons and a shortage of engineering and research people in government and industry were bringing rising demands on research organizations. Then he emphasized a conviction — "SRI has a national obligation to assist to the greatest extent possible."

The idea of an *obligation* was a new thought for the directors. The philosophy had been to work for government only when it served our main pursuit — building an organization for industrial research. The change was a powerful line of reasoning with the Korean War still troubling the nation.

The huge Willow Run facility in Michigan, built during World War II, was becoming available with a closedown of automobile production by one of the Kaiser companies. The Army wanted to start a vast development program on battlefield surveillance devices. Some 250 people would be needed even with half of the work subcontracted to industry.

Although the Institute was attracted to the project, some felt it would divert attention from our main pursuits. However, in the end the directors gave a go-ahead if a suitable contract could be developed. The decision soon became academic when the Signal Corps decided to work with the University of Michigan.

This decision did not disappoint anyone particularly. Some were delighted with a side result, one that was hoped for from the beginning. Management was told that "the policy limitations should not preclude consideration of major defense research programs." Whether right or wrong, this shift in policy lifted the gates on government contracts.

Another event in the autumn of 1952 had a significant impact on the Institute. It involved Stanford. Believing that the time had come to start doing something on assistance to the University, a suggestion was made that SRI begin paying a fee for services. Forbes agreed and plans were put in motion. The idea was right and proper and overdue — about $825,000 was sent to Stanford within a decade.

Visitors to Radiation Laboratory including **HAROLD STASSEN** viewing Cobalt source, far right.

On November 20, 1952 our new Radiation Engineering Laboratory was dedicated. Its centerpiece was a radioactive Cobalt 60 energy source in a "swimming pool" filled with 5,400 gallons of water. It was the largest radioactive source outside AEC installations and thus attracted widespread attention along with some public concern.

Research programs throughout the Institute were moving along quite well at the time. In addition to the Cobalt source, an X ray diffraction unit and an ion-scattering analyzer had been added in physical sciences. But all this was minor in relation to needs.

Engineering work — mostly electronics — was growing rapidly. More expansion was being planned for the next two years, especially in materials, industrial controls and instrumentation. Again, the operations were equipment limited.

The economics group also was growing apace. But even more was in the offing. Our plan was to double industry-sponsored research during the next two years. At the time, economics had a staff of 100 and in many ways was still a pioneering program among the research institutes.

The engineering group did indeed expand substantially during the next two years. Revenues rose by some 65% as had been predicted.

The economics forecast turned out to be far too modest; industrial revenues doubled within a year.

All this was hardly "gradual expansion" as some had called the September 1952 plan. But, it was certainly "progress."

The year 1952 as a whole was a high growth period. In all, 354 projects were undertaken for more than 300 clients. This was 65% more than for the previous year. Industry sponsored 227; 91 were for government and 36 were sponsored by SRI itself. The year began with 126 projects, 219 were added during the year, and 135 were carried over to 1953. The momentum was gathering force.

Work on the Los Angeles smog problem continued throughout the year. It centered on a

LIBRARY AT SCL PASADENA

variety of phenomena including chemical reactions in the atmosphere. A movie was released as one way of telling the public what was known about smog in the area.

Several other projects also received public attention. They included, for example, unitized electronic designs aimed at reducing maintenance costs, transistor studies and articulation testing of long-range radio transmissions. The Institute's physics group was involved in explosive phenomena work on a Nevada desert. Also, an economics report on maintaining U.S. production in the event of an air attack was featured by the national media.

NUCLEAR TEST IN NEVADA
or Man on the Moon?

All three research areas were involved in our self-sponsored work in 1952. They covered the waterfront, so to speak, from studies on polymer molecules to economics of the electronics industry. The main idea was still to pave the way for new projects with both government and business.

Two SRI people received special national recognition during 1952. John Granger, head of the aircraft antenna laboratory, was named outstanding young electrical engineer for the year. Then Doll, chairman of applied physics, was appointed national program director for a series of nuclear explosion tests in Nevada.

The main public emphasis within the Institute as 1952 came to an end was our role in providing facts to decision makers, particularly in the business world. ''Applied research is directed to the production of facts for the management equation ... formulation of the equation, its expression, and its solution must remain with management itself.''

The last part of this statement is, of course, a truism and was nothing new. Nevertheless, the idea that our main pursuit was to concentrate on facts — leaving interpretation to others — was too limiting. As time went on, the concept was allowed to pass away.

Everyone had hoped the cumulative red income figure would be gone by February, 1953. But, alas, some $14,000 remained at the end of the month; the goal was missed in March by a mere $1,130.

By the end of April another milestone had been passed. The operating deficit was gone; there was a black figure of $19,000.00 in the surplus account. After capital contributions, net worth was more than $900,000. There was no red ink anywhere.

This state of affairs was most satisfying to the staff and indeed to the directors. For once, the statements were mailed routinely to McBean rather than being delivered in person with explanations. He was quick to call — not with congratulations but rather an exhortation. ''Let's get the surplus up to $50,00 a month.''

Even with McBean's onward and upward urgings, the general feeling was that the Institute had justified the faith shown by both the directors and the Stanford Trustees in earlier years when one financial problem seemed to follow close upon the heels of another. The directors must have been reasonably satisfied; they decided to increase benefit levels in our retirement plan.

With a good bottom line, the Stanford Trustees seemed to relax a bit.

Several benchmarks came to the forefront during 1953. A social sciences initiative centered on industrial psychology, and training was taken but was later brought to an end for lack of business interest.

At the urging of one director, Stephen Bechtel, Sr., a relationship with the Ford Foundation was set up on work with newly-developing countries. The plan continued for several years with small industry development and other projects in India, Pakistan, Iran, Burma and elsewhere.

Some thirty international projects were in place at the time accounting for about 9% of our revenue. Bechtel, however, continued to call for more.

50% of commercial revenue and 25% of the total!

We finally came to about 40% and 20% but not until the end of the 1970s. In the meantime, our total revenues multiplied more than 25 times.

A major project was started in mid-1953 on the forest products industry. The later so-called Weyerhaeuser Report was widely distributed around the world and had a major favorable impact on the international industry.

Also, during the year, the Institute received publicity on a large techno-economic study involving the new "Big Inch" pipeline across Canada. Many others of the same type in other parts of the world were to follow.

A big financial event of 1953 was final payment on our $600,000 bank loans from early 1949. In business circles, this quickly became a symbol of "a new and stronger SRI."

A banker said "wonder of wonders — much, much more than had ever been expected; the Institute is now A-#1." Zellerbach merely said, "I told you good things would happen."

GROWTH
The Take-Off Days

Year	Staff	Revenue (Millions)	Surplus*
1948	204	$ 599	− 26.5%
1950	260	$ 1,990	− 2.9%
1955	1163	$10,029	3.2%

* 1951/1952/1953 − 4% − 5%

THE FINAL PUSH

The pace is pretty fast; there are so many plans.

— JOHN A. McCONE - 1954

IN 1953, AS WE WERE APPROACHING the end of a 15-month development period, the first of four more plans that were to follow was put in place. All this was to be an 80% expansion in a mere 24 months.

Each plan as it came along in rapid succession covered one year broken down by quarters. The first three were revised at six-month intervals; the fourth was replaced on the same schedule by a six-month and three-year plan. The Institute was on a fast path. This led one director (John McCone of Los Angeles) to say that the frantic pace was causing him to lose track.

McCone's comment was understandable. A drive was on to reach a new milestone. Even internally, it was not easy to match up plans with performance; plans were changing so frequently.

Nevertheless, the situation was exciting, and the senior group was exuberant about the chain of events. The directors were still worried, but no one was inclined to argue forcefully against a wave of success on both programs and finances that seemed to be occurring.

The first six-month plan called for virtually no revenue growth from the $6.2 million annual rate at the end of 1953. However, the surplus rate was supposed to go up (from 4.7% to 5.4% of revenue).

This apparent pause in growth fell on receptive ears in the boardroom: the date was December 14, 1953. All were glad to hear that SRI was embarking on what one director called a "consolidation." Thus, no one was really prepared for another upward thrust that would soon emerge.

As 1953 turned into 1954, there was much talk about reshaping our organization. Hobson had come to feel that the situation called for a new senior man as overall manager of research operations. Krause had been in this post but he wanted to move to a new and much-needed planning job.

There was no question in anyone's mind that Hobson was looking forward to a much larger Institute. He often said as much even in terms of "twice our present size." Even he did not think this would happen so quickly. Nevertheless, he was once again generating a growth mood among the staff

A.K. BEGGS
Forest Products Authority and future Vice President.

even while speaking now and then about a "consolidating phase." The handwriting was on the wall, but it was not as evident outside.

The new setup in the spring of 1954 included eleven Institute-wide committees. They brought more people into central management activities. Hobson was co-chairman (with Krause) of the main Management Committee, but in fact he was executive chairman in all possible ways.

COMMITTEES — 1954

Chairmen	Committees
J. E. Hobson	Senior staff—Management
R. A. Krause	Finance and facilities
W. E. Rand	Institute-sponsored research
D. L. Benedict	Staff education
W. J. Platt	Personnel
L. M. Richards	Publications
R. L. Woodcock	Associates Plan
W. B. Gibson	Relations with industry
C. Steffens	Institute reports
T. H. Morrin	Patent review

Even by April, 1954, only four months after the first of four plans had started, a problem was evident. It was not an unfamiliar one. Revenue had moved up quickly to a $7.0 million annual rate, but the surplus rate was declining.

The first two weeks of June 1954, were not easy times for the Institute. Belts were tightened all around the organization; all sorts of activities were slowed down or stopped. Everyone pitched in to get the job done.

Even with the spring setback, a $60,000 payment was made to Stanford against working capital advances. This was a big help in offsetting some of the Trustees' remaining concerns about the Institute. The other three short-term development plans were put in place on schedule in 1954 and 1955. A few numbers show where things stood at the end.

The accumulated surplus was more than $755,000 and net worth was almost $2.6 million. With a staff of 1,163, cumulative revenues of $35.0 million, and 217,000 square feet of floor space, the Institute had become a sizeable operation. Among other things, it had "hit the bull's eye again — $10 million in annual revenue.

We had grown some five times over in five years and were operating with a 3–4% surplus. The "critical mass" had dropped out of our lexicon.

All this brought on a feeling of great satisfaction around the Institute. It was not fully evident at the time, but the days of "induced growth" had come to an end. Although the Institute was to have many more years of quite rapid growth, it was not to be "driven" in the same way.

It was clear to everyone at the end of 1955 that "The Final Push" had been successful although at times a source of concern — and even anxiety — to some of the directors and Stanford Trustees.

All this had McBean's full support partly because the founder was always delighted to hear about new projects, clients, and finances.

Sterling and a few other directors were worried about the rapid pace of events. Their earlier concern about growth was based on finances. But during the Final Push, their worries had to do with possible impacts on quality.

Sterling, in particular, kept wondering and asking how quality could be maintained or increased with so much attention on handling an ever-higher volume. This was an understandable worry even though the Institute's reputation and quality of performance were growing.

The general attitude of the directors, particularly during 1955, is well illustrated by an exchange with Paul Davies of FMC when he asked how much the Institute would grow during the year. Upon hearing — "about 30% in staff and revenue" — he said without hesitation, "That doesn't sound like consolidation to me."

Then, he asked about the surplus, and upon hearing "about a 40% increase" promptly swiched gears with a humorous note, "That's the kind of consolidation I had in mind." □

L.M. RICHARDS
Chemist

CHARLES HAMMAN
Industrial Economist

With the complex of today's problems, the technique of a single science may be effective on some occasions while on others several acting in concert produce the most favorable results.

— E. FINLEY CARTER - 1955

AS SRI GREW AND DIVERSIFIED DURING THE TAKE-OFF DAYS, it delivered an increasing "payload," so to speak, to its many clients and communities — companies, governments and the general public, at home and abroad.

Programs and projects are the main vehicles through which the Institute's goals are pursued. High quality in professional work is the key ingredient.

Size and growth rates — whether in staff, buildings, equipment or other assets, or in revenues — are merely measures for the organization as a whole.

Even a summary of professional pursuits during the eight years from 1948 through 1955 is not feasible here. However, both program and project examples do appear in several chapters.

A few others appear in The Story of SRI, a journal published in 1966 on the occasion of our 20th Anniversary. They include, for example, new compounds for cancer chemotherapy, static suppressors for airplanes, new products from tallow, a railroad shock absorbing device, and shaped explosive charges for oil well perforation.

Also, highlighted are improved spinnability of cotton, helping developing countries become self-supporting, long-range planning systems for business, and an electronic accounting system for banks.

This last project (ERMA) was a large, Institute-wide endeavor — perhaps the most important from our early years. It was shown publicly seven years after our Engineering programs were started with the arrival of Thomas Morrin on September 1, 1948.

More than any other single project, ERMA was and still is a symbol of our "Take-Off" in professional work.

SRI's Kenneth R. Eldridge (left) demonstrates check sorter element of ERMA to Bank of America president, S. Clark Beise, September 1955

THE MONTEREY THEME

Images shape the future.

— FRED L. POLAK - 1955

DURING THE MID-1950s, a Dutch economist was promoting a large social sciences project known as Images of the Future. He sometimes used the words "the future in past tense." Polak believed that the future of a nation is governed largely by its images or ideas of the future. He thought they could be measured scientifically and used in planning.

The whole idea was controversial. However, it appeared for a time that an American publishing company might sponsor such a project on the United States.

Although this did not happen, Polak's theme had symbolic value. It came to the forefront in mid-1955 when our management group assembled for a weekend session at Monterey, California. The gathering was similar to one held in mid-1948. It had helped usher in the first rapid surge during our Take-Off Days.

Our situation was vastly different from what it had been seven years earlier. Sterling, the chairman was using the phrase — "a strong and productive position."

- The three basic program areas were firmly in place.
- National and international dimensions had been added.
- Some $1.8 million of "equity capital" had been received.
- A surplus was being generated.
- Net worth (capital) stood at some $2.6 million.
- A "critical mass" had been reached.

The staff count at mid-year was over 1,000 people; annual revenues were at the $10 million point. Research quality was increasing; projects were growing larger.

Three things emerged from Monterey — some "images" including six priorities, four decisions and a set of principles.

The priorities were more or less in the form of a "To Do" list beginning with research programs:

- More and more emphasis on quality.
- Growing interdisciplinary work.
- Greater selectivity on projects.
- More support for basic research.
- Added emphasis on public services.
- Rising international work.

A few points on organization and operations were included:

- More effective marketing.
- A better working environment.
- Longer-range planning.
- Greater efficiency.

To all these, four perceived investments were added:

- More facility improvements.
- Rising equipment outlays.
- Some staff education/training.
- A new headquarters building.

Also, the idea of further assistance financial and otherwise to Stanford was encompassed.

These and other images or needs were discussed at length. All was then put in a financial framework with Herbert taking the lead. Four group decisions were taken.

- Staff and revenue growth rates "slowed down" from 30–40% per year to "reasonable Bounds" of 10–15%.
- A 50/50 government/commercial ratio.
- A higher surplus rate — from 3% to 4½% or higher.
- Financial self-sufficiency.

These decisions were made with some "special opportunities" in mind, a possible Laboratory of the Sun in Arizona, a nuclear reactor in Northern California, and a Forest Resources Laboratory in the Pacific Northwest. They did not come about but, anyhow, they were to be financed separately.

Also, an SRI-Stanford Basic Research Center and a possible SRI-Mellon affiliation were under consideration along with many special public service projects. Associates or other money was to be involved.

The Institute might well become self-sufficient for "normal operations," but, even with borrowings, it certainly could not handle everything the group wanted to do. A headquarters building was put in place three years later with help from a long-term loan.

With some more Associates' money in the till for equipment, basic reasearch and public services, and with a higher surplus, the Institute was soon able to "make its own way" as the directors had intended in a 1951 policy.

However measured, growth in an SRI-type organization is highly important; appropriate rates are the product of many factors including working capital, equipment and space requirements.

During the decade after Monterey, the Institute staff grew at an annual average 10% rate; revenue rose at 18%. These rates were too high for comfort. A sizeable staff reduction was necessary in the 1960s. The two decades following 1955 saw our annual growth rates stabilize at about 5% for staff and 12% for revenue.

The third product from Monterey was a set of principles on the Institute's obligations and opportunities.

PRINCIPLES

- Spurred to an early maturity by unprecedented demands of war and peace, organized research has not fully developed the operating principles by which many other professions and activities are guided.

- Still, in one single, hurried generation, a number of objectives, policies and procedures have been defined. In particular, it has become apparent that a public service, applied-research corporation must meet several distinct but interdependent responsibilities.

- It must make available and it must continuously perform contract research services of the highest professional quality, without compromise, without prejudice, and without preference.

- The solution of specific scientific, technical, and economic problems under these strict standards is the very first obligation of the institution and will establish and maintain its ability and its integrity.

- It must dedicate its skills, experience, and a full measure of its resources to public service on an ever-expanding scale.

- It may direct its energies toward developing human, material, or financial resources, the strength and capacity of a geographic or an economic segment and the solution of scientific and economic problems of broad public consequences.

- Recognizing that these functions should not be separated, it must move toward an integration of its policies and capabilities into a single, co-ordinated unit.

- Thus, it may serve whole areas of public interest — geographic, scientific, industrial, educational and government communities — in research activities contributing to the public welfare.

- It must constantly and increasingly encourage its several communities of interest and contact, and also its clients, to new undertakings, new achievements (and) new perspectives.

Research leadership in science, engineering and economics is a decisive factor in stimulating individual companies, industries and government agencies to new concepts, progressive policies, and sound actions.

Each of these charges — project service, program planning, public leadership — is demanding and challenging in itself, but none of them casts more than its own shadow independent of the others.

Each, however, can lend substance, life, strength and vision to the others. Together, they offer programs of usefulness, improvements, and renewed vitality.

The application of basic scientific knowledge is a distinguishing characteristic of modern society. It is fundamental to the social, political, economic and mechanical accomplishment of our generation.

Applied research organizations, therefore, have a direct responsibility to support basic scientific research and investigation.

- Basic research and the industrial technology that springs from it are vital both to the prosperity and security of our own country and to human values everywhere.

- Scientific training and education (the preparation for creative careers) are linked inseparably to basic research achievements.

- The challenge of exploring new scientific knowledge and new approaches to application of such knowledge must be brought to inquisitive, bold young minds by every means available.

The responsibilities and the opportunities of the public service, applied research and institution are unmistakable.

- It must serve industrial, governmental, regional, and scientific interests.

- It must support advancement in all sciences.

- It must contribute to scientific education and the public welfare wherever and whenever it can.

- It must, on its own, create and enhance opportunities for such service. □

First study science and then follow the practice born out of that science.

— LEONARDO DA VINCI

GOOD NEWS FROM SRI !!!

Stanford Trustees Richard E. Guggenhime (left) and David Packard, (right) with
Frederick E. Terman, University Provost. Packard and Terman also SRI directors.

These principles — over Jesse Hobson's name — appear in our annual report for 1955.
He was the main author and he wrote:

These principles are fundamental to Stanford Research Institute.

Also, he said that "the staff has accepted them with enthusiastic and effective
understanding ..."

Circumstances and policies change from time to time. But, these were the "images" as
the Take-Off Days moved into the Upsurge Years.

There was no long-range plan from Monterey. Even the four decisions covered only a
few years. Nevertheless, a new theme soon pervaded the Institute.

Pride in the institution was at an all-time high; confidence and enthusiasm for the
future were evident everywhere. If the second stage in our development was passing to a
third, it was doing so on a high note.

Polak could not have measured it, but it was there for all to see and feel.　■

The Open Forum

– INSTITUTE DEVELOPMENT AND PUBLIC SERVICE –

A research institute should take the lead in making useful information available to its publics.

— VANNEVAR BUSH - 1954

WHEN THE INSTITUTE'S VIGOROUS THRUST BEGAN IN 1948, it was apparent that something had to be done to promote the concept of contract research along with SRI as a new entrant in the field.

Presentations were made to many groups, public and private. Brochures were widely distributed; many meetings were held within business and government.

All this was helpful, but given our development needs, it was not enough. Ways had to be found to ''spread the word'' more rapidly. Platforms were needed within the Institute's various publics.

To this end and as a public service, a series of SRI forums was launched. The emphasis was two-fold — presenting economic, scientific and technical information and making the Institute's interests and capabilities known to invited participants.

Some forty events were held during the following decade. More than 6,000 people were involved. Many staff members made presentations and led discussions in their professional fields.

These forums were helpful in project development as well as a public service. They played a key role in making the Institute and its programs known in the American West and then nation-wide and around the world.

L TO R: **ASTON O'DONNELL** AND **MERRITT L. KASTENS**
SRI Presentations at a 1954 Energy Forum

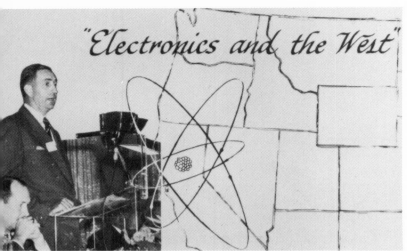

ADDRESS BY DAVID PACKARD.

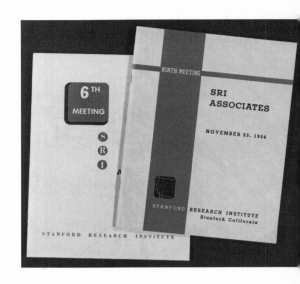

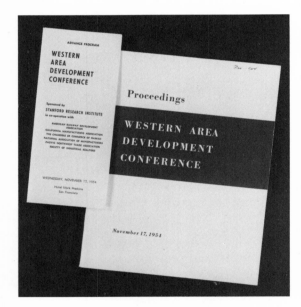

Are there 88 people for dinner? Time to be seated, gentlemen.

McBEAN-BECHTEL DINNER
in Henry Luce's Honor — The IIDC.

Several of these events including two in the energy field in 1954 and 1955 were "world class" in both substance and participation.

The early movement was at its zenith in the mid-1950s. It was inspired in part by Vannevar Bush's comments in Los Angeles during a special event in the series. Bush was a leading statesman of American science.

The forum approach continues today in various forms and in diverse fields. Leadership on the global scene is by the Institute's World Business Division and SRI-Washington.

The first International Industrial Development Conference — now known as "the IIC" has become one of the world's most prestigious business conferences, each attended by some 500 senior executives from more than sixty countries.

Over the years, the Institute's forums have certainly helped make SRI a "household name" among its publics in both business and government. Whatever success may have been achieved in this respect arose first of all from high-quality professional work in SRI's research and advisory pursuits. ■

PRINCIPAL EVENTS
— The First Decade —

Northern California Research Conference (San Francisco)

> January 12, 1949
> January 11, 1950
> April 6, 1951

National Air Pollution Symposium (Pasadena)

> November 10–11, 1949
> May 5–6, 1952
> April 18–20, 1955

Symposium on Automatic Production of Electronic Equipment (San Francisco)

> April 19–20, 1954
> April 22–23, 1955

Western Area Development Conference

> November 17, 1954 (San Francisco)
> September 8–9, 1955 (Portland, Oregon)
> October 31–November 1 (Phoenix, Arizona)

Atomic and Solar Energy

> April 4–5, 1954 — Atomic Energy Forum (San Francisco)
> November 1–5, 1955 — World Symposium on Solar Energy (Tucson & Phoenix, Arizona)
> January 21–22, 1957 — Solar Furnace Symposium (Phoenix, Arizona)

Social Sciences Seminar (San Francisco)

> March 13, 1953   March 23, 1955
> May 11, 1954   April 4, 1956

Industrial Economics Conference

> January 30–31, 1956 (Los Angeles)
> January 21–23, 1957 (San Francisco)
> January 13–15, 1958 (San Francisco)

High Temperature Symposium (Berkeley, California)

> January 25–27, 1956

Special Luncheon Programs — Associates Plan

> November 14, 1951
> (San Francisco — David Sarnoff)
> January 20, 1954
> (Los Angeles — Vannevar Bush)

World Tourist Symposium (Honolulu)

> November 18–19, 1957

Associates Day Programs

> November 17, 1949   November 23, 1954
> October 24, 1950   November 9, 1955
> June 17, 1951   November 14, 1956
> November 20, 1952   December 4, 1957
> November 19, 1953   November 20, 1958

Research Management Tours (Associates Plan)

> May 5–19, 1953 (Southern California)
> April 28–May 1, 1954 (Pacific Northwest)
> March 8–12, 1955 (Northern California)
> May 1–5, 1956 (Salt Lake City/Denver)
> May 13–17, 1957 (New Jersey)
> September 21–October 3, 1958 (Europe)

International Industrial Development Conference (IIDC) (San Francisco)

> Announced in 1955 to be held, October 14–18, 1957, in cooperation with Time-Life International. Subsequently co-sponsored every four years with The Conference Board of New York.

A Lighter Vein

In the Market Place

Even with the growing American and world economies during SRI's early days, acquiring clients was no easy task. The Institute was not exactly a "household name" in business or in government. Our "track record" was very short.

Everything had to be promoted simultaneously — the values of contract research, SRI as a new institute, and project ideas. The staff was on "double time." However, there were some light moments along the way:

FROM BUSINESS

- We already have a laboratory; it does our inventing.
- An economist here handles such things for us.
- I graduated from Stanford but SRI is news to me.
- The kinds of things you talk about are secret inside the company.
- It's unlikely, but we'll call if something comes up.
- Can you post a bond and guarantee results?

FROM GOVERNMENT

- We can't find your name on the approved list.
- Better talk to your Senator first.
- Stamford (Connecticut) is OK, but Stanford (California) is too far away.
- Your 30% overhead is *far* too high.
- Where did you get your equipment?
- We'll send some people to work at your place.

Two Letters Received

WHO!

- Dr. James Goodenough, Stanford University, Menlo Park, California — Dear Mr. Good: "We greatly appreciate your attending the meeting about SRI. We did not know you founded it. But, again, Mr. Zellerbach, we thank you ..."

CADENCE!

- Dr. Weldon B. Gibson, Stanford Economics, Stanford Research Institute, Stanford University, Stanford, California — Dear Dr. Stanford!!

Words from the Founder

Atholl McBean was a forceful person; the Institute was "the apple of his eye." He left no stones unturned in its affairs; he was colorful without even trying. He was often tough and arbitrary, as well as impatient and insistent. But, he had a sense of humor.

- Budget or no budget, tell the architect to fix up the patio and send the bill to me. (A month later — Here is the bill for payment — hope you like what he did.)
- I hear that fellow is not interested in SRI; he's *all* wrong; I'll straighten him out!!!
- What's all this about a project in Italy? I better go over there (he did) and tell them about founding SRI.
- Ninety days to do that project? That's too long; he wants results right away.

- Your full name is OK and "Dr." is just fine, but we call you "Hoot." Let's use a better name; what do you suggest?" The response — Well how about Dr. Hoot? The reply — I'll think about that — on second thought — forget it.
- You have *two* choices — break even now or break up later!!
- Get the surplus up; don't let the banks get nervous.
- A retirement plan? We've hardly started!!

A Global Network

— AN EARLY START —

*A more distinguished group of world business leaders has
never before been created; I am honored to be included.*

— HENRY R. LUCE - 1955

IN ADDITION TO THE DIRECTORS, many well-known senior executives around the
world have long provided advice and assistance to SRI in connection with its international
activities.

They have been most helpful on such endeavors as the International Associates Program,
the quadrenniel International Industrial Conferences in San Francisco, and many
other worldwide events for business and industry (e.g., in London, Tokyo, Singapore,
Sydney, Mexico City, New Delhi, Menlo Park (California), Moscow and Hangzhou (China).

Also, they have helped on various institutional and project development activities
including in some cases the opening of SRI offices outside the United States. Many of their
companies have been, and are, project clients.

Building this informal global network began during the Institute's Take-Off Days. The
group has changed over the years but even during the late 1950s some 250 chairmen, presidents,
managing directors and other executives in high positions were involved.

A similar network is helpful to SRI in the 1980s. It operates in connection with our
World Business Division. The number of people involved (even in the 1950s) is far too great
to list by name.

Since the beginning, the ever-changing group has given high service to the Institute all
of which has been — and still
is — greatly appreciated.

Identifying a few people
from the early global network
merely illustrates the high
standing of the group and its
worldwide composition.

A STRONG TRIO
L to R: **MARCUS WALLENBERG** (Sweden)
CRAWFORD GREENEWALT (U.S.) and
CHARLES MALIK (Lebanon)

HIS MAJESTY, KING FAISAL

EDWARD S. PRENTICE
IIDC Program

GEORGE W. BALL
Later U.S. Under Secretary of State

DAVID ROCKEFELLER

S. D. BECHTEL, SR.

A STAUNCH SUPPORTER
HERMANN J. ABS (Germany)

THE CHAIRMAN AND AN EASTERNER
L to R: **J.E. WALLACE STERLING** and **HAROLD H. HELM** (U.S.)

INTERNATIONAL INDUSTRIAL DEVELOPMENT CONFERENCE

IIDC Banquet — Fairmont Hotel

May our work lead to greater understanding among the nations.
— E. Finley Carter - 1954

Some Quiet Advice From Taizo Ishizaka

Henry Luce
Conference Chairman

A New Zealand Group
Jack Radford, Frank Renouf, Sir James Fletcher, and son **J.C. Fletcher** (later also Sir James).

Frances O. Bohley
International Secretariat

OL **H. Ebtehaj** (Iran)

GEORGE LIEN YING - CHOW (Singapore)

EDGAR F. KAISER
An Energetic Leader

L to R: **PRESIDENT SUHARTO, JULIUS TAHIJA,** (Indonesia)
the author, and **A.W. CLAUSEN** (U.S.)

A SESSION IN MANILA

L to R: **WASHINGTON SYCIP, ROBERTO VILLANUEVA,** and friends.

SIR SIK-NIN CHAU (Hong Kong)

EUGENE R. BLACK
President, World Bank

YOSHIZANE IWASA (Japan)

Epilogue

We are building an institute.

— AN SRI STAFF MEMBER - 1955

T HIS BOOK IS BEING PUBLISHED during a "double anniversary" year, the 60th and 40th, for SRI.

It was in 1926 that Dr. Robert E. Swain at Stanford University first took his idea about a new research institute to Herbert Hoover, Stanford's most distinguished alumnus.

Although the circle of supporters widened during the balance of the 1920s and through the 30s, nothing else happened because of the Great Depression. Then, in 1939, Swain took another initiative within the University and among a few business friends. Unfortunately, everything had to be put "on the shelf" because of the outbreak of World War II.

In 1945, a group of western business leaders under the leadership of Atholl McBean in San Francisco entered the picture. Events moved rapidly during the next several months until the Institute was incorporated in the autumn of 1946. Two years later, the Founding Years came to an end and the Take-Off Days began.

As indicated earlier, the full story of our Founding Years appears in a 1980 book. This one deals only with the seven or so formative years that began in 1948. The period is important in that several dimensions, features and initiatives were added to the young institute.

The basic structure for an SRI affiliated with Stanford can be outlined briefly. It was to be an independent, nonprofit, scientific, tax exempt, public service organization operated separately from the University.

The key tie between the two institutions called upon the Stanford Trustees (acting as general members of the Institute) to elect our directors. Also, the president of the University was to be chairman of SRI's board. Thus, ultimate control over the Institute was to be in the Trustees' hands with residual ownership rights in the University in event of our dissolution.

This was a conventional arrangement under the circumstances. However, the new Institute was to be independent of any business or governmental organizations thus helping to insure objectivity in all its operations.

The tax-exempt plan was included so the Institute would be eligible for tax-deductible gifts by donors. Also, our parent was itself tax exempt as a University and did not wish to create a regular profit-making entity.

Another reason was to permit SRI to be exempt from taxes on income associated with its tax-exempt purposes. Still further, our founders believed that the non-profit, tax-exempt status would be helpful even though conventional equity capital would not be available.

Another important foundation emerged from the Founding Years. Our charter included several public service purposes among them being — to maintain a scientific research center, promote economic and industrial development (especially in the American West) and contribute to peace and prosperity for mankind.

Also, the Institute was to assist Stanford in various ways and otherwise serve the public interest and welfare. Both pure and applied research were included in its pursuits, but the main intent was that SRI would work under contracts with other organizations, public and private.

Our founders felt quite rightly that such matters as organization, particular fields of research, financing and other policies as well as features for the "Stanford subsidiary" should be left to the future.

On this basis, the Institute began on a limited basis immediately after its founding and continued this way through 1947 and into 1948 when a vigorous thrust ushered in the Take-Off Days.

One key change in our basic foundations occurred later on when Stanford and SRI mutually agreed to separate. In essence, this was done by the Institute's directors also becoming general members and then operating on a self-perpetuating basis.

EARLY VISION

- The concept of "applying science for useful purposes" originated at least four centuries ago during the Age of Commerce and Discovery.
- Francis Bacon believed that the world's attention should be turned from a medieval emphasis on deductive reasoning to the Kingdom of Man and to human society and its many problems.
- He contended that this could best be done through the applied sciences and that the chief task for mankind was to make the world a better place for human habitation...
- Bacon also believed that one of the main objectives of research should be to create "a rich storehouse for the glory of the Creator."
- This dedication led him to create Salomon's House — a foundation devoted to "enlarging the bounds of human empire." Thus, we find the forerunner of present day institutes and research foundations.
- Even Einstein in his quest for new knowledge often expressed concern about the great unsolved problems of human endeavor and once counselled an audience to "never forget this in the midst of your diagrams and equations..."
- These expressions — were placed in modern focus some seventy years ago by an Englishman, J. Arthur Thompson. He wrote about "bringing the light of science to bear on man's problems all along the line, on health of mind as well as of body, on education as well as on agriculture, on ethical development as well as on industry, on eugenics as well as on utopias.

— Newcomen Address on SRI (author) - 1967

This change also included a new name — from Stanford Research Institute to SRI International — but with no change in other foundations from the Founding Years. The Institute continued to be widely known as SRI, as it had been since 1946.

As the Take-Off Days got under way several features or dimensions for the fledgling institute were introduced. All were modified along the way in keeping with circumstances and experience.

FEATURES/DIMENSIONS

- A *system* of contract operations with both government and business was created.
- Moves were made for the organization to become fully *national* and then *worldwide* in scope as soon as feasible.
- A *self-sponsored* research program (including fundamental scientific investigations) was initiated.
- An *Associates Plan* designed to provide the equivalent of equity capital was put in place.
- Three basic *program areas* were selected, the physical and life sciences, engineering (mostly electronics) and economics-management, along with other social sciences.
- A long-drawn out move to acquire our Menlo Park headquarters site was initiated.
- Several *offices* and research *groups* mainly in the U.S. West away from headquarters were created.
- The founding *board* increased its numbers and worked out a system for policy guidance and support.

Also, between 1948 and 1955, several basic initiatives and policies greatly affecting the Institute's present and future were put in motion.

INITIATIVES/POLICIES

- Concepts of teamwork and multidisciplinary approaches in organized research and advisory services.
- Greater selectivity on programs and projects along with increasing quality in all professional endeavors.
- A never-ending search for purposes and strategies in keeping with changing environments.
- Initial basic financing through borrowings and then seeking the equivalent of equity capital.
- Rapid early growth in staff and contract revenues aimed at reaching a ''critical mass'' at the earliest possible time with lower-growth planning thereafter.
- ''Sound business principles'' with an emphasis on generating higher returns for internal investments.
- Joint programs with Stanford.
- Self-sufficiency (including appropriate borrowings) for regular operations.
- Basic principles underlying activities deemed to be primarily in the broad public interest.
- A reasonable balance between work for business and for government.
- Growing diversification in relationships within both business and government sectors.
- A system for avoiding conflicts of interest with Associates and clients.
- Guidelines for handling controversial projects.
- A mechanism for retaining some patent and royalty income.
- A strong and coordinated marketing program.
- Financial and other assistance to the University.

Some of these features and policy initiatives (e.g., the Associates Plan) were highly successful even within the Take-Off Days; others, such as the balance between government and industrial revenues, were not so successful. Still others (e.g., the search for purpose and strategy) were simply the first steps in a long continuing process.

In retrospect, several of these topics may appear routine and inherent. However, SRI was in its formative times and in many respects was "feeling its way."

The subtitle of this book implies that some right steps were taken at the right times during the 1948–1955 span of years. This does not mean that *all* were right and at the right times. More could and perhaps should have been done. Even so, it is fair to say that the "batting average" was reasonably good for a new Institute with limited resources and experience.

Still another set of basic forces affecting the Institute's future was brought to play during our formative years. They cannot be easily measured but, nevertheless, they certainly were present.

A wave of high energy and enthusiasm pervaded the organization. Strong entrepreneurship arose in creating new programs and projects within an increasingly unified organization. Various moves were made to "improve the working environment" and to "enhance external images" of the Institute.

As might be expected for a young and relatively small organization, (at least by later standards), many steps were taken along the lines of creating an "SRI Family." This idea was especially strong during the early 1950s.

Staff members in the services were as much a part of the "family" as were those in research endeavors. Among the best known and most highly respected "professionals" of the times were our photographer, glass blower, some equipment technicians, and two first-rank carpenters in the maintenance crew. They, too, had great pride in the growing institute.

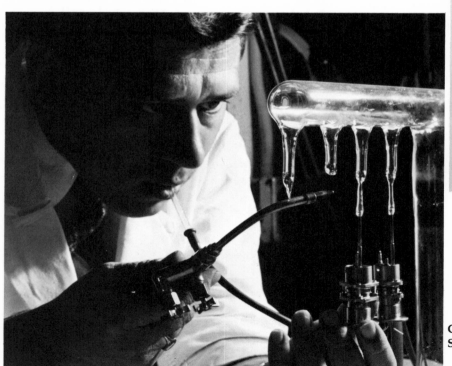

TECHNICAL PHOTOGRAPHY
Walter Lawton

GLASSBLOWING SPECIALIST

One of the latter gave voice to this feeling during a visit by a distinguished European in mid-1955. Seeing one of our carpenters busily at work atop a temporary barracks-type building, the visitor asked: "What are you doing."

Some response such as "repairing the roof" might have sufficed. But, instead, he replied, "We are building an institute."

Later, during a speech before a large audience in the Waldorf Astoria in New York, our guest repeated the exchange to illustrate the motivation he felt he had found within SRI.

To whatever extent his assessment may have been justified, the idea of helping "build for the future" has pervaded the Institute's staff since its beginning.

This is not, however, a book about the post-1955 years, the present or the future. This must await another day. It may well be that in time the upsurge years will or can be divided into two stages — one from the mid-1950s through the early 1970s during which the separation between the Institute and Stanford occurred, and one for the balance of the decade known, perhaps, by "A New Independence" theme.

Whatever may be appropriate in this respect, an added stage surely began in the early 1980s. It can easily bear "A New Horizon" name. New purposes, goals and planning are in the forefront.

SRI is a dynamic organization today as before and promises to continue so for a long time to come. It is forward-looking; it has a strong conceptual base; it keeps "in tune" with changing times; its reputation grows higher year by year; the quality of its output rises steadily. And, its guidelines to the future are clear and concise.

SRI WILL ...

- Continually strive to be a leading science and knowledge-based research and consulting organization working with governments and businesses world-wide.
- Be seen as a center of excellence in terms of professional standing, methodologies and experimental facilities.
- Continue to provide a leadership role in addressing and solving world business, economic and social issues.
- Capitalize on its intellectual properties through patent and commercial opportunities.

— AND IT IS —

- Committed to growth and improved financial performance in order to have a more significant position in our markets and in the advancement of our other goals.

These *cornerstones* authored by Dr. William F. Miller, (SRI's president and chief executive officer) are fundamental in our continuing search for purpose and strategies.

They can and surely will help lead the Institute to and through an exciting and productive stage during many years to come.

A FEW IN THE "SRI FAMILY" . . .

EARLY PERSONNEL OFFICE

AN OPEN HOUSE TOUR

PUBLICATIONS
- Charles A. Scarlott -

REPORT PRODUCTION DEPARTMENT
L to R: Felix Natis, Charlotte A. Matthews, and Raymond Andersen,
— discussing a technical drawing.

EXPERT MACHINIST
- Wilfred "Pop" Walters -

POULTER LABORATORY
- Margaret Ray -

SRI FAMILY OPEN-HOUSE — IRMA CHECK SORTER

MAIL FROM CLIENTS!

MODEL SHOP — ANTENNA LABORATORY

ENGINEERING PICNIC

BENIAMINO "BENNY" BUFANO
Artist in Residence for a few hours!! A sculptured head on "exhibit" next to Fred Kamphoefner, (far left) July 1955.

FRANK LLOYD WRIGHT
Architect extraordinaire …
his famous hat and walking cane
on fireplace mantel in an early
SRI clubhouse. J.E. Hobson (center)
August 1955

LILLIAN GILBRETH
Production Management Specialist …
Out under the bay trees, September 1956

FORUM ORGANIZER
Rogers Cannell

Thus, "We are building an ... institute" — with two adjectives inserted — applies today. The adjectives are "ever stronger."

Whatever may have happened during our Take-Off Days, some right steps are certainly being taken at the right times in the mid-1980s.

I joined SRI at its beginning; my enthusiasm for it was unbounded; I feel the same way today.

Although speaking in a light tone, Atholl McBean was certainly quite right when he said in 1956:

> *The Institute has a great future; we know where it is and how it got there;*
> *look to the future; be confident; improve quality; work hard; be enthusiastic;*
> *and keep moving — but take some new bearings along the way!!!*

SRI does indeed have plans as it looks to a New Horizon. ∎

A NEW FEATURE

IN MID-1955, when the Institute moved to a financial self-sufficiency policy, one exception was in the forefront. It involved basic research.

Early in 1954, a decision was made to provide more money as soon as possible for fundamental investigations in the sciences, engineering and economics-management. The idea was to strengthen the organization's "scientific base."

This money was to come from the Associates Plan, overhead allowances and net earnings. The idea was to create a small basic research group in each of the Institute's three main divisions. Each group was to have maximum freedom in selecting projects with guidance by a small program committee. There was to be a flow of senior people between basic and applied work.

Some step was greatly needed; very little money was being spent for the purpose. The goal was an annual outlay of $200,000 or so. There was

widespread support for the plan within the Institute and at board level and especially by Atholl McBean. Ralph Krause was the principal architect.

As planning got under way, Hobson moved the initiative to a much larger scale with implications for Stanford University and the nation. Douglas Whitaker, the University's Provost, and a few other faculty members soon entered the picture.

With McBean's full support, Hobson first proposed that some sort of SRI-Mellon Institute affiliation be created for basic research purposes.

Meetings were held with Mellon's directors but nothing feasible could be developed. Hobson then moved things in another direction — creating a national fund to support work in a few basic research centers in leading universities (including Stanford) and at Mellon.

Several hundreds of thousands of dollars were to be involved. SRI was to participate in some way in the Stanford Center and would receive some grants for its own basic research. McBean was anxious to move ahead with industry on fund raising. A special SRI board committee was created to help guide the overall ''project.''

A possible plan was widely discussed within business, government, university and other circles during 1954 and the first half of 1955. Some financial support was to come from the federal government in the form of overhead allowances in R&D contracts wherever placed and also through tax credits for industry based on total R&D spending. Also, some support was to come from SRI earnings.

For various reasons (perhaps obvious in retrospect), the plan encountered one obstacle after another. Even Stanford was reluctant to support the concept of a relatively independent entity within its structure. Government showed little interest in the tax credit idea.

Nevertheless, Hobson and McBean still wanted to do something. Thus, on March 29, 1955, a long-drawn-out day-long senior staff meeting lasting through much of the night was devoted to the initiative. This and a report by the board committee soon centered things on SRI and Stanford alone. We were not in a position to launch a large-scale effort.

The new plan called for a Stanford Fund and also a Stanford Center for the Natural Sciences and Mathematics. Funds were to come from both contributions by industry and Institute earnings. A sizeable annual budget was involved — upwards of $250,000 per year plus various facilities and services from the University for the first two or three years.

Although emphasis by this time had shifted from basic research at SRI to the national scene and then to Stanford, it appeared by mid-year that something would soon be set in motion.

However, little happened during the balance of the year. The plan had limited appeal within business, and Stanford itself had come to feel that only a grant-type entity should be involved. McBean lost enthusiasm when it became clear that the fundraising should move into the University or at least away from SRI.

By year end the two-year exercise had come to an end. Hobson had left SRI; Frederick Terman had become the University's Provost; McBean's interest within SRI turned elsewhere.

Although he was no longer to be involved, Hobson made a final plea of sorts for what had become a personal but laudable obsession. His words appeared on December 31, 1955, under the byline, ''A Bow to Basic Science.''

> ''The situation is simply this: our national existence is critically dependent upon an ever-increasing supply of fundamental knowledge; present mechanisms are not geared to fill the need; neither traditional European sources of basic data nor our own efforts at basic research are adequate. New concepts, new approaches must be found.
>
> ''Although industry is ultimately the chief consumer of basic research, it should be recognized that applied industrial research is the middleman drawing heavily on supplies of knowledge and gifted scientists. Applied research should somehow pay for basic research, its raw material, and such payment should be considered a normal part of the cost of applied research.''

TENTH ANNIVERSARY — 1956
From Take-Off to Upward Surge.

PLANNING A HEADQUARTERS BUILDIN
L to R: Frank Burrows – contractor,
William Stockwell and Jess Stanton – archit

ALLEN M. PETERSON AND THOMAS H. MORRIN
Select site for Big Dish antenna
on Stanford Campus.

THE BIG DISH

Whitaker at Stanford had said earlier in the year, ''Let's get on with SRI's idea on basic research.'' Terman closed out the initiative as he became the University's provost, an SRI director, and the board's vice chairman.

> *Let's move on to SRI supporting its own basic work, then helping Stanford as it can on departmental programs of mutual interest.*

As mentioned elsewhere in this book, this is what happened after the Take-Off Days The account here is significant only because it was a well-intentioned, even if unsuccessful, episode during our early history.

In retrospect, the best plan would have been to step up the Associates Plan right away and devote more money, at least for a while, directly to basic research within SRI. Assistance to Stanford in the order of $50,000 to $100,000 per year might still have been feasible in mid-1955 as was proposed at one point by the University. □

The Printouts

WITH SRI's ANNUAL REVENUES MOVING UPWARD from $200 million in the mid-1980s (along with net income in the 3% — 5% range) and with total assets at well over $110 million, the equivalent numbers for the mid-1900s seem rather insignificant.

However, figures on the financial statements at the time and particularly their rates of increase were highly significant. The important point is that they were changing in the right direction.

The numbers for each month were being watched in great detail. With red figures on the income statement and also deficits on the balance sheet, a drive was on during the early Take-Off Days to change their color.

By mid-1950 black figures began to appear on the monthly printouts. They were small but they signalled a new day in finances. In 1955 the deficit on the balance sheet had been changed to a healthy surplus. The Institute was essentially self supporting.

INCOME AND EXPENSE

1947	1950	1955		
$231,806.08	$1,990,484.89	$10,029,278.50	—	Project Revenue
180,128.07	1,234,606.59	5,872,747.18	—	Project Costs
$ 51,678.01	$ 755,878.30	$ 4,156,531.32	—	Gross Income
94,525.31	813,901.51	3,831,175.30	—	Overhead Costs
$(42,847.30)	$ (58,023.21)	$ 325,356.02	—	Oper. Income*
(53.66)	—	—	—	Other Inc./Exp.
$(42,793.64)	$ (58,023.21)	$ 325,356.02	—	Net Income (Surplus)

The surplus for July was not exactly a comfortable one, but it was a welcome change from the past. The Institute had demonstrated that its Take-Off could be sustained.

BREAK-EVEN — JULY 1950

$160,022.51	—	Project Revenue
99,294.19	—	Project Costs
$ 60,728.32	—	Gross Income
$ 58,795.29	—	Overhead Costs
$ 1,933.03	—	Operating Income
$ 396.60	—	Other Income
$ 2,329.63	—	NET INCOME (Surplus) to Capital

*From minus 3% of revenue in 1950 to a plus 3% in 1955.

Whatever you do, complete it on time and within budget; get in the habit.

— S.D. Bechtel, Sr.

DEBITS AND CREDITS

The year-end printouts led one banker to accept the ''current'' ratios but to
inquire about the ''acid tests'' (cash versus current liabilities).

Assets

1947	1950	1955		
$ 450.00	$ 106,982.22	$ 266,328.20	—	Cash
114,460.61	436,650.93	2,272,322.42	—	Accounts Receivable
21.54	47,327.21	155,639.87	—	Inventories
20,768.68	388,487.12	1,919,932.97	—	Plant/Equipment–Net
1,501.96	40,466.77	158,897.04	—	Other
$ 137,202.79	$1,019,914.25	$4,773,120.50		TOTAL

Liabilities and Net Worth (capital)

1947	1950	1955		
$ 133,156.68	$ 344,400.59	$1,093,489.95	—	Current Liabilities
—	950,000.00	1,100,000.00	—	Long-term loans
$(133,156.68)	$1,294,400.59	2,193,489.95	—	Total Liabilities
$ (51,237.87)	$ (451,486.34)	$ 755,060.59	—	Net Income (Surplus)
$ 48,000.00	177,000.00	1,824,569.96	—	Contributions–Net
$ (3,237.87)	$ (274,486.34)	$2,579,630.55	—	Net Capital
$ 137,202.79	$1,019,914.25	$4,773,120.50		TOTAL Liabilities and Capital

As with many other organizations, the Institute had some financial problems in later
years but none as tight as those during the early and middle Take-Off Days.

Calendar of Selected Events

THE FIRST DECADE

1946 – 1956

1946

September 1 — First executive director (Talbot) appointed
November 1 — Guayule rubber project begins
November 6 — Articles filed with State of California
December 13 — Stanford Trustees adopt charter.

1947

January 8 — Founding directors meet at Stanford
May 21 — Staff moves from Stanford to Menlo Park
May 31 — Smog research project starts
July 1 — Aircraft industry project begins
December 31 — Talbot Resigns — Transition begins.

1948

March 1 — Second executive director (Hobson) appointed
April 6 — Vigorous development plan approved
September 1 — Air Research Laboratory opened (Pasadena)
September 1 — Directors-Chemistry and Engineering arrive
September 24–26 — Senior staff meeting (Aptos, California).

1949

January 5 — Field demonstration — Poulter Method — Geophysical Exploration
January 12 — Northern California Research Conference
January 25 — Re-financing plan adopted
February 17 — First Associates Plan initiative
May 13 — International Plan announced
May 17 — Los Angeles Office opened
July 1 — Taku Glacier project begins
October 31 — First financial breakeven
November 10–12 — 1st National Air Pollution Symposium
December 21 — Technical Advisory Committee appointed.

1950

April 20	—	Stanford opens negotiations — Stanford Village land
June 21	—	Search for purpose/strategy begins
July 31	—	Sustained surplus operation begins
August 17	—	Holland Report completed
December 2	—	RFC Loan application submitted.

1951

April 26	—	Second development plan started
May 9	—	Italy project (mechanical industries) launched
August 2	—	RFC loan approved and then declined
November 14	—	''Million Dollar'' Associates Plan Luncheon, San Francisco
November 30	—	Positive net worth (after donations) first achieved.

1952

May 5	—	Washington Office opened
May 5–6	—	2nd National Air Pollution Symposium
July 23	—	Proton bombarder installed
November 30	—	Radiation Engineering Laboratory dedicated.

1953

April 30	—	Cumulative deficit offset by earned surplus
May 15	—	SRI movie on air pollution research released
August 31	—	Final payment — 1949 bank loans
October 3	—	Mountain States Division (Office) opened (Phoenix, Arizona)
October 16	—	Stanford payments plan adopted — 1954 start
November 1	—	Mt. Lee antenna laboratory (Hollywood) acquired
December 14	—	Patent policy/system adopted
December 15	—	Two-year 80% growth plan adopted.

1954

January 20	—	Vannevar Bush Luncheon — Los Angeles
April 1	—	Pacific Northwest Office opened (Portland, Oregon)
April 19–20	—	1st Symposium on Automatic Production (electronic equipment)
September 30	—	Hawaii Office opened (Honolulu)
October 1	—	General Manager for Research (E. Finley Carter) appointed
November 17	—	1st Western Area Development Conference.

1955

April 4–5	—	Atomic Energy Forum — New Industrial Frontier
July 16–18	—	Senior Staff Meeting (Monterey, California)
July 29	—	First Stanford Village Land (30 acres) purchased
August 2	—	Financial self-sufficiency plan started
September 22	—	ERMA (Electronic Recording Machine Accounting) announced
November 1–5	—	World Symposium on Applied Solar Energy (Arizona)
November 9	—	10th Associates Day Meeting
November 15	—	European Office (Zürich) announced
December 31	—	A milestone reached — 1,163 staff; $10M revenue.

1956

January 21-22	—	Solar Energy Furnace Symposium
March 31	—	Third Executive Director (E. Finley Carter) appointed — became president March 26, 1959
June 22–23	—	Southern California Laboratories (Pasadena) opened
July 18	—	First IIDC-SF announced for October 14–18, 1957
October 3–4	—	10th Anniversary Program (San Francisco).

Highest dedication to his profession, colleagues, SRI, and international understanding.
— DONALD R. SCHEUCH - 1986

E. FINLEY CARTER *
SRI from 1954 to 1965

*See page 126.

The Chapters*

1. Prologue   Pre-1949

A perspective on the Founding Years and Take-Off Days for a new western institute and its rapid development starting in 1948.

> Initiatives at Stanford University and from San Francisco — operations begin in late 1946 — the first Talbot year (1947) — a new executive director.

The leaders: Atholl McBean, Alvin C. Eurich and J. E. Hobson.†

2. The Sister Institutes   1948

The family of endowed and non-endowed American research institutes and their rapid growth during the years immediately following World War II.

> Promotion of contract research — rise of the regional institutes — events on the world scene — an economic upsurge in the USA — national R&D spending — institute leaders — a meeting in Chicago — the Four Horsemen.

Four central figures: Edward R. Weidlein, Clyde Williams, Harold Vagtborg and Charles N. Kimball.

3. The Nick of Time   1948 and early 1949

A vigorous development thrust featuring rapid growth from the spring of 1948 through the balance of the year and leading to a severe cash shortage following by refinancing.

> The second executive director takes immediate charge — a development program launched on five fronts — beginnings of a new organization — three basic program areas put in place — search for a re-financing plan — loans from a client, Stanford University and six banks.

Some principal people: J. E. Hobson, Thomas C. Poulter, William E. Rand, Carsten Steffens, George R. Herbert, Atholl McBean, Alvin C. Eurich, Charles R. Blyth and William L. Stewart.

---

* See Table of Contents page v.

† J. E. Hobson is a principal in all the chapter accounts; his name is not repeated with the digests that follow. The author was much involved in events of all chapters but his name is not listed below. George R. Herbert played a key role throughout the 1948–1955 period.

4. Broadening the Base
1949

Greater selectivity in growth and rising emphasis on quality of professional work.

Five research departments — an internally-sponsored research program — a Precision Gage Laboratory — a plan for international work — beginnings of the Associates Plan — First National Air Pollution Symposium.

A few key participants: J.E. Wallace Sterling, Thomas H. Morrin, Donald B. Benedict, Paul J. Lovewell, Edward W. Doll and Raymond H. Ewell.

5. A New Drive
1949

A concerted move to reach a financial breakeven by October, 1949.

Pricing on research contracts — the government/commerical ratio — project diversification — first royalty income — some fund-raising plans — expense reductions — further rapid growth — rising equipment needs — and a temporary surplus rate.

The helping hands: John F. Forbes, M. E. Spaght, George R. Herbert, Ralph A. Krause, Emery Bator and division directors.

6. An Expanding Board
1949-1955

The founding directors and their dedicated service to a fledgling institute striving to become a significant institution in the American West, then for the nation, and later on a worldwide basis.

The first eleven directors — early 1949 additions — further expansion in numbers — circumstances and services — a new chairman from Stanford — honor and recognition.

Some leaders of the cause: Charles R. Blyth, Paul L. Davies, Alvin C. Eurich, Atholl McBean, Donald J. Russell, Stephen D. Bechtel, Sr., J. E. Wallace Sterling and Edward W. Carter.

7. A New Target
1950

A commitment to achieve a continuing and then rising suplus operation by mid-1950.

Some shortfalls — alternative plans — the government/commercial ratio — a tight squeeze — results on target — a self-sufficiency goal — an exchange about the future — and a foreign project upcoming.

Leaders of the exercise: George R. Herbert, William E. Rand, Carsten Steffens, all department heads and John F. Forbes.

8. A Search for Purpose   1948-1955

A never-ending study on basic purposes, goals, objectives and strategies consistent with the Founding Charter and changing circumstances.

A new policy statement — contract research pursuits — obligations to Stanford University — public services — sound business principles — service to government — and western U.S. economic development.

Some guiding hands: J. E. Wallace Sterling, John F. Forbes, Atholl McBean, Carsten Steffens, Morris M. Doyle and Donald J. Russell

9. An Outside View   1950

An outside report on organization, policies and operations for the board of directors.

A critique on planning — comparisons with other institutes — the SRI ''building blocks'' — more capital and further growth needed — recommendations to both the directors and management.

The author: Maurice Holland (industrial research consultant).

10. The RFC Episode   1950-1951

A year-long negotiation for a capital loan from the U.S. government.

Changing the law to include non-profit organizations — help from Senator Nixon — frequent re-submissions — timid actions in Washington — President Truman's reaction — loan finally approved — declined by SRI — new impetus on fund-raising.

Principal negotiators: James Drumm and George R. Herbert.

11. Some Equity Capital   1951-1955

A program to obtain $1.5 million (as the equivalent of equity capital) from American companies through an Associates Plan.

Development Committee of the Board — planned use of funds — relationships with Associate companies — the Million Dollar ''Kick-Off'' Luncheon in San Francisco — Coordination with Stanford University — and goal achieved.

The prime movers: Atholl McBean, Alvin C. Eurich, Louis B. Lundborg, David Sarnoff and Carl Titus.

The Associates — Never ever forget what they have done.
— R. GWIN FOLLIS - 1955

12. A Village Home   1953-1955

A joint effort with Stanford University, the City of Menlo Park, California, and SRI to acquire a permanent homesite in Stanford Village, Menlo Park, California.

A World War II military hospital — leased by Stanford for student housing — surplus property under the Lanham Act — purchased by SRI — obligations to remove temporary buildings — a church re-located — a world headquarters building.

The acquisition team: George R. Herbert and Matthew Stafford, with Dwight Adams from Stanford and Mayor Charles Burgess of Menlo Park.

13. Area Outposts   1949-1955

A buildup of offices and research groups away from headquarters in Menlo Park, California.

Los Angeles, Pasadena, Washington, D.C., Phoenix, Portland and Hawaii.

Among the leaders: A. M. Zarem, Fred B. Ortman, Carlton L. Green, Robert B. Englert, Patrick M. Dowling, William E. Hosken, William S. Royce and George T. Hayes.

14. The Second Stage   1951-1955

The gathering forces and a rising thrust from mid-1950 through 1955 as the organization reached a "critical mass" in size, embraced principles of service, performance and leadership and continued on a self-sufficient basis.

A long-delayed plan — from red to black — a pause for cash — the bottom line — the final push — new growth policy — and the Monterey theme.

The planners and doers: the executive director, the chairman, George R. Herbert, and other administrative and professional leaders during the Take-Off Days.

15. Epilogue   1948–1955

A perspective on events throughout the Take-Off Days leading from a tiny western research institute in 1948 to an organization of more than 1,000 people and $10 million in annual revenues by 1955.

The physical and life sciences, engineering and economics-management sciences — new dimensions on a national and international scale — and emphasis on public services — the Associates Plan, a permanent home in Menlo Park, branch offices in the U.S. West and elsewhere — rising quality of professional work — and the beginnings of an upward surge by a maturing institute.

Key contributors: The professional and service staff.   □

Postcript

IF PARTICULAR DATES ARE TO BE SELECTED, SRI's Take-Off days began on April 6, 1948, and ended on December 31, 1955.

At the beginning, other take-offs were under way. The American people were building a new future following the Great Depression and World War II. With partners abroad, the nation was striving for a new world order.

In addition, R&D was becoming a new force in both business and government. The research institute movement was gaining momentum.

An Academy Award winning RKO movie, ''The Best Years ...,'' was symbolic of the times. Some twenty years later, Joseph C. Goulden in a book by the same name wrote about the euphoria of the times.

To one who has been involved with and within SRI since its Founding Years, our Take-Off most certainly was ''good'' if not the ''best.'' All is relative, but it was a formative and exciting time.

A few lines depict what was happening with great impact on our future.

THE ENVIRONMENT

- Sky-high enthusiasm in a great cause.
- Vigorous moves to a critical mass.
- Widening horizons — national and global.
- A search for purpose in the public service.
- Rising quality in professional pursuits.
- All-out support by the governing body.
- Bold actions on the financial front.
- High energy from a youthful staff.
- New dimensions for a research institute.
- Great faith in the founding visions.

OPERATIONS

- Creating a system for later perfection.
- Entrepreneurship as a driving force.
- Never-ending equipment shortages.
- A drawn-out solution on a village home.
- Onward to an upward surge.

Suffice it to say that some important things did happen as SRI ''geared up'' for the long pull. In retrospect, some right moves were made. Many better ones were to follow — and are still occurring.

This is why SRI with each passing year since its origin has become an increasingly *"significant international institution."* This is what one director, S.D. Bechtel, Sr., said in the early 1950s should happen.

In a 1945 book, "I Was There," Edwin Layton wrote definitively about some aspects of World War II intelligence in the Pacific. Many others agree with him.

But when one writes as a participant in past events, there can always be varying interpretations by others who were "there" or who later study the times.

I was "there" during our Take-Off Days. I have attempted in this book to remove the possibility of differing interpretations as I know them from the record and from recall. It is best, however, to end my account by adding to Walter Cronkite's well-known words,

"And — That's how I think it was."

WELDON B. GIBSON

Menlo Park, Calfornia - 1986

SRI STAFF

The Extended Family
———— Builders of the Institute ————

1,163 — December 31, 1955
2,033 — Total I.D. cards issued*

2,918 — December 31, 1985
20,503 — Total I.D. cards issued*

———————
* An I.D. card is issued upon employment.
Numbers are cumulative since SRI's beginning.

See page 212.

Europe will re-industrialize; it is in the "West;" SRI should play a role in its future.
— J.D. ZELLERBACH - 1951

Index

Pages on Stanford Trustees, SRI founders and directors, sciences, engineering, economics—management, international and key staff members are too numerous to list fully. See, e.g., Board of Directors, Special Service, Colleagues, Chairmen and Presidents and Chapters (Digest).

Plus

SPECIAL RECOGNITION

to

MARTIN GOLAND, Southwest Research Institute
GEORGE R. HERBERT, Research Triangle Institute
CHARLES N. KIMBALL, Midwest Research Institute

and the

SRI PROFESSIONAL STAFF

THE WIDENING CIRCLE

OUR TAKE-OFF DAYS ended on a high note—on principles, substance, growth, finances and other features. The momentum continued—and still does—including facilities, research and public service.

The staff has tripled to some 3,000; annual revenues have multiplied more than twenty times to well over $200 million, 40% commercial and industrial and 60% from the U.S. Government.

There are now thirteen divisions spanning engineering, the sciences (physical, life and social), economics-management, world business and international-domestic policy.

Hundreds upon hundreds of projects are undertaken each year for business and governments around the world. Offices and in some cases research groups are maintained in New York, Chicago, Washington, D.C., Croydon (U.K.), Paris, Milan, Frankfurt, Stockholm, Zürich, Tokyo, Singapore and elsewhere.

The circle widens further. Since 1957, more than 150 world business sessions have been held under SRI auspices (in whole or in part) on the six continents. Hundreds of companies have been involved. ☐

A FEW EXAMPLES . . .

WORLD CLASS EVENTS

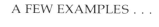

SAN FRANCISCO
Every four years

DJAKARTA
1967

MOSCOW
1974

SYDNEY
1978

HANGZHOU
1981

. . . SOME SRI SPEAKERS

E.F. CARTER

C.A. ANDERSON

E.H. WASSON

W.B. GIBSON

H.E. ROBISON

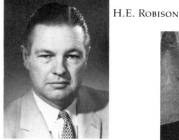
J.R. NATER

W.F. MILLER

What they had to say must wait another day !!

. . . Finis   213

SRI is moving ahead energetically; a strong base for the future is being created. The pace must be maintained.

SRI
The Take-Off Days

MID-1900s

Key Steps

May our

Europe will re-industrialize; it is in th

... to promote the general interests of International exchange ... in resear

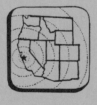

The West — Our country's future is here. Think big thoughts about the Wes

Whatever you do, complete it on time and within budget; get in the habit.

EQU

BREAK-EVEN

PURPOSE / GOALS

On growth — let it first be in quality.

REFINANCING

VIGOROUS THRUST

SCIENCE / ECONOMICS / ENGINEERING

1948   1950